Renaissance Utopias
and the
Problem of History

Renaissance Utopias and the Problem of History

Marina Leslie

Cornell University Press

ITHACA AND LONDON

First published 1998 by Cornell University Press.

Printed in the United States of America

Library of Congress Cataloging-in-Publication Data
Leslie, Marina.
   Renaissance utopias and the problem of history / Marina Leslie.
      p.   cm.
   Includes bibliographical references and index.
   ISBN 0-8014-3400-9 (cloth)
   1. Utopias—History.   2. Utopias in literature.   3. Literature and
history.   4. European Literature—Renaissance, 1450–1600—History
and criticism.   I. Title.
HX806.L47   1998
321'.07—dc21   98—17865
                                                                   CIP

Cornell University Press strives to use environmentally responsible suppliers
and materials to the fullest extent possible in the publishing of its books. Such
materials include vegetable-based, low-VOC inks and acid-free papers that are
also recycled, totally chlorine-free, or partly composed of nonwood fibers.

Cloth printing   10 9 8 7 6 5 4 3 2 1

Contents

Illustrations

Acknowledgments

My interest in utopia first took root long ago when as an undergraduate I had the great good fortune of studying Renaissance literature with Harry Berger, Jr., in that locus amoenus among state institutions, University of California at Santa Cruz. If anyone is to blame for my early and persistent confusion of a career of scholarship and teaching with utopia, it is he. I would like also to thank John Hollander, who served as my advisor at Yale and encouraged and restrained my utopian musings in the early stages of this manuscript. The careful reading of Thomas M. Greene, Lawrence Manley, and Susanne Wofford helped both to bring that project to a close and to suggest the outlines of its new incarnation in this book. The generous support of a Charlotte W. Newcombe fellowship and a Northeastern University Junior Research Grant offered precious time to work. Over the years a number of mentors, friends, and colleagues have shaped my thoughts on utopia and given it a worldly referent, these include: Deborah Beard, Frank Blessington, Kate Brogan, Mary Baine Campbell, Kevin Dunn, Margaret Ferguson, James Holstun, Kathleen Kelly, Lee Cullen Khanna, Lawrence Manley, Mary Pat Martin, Stuart Peterfreund, Barbara Rodriguez, John Rogers, Katrina Van Valkenburgh, and Joseph Westlund. My students at Northeastern have helped to inspire and test my work in progress in the crucible of the classroom. Philip Cavalier and Catharine Ferguson, in particular, deserve both praise and thanks. A special debt of gratitude is owed to David L. Clark, Mary Loeffelholz, Jaya Mehta, and Edward Schiffer for challenging and sustaining my work at every turn. Phyllis Leslie has been a maternal font of utopian inspiration, and I hope this book can serve as a tribute to her and to the memory of my father, Harry Leslie. I want particularly to thank Bernhard Kendler of Cornell University Press for his support of this project, as well as the two anonymous readers for their wonderfully lucid and enormously helpful comments.

Earlier versions of Chapters 2 and 5 appeared as "Mapping Out Ideology: The Case of Utopia," *Recherches sémiotiques/Semiotic Inquiry* 12 (1992): 73–94; and, "Gender, Genre, and the Utopian Body in Margaret Cavendish's *Blazing World*," *Utopian Studies* 7.1 (1996); 6–24. I am grateful to both journals for permission to reprint.

Finally, this book is for Hugh Baxter, whose judicious interventions, winning distractions, and unfailing companionship have made a world of difference in this book as in everything.

MARINA LESLIE

to escape. But whereas utopia has proved fertile terrain for historicizing readings, the genre turns out to be very unstable ground for charting out the relation of the literary text to its historical context. Even a cursory glance at the literary history of utopia's meanings and uses can begin to suggest the nature of the difficulty.

Defining Nowhere and Other Utopian Projects

From its origins a linguistic, topical, and generic oxymoron, utopia has always called for and frustrated attempts at definition. It is clear that utopia has meant many different things, and what I want to do here and throughout this book is to keep the variety of utopia's historically and textually specific definitions in play rather than choose definitively among them. Instead of reading utopia as a fixed, semantic site whose fullness (sufficiently expansive to account for any and all particular meanings) will be revealed to the careful reader, I want to consider utopia as a kind of edgy, multiple, and palimpsestic way of reading.

Several intractable problems have plagued utopian semantics, perhaps the most immediately apparent being the practical difficulty of balancing the requirements of adequate inclusiveness and formal intelligibility. Utopia was from its inception a hybrid production, and More's originary *Utopia* fuses a number of poetical, rhetorical, and historical genres. *Utopia* belongs to what Rosalie Colie calls, in her analysis of Renaissance genre systems, the *genera mixta,* or mixed genre, which she characterizes as "a mode of thought as well as of poetry" and describes under the rubric "inclusionism."[1] More "includes," and in so doing he transforms a number of literary topoi and their conventions: imaginary voyage, *speculum principis,* model commonwealth, dialogue, satire, paradoxical encomium, epideictic oratory, and so on. Francis Bacon and Margaret Cavendish, whose utopias I will also be examining, blend their own generic olios to produce texts that depart in form, content, and tone both from More and from each other. Even those features that my selected utopian subjects share—dialogue, for example, or the framing device of the imaginary voyage—are not regarded by utopian scholars as formal requirements of the genre. Different utopias have been structured by entirely different formal patterns, and utopian bibliographers have drawn the line between approved and nonapproved forms in different ways and according to entirely different and often quite personal

Introduction

A map of the world that does not include Utopia is not worth even glancing at, for it leaves out the one country at which Humanity is always landing. And when Humanity lands there, it looks out, and, seeing a better country sets sail.

—OSCAR WILDE, "The Soul of Man under Socialism"

Long a favorite epigraph of utopian writers and critics, this passage from Oscar Wilde's essay "The Soul of Man under Socialism" is more often invoked ringingly than inspected closely. Nonetheless, the course to utopia that Wilde charts here is neither direct nor without obstacles. Are we to understand the shifting features of the ideal map Wilde describes as abstractly inspirational or as a metaphor grounded in imperialistic practice, whereby the seekers of utopia deplete one desired territory only to fix their desires on another? When considered a century later, the ironies and ambiguities of Wilde's 1891 essay in defense of socialism seem to proliferate rather than to resolve themselves in view of a world map whose boundaries are at the present moment radically protean. But are the shifting maps of history relevant to deciphering what the literary utopia attempts or achieves? And even assuming an affirmative answer, how does one measure the distance or proximity of these domains?

Negotiating the narrow divide between idealism and ideology in utopian discourse is nowhere more pressing (or more perilous) than in the attempt of contemporary critical practice to get a fix on the genre in the early modern period. Recent readers, no longer content to treat utopia as a straightforward social blueprint, generally agree that utopia constitutes a complex textual practice enmeshed in a web of historical contingencies to which it cannot but draw attention even as it struggles criteria.[2] Neither diachronic nor synchronic approaches to utopia seem to yield the unified definition on which all can agree.

Complicating any definition of the proper domain of utopia is the matter of utopian reproduction and the peculiar way in which utopia functions as a literary genus. More's *Utopia* inaugurated a novel form that was widely imitated and quoted. Yet, ironically, perhaps the most reliable feature of subsequent utopian texts (or, for that matter, dystopian texts) is an explicit or implicit rejection of the model offered by every other utopia. Each utopian fiction enacts a deliberate revision and reworking of its predecessors to establish a new model commonwealth in a new site, generally declaring all other utopias mere dreams and fancies in the process. By the same token, literary quotations that assimilate previously established utopias almost invariably empty them of what we might regard as their utopian content. Thus, for example, by incorporating Utopian geography into the literary landscape of *Pantagruel*, Rabelais renders null in the process its utopian function—which is, of course, precisely the point of its inclusion.[3] Robert Burton's "personal utopia" in *The Anatomy of Melancholy* follows the utopian paradigm of rejecting all others' utopian visions; however, instead of asserting the reality of his utopia, Burton arrogates the utopian pattern entirely to its patron by limiting its social efficacy to a completely subjective realm: "I will yet, to satisfy and please myself, make an Utopia of mine own, a New Atlantis, a poetical commonwealth of mine own, in which I will freely domineer, build cities, make laws, statutes, as I list myself. And why may I not?"[4] The ensuing catalog of the efforts of Plato, More, Andreae, Campanella, and Bacon deliberately trivializes Burton's own utopia, as well as those he names, by reiterating those links that utopia must suppress—that is, its purely literary origins and ontology. Echoing the conclusion of More's *Utopia*, Burton asserts that "utopian parity is a kind of government to be wished for rather than effected" (101). In this context, however, such quotation debilitates rather than replicates utopia as genre, even as it ironically discredits utopia by the authority of the original.

These examples should not, of course, be taken to suggest that satiric inversion is utopia's undoing. Utopia's intimate connections to satire have an ancient history—indeed, a prehistory—whose origins Robert C. Elliot traces to Saturnalian rituals.[5] Darko Suvin observes that utopia "takes up and refunctions the ancient *topos* of *mundus inversus:* utopia is a formal inversion of significant and salient aspects of the author's world which has as its purpose or telos the recognition that the author (and reader) truly live in an axiologically inverted world."[6] Insofar as utopia is always already inverted, the relation between utopia and dystopia cannot be readily described as inversion or opposition. As Alistair Fox and others have pointed out, More's *Utopia* serves as the prototype for both genres.[7] Even texts that divide much more clearly between earnest utopian reform and cynical dystopian satire not only share a critical posture with respect to the old world, but also often employ the same formal patterns, framing devices, and themes as well.

Clearly, whatever we recognize and distinguish as "utopian" does not inhere exclusively—or even reliably—in its formal design. James Holstun has argued that utopia can be understood "as simultaneously a literary form, a political rhetoric, and a social practice."[8] To demonstrate Utopia's extraliterary impact, Holstun points to Vasco de Quiroga's attempt to bring Utopia's social design into actual practice as a way of organizing the conquered Indian population of New Spain. Holstun argues persuasively that even if this early modern project of social engineering is a "misreading" of More, de Quiroga's hospital pueblos cannot be excluded from "the history of utopia proper," despite the bias of those who view "utopian practice" as a "contradiction in terms" (8–9).

The very elusiveness and expansiveness of utopia have inspired a number of utopian compounds, the utopian "dream," "impulse," "mode," "ideal," "spirit," and so forth, which describe utopia as the manifestation of some deeper structure, behavior, or human need. Yet even these broad and seemingly inclusive definitions of utopia often lead directly into the heart of specific disciplinary interests (literary, historical, psychological, sociological, political, philosophical, or theological, to name the principal fields), whose purview is methodologically "interested" and determined.

There is, finally, a more fundamental problem in defining utopia than the difficulty of tracing the descent of the genre or developing a definition expansive enough to embrace all that utopia *has* meant. The problem, rather, derives from the premise that the *true* definition of utopia governs what it *should* mean now, historically, and in the future. The slippage from descriptive to prescriptive definitions is endemic to utopian scholarship of every stripe; and, indeed, the history of utopia's uses makes this confusion difficult to avoid. The establishment of an ideal definition is itself a utopian construction that covertly polices its borders by displacing its own negative (or dystopian) "other" onto those utopian fictions that it rejects.

The regulation of utopia according to ethical criteria has generally followed a paradoxical protocol. The "false" utopia is alternately deemed (a) an impossible fancy, or (b) an all-too-plausible social (political, historical) nightmare. Conversely, the "true" utopia offers (a) the unattainable ideal toward which we must perpetually strive, or (b) the realistic end of all human struggle. These twinned, if mutually exclusive, alternatives have generally been taken as a sign of the eternal relevance of utopia as promise or as warning. Nonetheless, even the most unabashedly ahistorical evaluations of utopia (or dystopia) must necessarily vacillate between the antipodal positions of historical impossibility and historical imminence. One simply cannot think utopia without measuring it against history. And yet the archaeology of utopia has produced a wealth of contradictory evidence about its historical situation.

Nowhere in History

It is perhaps unsurprising that both Marxist and new historicist critics—working out of those contemporary critical practices most explicitly committed to reading literature against history—have been interested in reading Utopia "historically." What is less immediately clear is how or why the literary utopia came to serve not simply as one form among many available for reading history but as a privileged form, or even a methodological paradigm. Recent critical claims for the paradigmatic function of the utopian genre as a mode of history-making are particularly intriguing, as the same utopian texts have been enlisted to illustrate very different historical allegories. Indeed, utopia seems *peculiarly* susceptible to an extraordinary range of incommensurable characterizations—from radical social critique to ideologically entrenched exercise. Utopia remains at once transparent and opaque. Its engagement with history is taken to be self-evident, while the effects of that engagement elude measure.

Utopian fiction, perhaps most often characterized historically as ahistorical (static, escapist, and so on), would seem to offer an unlikely focus of intense historicist scrutiny, even for those who would heed Fredric Jameson's rallying cry, "Always historicize!"[9] It has not, however, been regarded as innocent that utopia's invention (or rediscovery) by More coincides with the birth of capitalism and the dawning of an age of colonial expansionism even by readers who succeed in avoiding the grosser anachronisms of reading *Utopia* backward against a history it can only dimly anticipate. Several of *Utopia*'s most salient features—its narrative of discovery, its secular rationalization of the social order, its attack on greed and the devastation of the landed peasantry—all announce the text as an important commentary on contemporary events and models of inquiry. Yet it is difficult to avoid tautological proofs when "demonstrating" the degree to which More's originary *Utopia* and its literary descendants reflect or deflect, anticipate or produce history. Underlying recent attempts to locate utopia in history is the often unexamined question of what counts as historical evidence, or even what counts as history—a particularly vexing problem in tracing connections between utopian texts and the sociopolitical context they are variously assumed to escape, to challenge, to idealize, or to disguise.

The notion that utopia is either a mimetic or a prophetic practice has clearly fallen out of favor. We no longer expect academic readers, at least, to use these texts to argue for the existence of a lost Atlantis, no matter how enduring such representations are in popular genres. Nonetheless, reading utopia against history has always necessarily and logically depended on reading *literally,* whether history is invoked to verify or debunk utopia's content or to assess the complex operations or efficacy of utopian representation. For their part, utopian texts do nothing to discourage literal readings; indeed, they demand them, whether such readings are topical, anachronistic, or proleptic. To read utopia literally, according to the "sensus historicus," is to read critically, to measure the word against the world.

The historical relationship between history and utopia has reflected not only the vicissitudes of the literary genre but also the history of history as a philosophical practice and a critical discipline. For Hegel, utopia, as the resolution of historical struggle, was not so much unimaginable as it was unnarratable. History's dynamism and utopian stasis were not antithetical in any productive dialectical sense but, rather, served as mutually exclusive principles. Where utopia was, history was not: "The History of the World is not a theatre of happiness. Periods of happiness are blank pages in it."[10] Despite the optimism of Hegel's rationalist universal history, his theory of social evolution and the continual process of self-transformation and self-transcendence in the realization of the "World-Spirit" or *Geist* emphasizes progress as/in struggle. Paradoxically, the teleological emphasis of Hegel's idealism made the utopian principle expressed by and in *Geist* both the ends and the end of history.

To follow the development of history as a discipline is to trace the permutations of its anti-utopian bias. As Hayden White has argued, the development of a historical method, conceived of as objective and empirical, to replace a philosophy of history, conceived of as metaphysical, opposed "a properly disciplined historical consciousness to utopian thinking in all its forms (religious, social, and political)."[11] Not only did this new historical consciousness "make realism effectively identical with anti-utopianism," but it also required what White terms the "rigorous de-rhetoricization" of historical thinking so that history might be clearly distinguished from fiction (65). The paradox here, of course, is that the anti-utopian, anti-rhetorical bias of traditional history led directly to its most "utopian" aspects, making it an article of faith that history might be transparent, objective, and without or above politics. The historicism outlined by Ranke in the nineteenth century declared that the objective of history was representing the past as it really was, claiming (if not always achieving) a rigorous scientific model for the discipline. More recent "historicisms," no less committed, it should be said, to getting the story straight, have pointed out the inherently fictive or imaginative construction of all narrative history. But the new historicist (not entirely new) emphasis on the rhetorical construction of history has inverted the emphasis rather than disturbed the traditional antithetical relationship between history and utopian thinking outlined since the early nineteenth century. Where the new historicism has regarded traditional history's "utopian" aspiration toward a perfect objectivity and transparency as a species of ideological occlusion, utopia has been held up, or exposed, as the "repressed" of history, a false front cloaking (and alternately disclosing) a dark secret. Utopia as such does not lie within history; rather, it gives the lie to history.

The persistence of this construction of the antithetical relationship between history and utopia in the philosophy of history since Hegel, and most famously and influentially worked out by Marx, has had the enduring effect of obscuring utopia's intimate links with early modern historicisms. Recent criticism has seized on the English literary utopia as a site for working out England's imperial ambitions or anxieties, although it has not always attended to the importance of the utopian locus for working out theories of historical transformation, from which such ambitions or anxieties would derive. Theoretical satisfaction has continued to depend on reading utopia *against* history (as its dialectical double) rather than reading utopia itself as a commentary on historical process and methodology. The concern of this book is to consider history not as the answer to or antithesis of utopia but as a question explicitly posed by and in Renaissance utopian fiction. My interest here is to examine the problem of history as it is raised by three early modern authors *within* their utopian fictions.

Utopia in the sixteenth and seventeenth centuries, I would like to argue, is best understood not as a self-reflexive retreat from history or a self-annihilating exposure of it but as a critical practice investigating the historical subject in the interrogative mode. I begin with the premise that utopian fictions, by their very nature as figurative attempts to re-form the world-as-it-is, necessarily dramatize historical crisis. I wish to argue further, however, that historical crisis serves not simply as the backdrop or context of utopian fiction but as a mode of representation. The historical crisis that the literary utopia represents is, in short, a crisis of representation. To put it another way, utopia, to be effective either as a narrative or model, must show how history is made up—in the double sense of "constituted" and "fictionalized"—in order to show how it can be made over. This concern was not restricted to early modern utopian authors. Although history as a discipline or method had attempted to distinguish itself from poetry since Aristotle at least, it was a commonplace in the Renaissance to argue that history had emerged from, and continued to be indebted to, poetic forms. History's links with grammar, rhetoric, moral philosophy, ethics, and politics were even more clear and suggest other disciplinary connections with utopian discourse. Even if history would inevitably distinguish itself from fiction (utopian or otherwise) by its claims to represent actual events and persons, it is important to remember that virtually all defenses of historical narratives held verisimilitude as useful or desirable in direct proportion to its ability to inspire, instruct, warn, or otherwise change the future behavior of men.

This book fouses on the models for historical transformation engaged and revised by three early modern utopias: Thomas More's *Utopia*, Francis Bacon's *New Atlantis,* and Margaret Cavendish's *Description of a New World Called the Blazing World (Blazing World)*. My interest is not in reading utopia *against* history where history serves as utopia's factual base or extratextual datum. I propose, rather, to investigate utopia's investment in, and enactment of, historical process and method, for it is only in understanding how More, Bacon, and Cavendish engage and revise the textual models for historical transformation available to them that we can begin to assess their specific narrative strategies for mediating between fiction and reform.[12]

Rather than attempt to measure the ability or failure of utopian discourse to dismantle or promote narrowly defined ideological agendas, I would like to take the discussion of utopian method and ideology to another register altogether. It strikes me that the methodologies that receive the least attention in the debates about utopia are those expressed, explored, and revised in the fictions themselves. So that while utopia has with increasing frequency been taken as a figure for history in which history serves as the absent referent, the representation or figuration of history within these early modern texts has gone largely unexamined. If utopia is for More an art, for Bacon a science, and for Cavendish a performance, this will have everything to do with the methodological preoccupations and prejudices out of which each of their texts is produced. And in all three texts, the emphasis on method pertains as much to the procedures of exposition and persuasion as to the procedures under investigation and inquiry. Bacon claims in *Advancement of Learning* that "knowledge. . . . ought to be delivered and intimated, if it were possible, in the same method wherein it were invented." The concession "if it were possible" has provocative implications for the structure of the *New Atlantis,* which offers the imaginative locus of the seamless congruence of the invention and the delivery of knowledge.

Each of these utopias is constructed as a liminal state, situated somewhere beyond the boundaries of knowledge in the very moment of discovery, explication, and potential application. The utopian voyage will necessarily traverse the distance (and ultimately realign the relation) between ideology and fantasy as the reader is directed to locate himself or herself in these texts, which deliberately refuse exact location. More, Bacon, and Cavendish are, nonetheless, vitally interested in imagining the possibility of intellectual traffic back and forth between Utopia and Europe, an exchange that is understood by each of these authors to transform both places. I propose, then, to examine the crises of method that drive and constrain More, Bacon, and Cavendish to figure utopia.

Because utopian writing offers itself as the imaginary solution to the crisis that informs and impels it, this crisis often turns up missing as the obvious content of utopian writing. In the chapters that follow, I discuss how new historicist, Marxist, and feminist criticisms have variously constructed this conspicuous absence and supplemented it with different theories of (or assumptions about) history, consequently producing very different readings of utopia. My concern, then, is to look at and begin to differentiate between all the different kinds of history-making involved, both in the early modern utopian texts and in the theories that struggle to register and account for their engagement with history.

By taking every reading of utopia to be as historically symptomatic as the literary production it assesses, this book incorporates a dual focus, integrating readings of three English Renaissance utopias with an analysis of the history and politics of reading utopia. The very invisibility of early modern utopian constructions of history may begin to suggest the degree to which they relate to and impinge on the narrative structure(s) of history assumed by critical theory today.

The provisional history I offer here, tracing utopia's shifting location in the historical imagination, begins by foregrounding the complex dialectical relationship of utopian writing to utopian reading in recent critical practice. Chapter 1 focuses on two of *Utopia*'s most famous readers, Stephen Greenblatt and Fredric Jameson, to discuss why and how new historicist and Marxist criticism has seized on the literary utopia as a paradigm for reading historically.

Chapters 2 and 3 examine More's *Utopia* as a humanist paradigm for historical revision. Focusing on the most concrete assertions of *Utopia*'s status as humanist historical document, these chapters treat in turn two of the text's accompanying figures: the map of Utopia and the Utopian alphabet. The woodcut map by Ambrosius Holbein, and the alphabet attributed to Peter Giles, along with the prefatory letters by some of the most renowned humanists of the era, serve as "evidence" (however archly offered) of the existence of Utopia. But these "documents" raise in turn the question of the best way in which Utopia is to be represented, and whether that representation is best understood as a project of historical recovery or as the exploration of a history that still remains to be charted out. This tension between reading backward against origin or forward against performance is staged throughout More's text. I pay particular attention to those passages in *Utopia* that represent the crisis of historical transformation brought about by moments of cultural contact.

Chapter 4 argues that the revisionist history of Francis Bacon's *New Atlantis* reconstructs rival historiographical traditions by combining the models offered by universal history and civil history. Although the religious idiom of the *New Atlantis* has generally been regarded as an anachronistic embarrassment or pietistic window dressing, in fact, the *New Atlantis* explicitly offers itself as fulfillment of prophecy and seems to base its scientific authority in miracles. And it is only, I argue, by taking quite seriously the construction of Bacon's text as a kind of parable that we can begin to answer the most basic questions about the form and function of history in this utopia.

The final chapter turns to Margaret Cavendish's *Blazing World*. By tracing Cavendish's attempt to rewrite the historical positioning of the female subject against the long history of Cavendish's reception, I want to outline the complex interaction between Cavendish's poetics of history and the history of feminist revisionism. Although *The Blazing World* has been revived and read principally as a feminist utopia, it has not always been legible as either "feminist" or as "utopian." It is the intersection of these terms in contemporary critical practice that I am particularly interested in exploring. Cavendish has been treated as an ambiguous champion of female rights, as her conservative royalist politics made her a passionate defender of traditional hierarchies and put her at odds with the utopian social fantasies of the English Revolution. Her royalist sympathies notwithstanding, it was the Civil War that provided the context for her allegorized refiguring of gendered hierarchies. *The Blazing World* is fraught with such contradictions, affecting both its production and its reception. This suggests a double crisis for feminist reconstructions of history that can be traced from the seventeenth century to the present.

It is important to make distinctions between the various historicisms suggested by early modern and current critical practice and history as extratextual datum, although the intersections between these are necessarily complex and dialectical. My intention here, however, is to seize the inconsistencies and account for them rather than posit a unified field of "history" against which these texts are read or corroborated. Seeing history as alternately produced by (or residing in) the copia of language, the positivism of science, or the transformative malleability of performance can be read not just backward against More, Bacon, and Cavendish, respectively, but forward against the various strategies of reading, recovery, and revision embedded in the historicizing impulses of current literary theory. This is the double vision that produces even as it annihilates all those hauntingly familiar and brave new worlds.

Chapter One

Praxis Makes Perfect:
Utopia and Theory

History is probably our myth. It combines what can be thought, the "thinkable," and the origin, in conformity with the way in which a society can understand its own working.

—MICHEL DE CERTEAU, *The History of Writing*

Utopia meets history, in the terms described here by de Certeau, at the border of the "thinkable." Both are social myths whose operations mutually depend on the ability of narrative to articulate and obscure their operations if they are to be effective—that is, to transcend their mythic origins. But how are we to read myths that would not, ideally, be taken as such? Hayden White has described the function of historical narratives in terms that might as easily apply to utopian narratives, arguing that "rather than regard every historical narrative as mythic or ideological in nature, we should regard it as allegorical, that is, as saying one thing and meaning another" (45). As allegories of history, poised at the boundary of what has been thought and can be thought, utopian fictions call on all our exegetical ingenuity and sustain a variety of often seemingly incommensurate interpretations. It is certainly worthy of notice, however, that whereas More's slender *Utopia* has supported a vast amount of criticism and commentary, the *New Atlantis* and *The Blazing World* have, until quite recently, generated relatively little critical commentary, albeit for quite different reasons. The *New Atlantis* has, historically, been treated as a transparent text and read quite literally against the Enlightenment history it was seen to anticipate, or even, in part, to produce. By contrast, *The Blazing World* was deemed, by those few who were acquainted with it, an opaque text, inevitably private in its fantastic visions, and therefore quite unreadable.

It is not, however, a coincidence that these two texts, for all their differences, have recently attracted a great deal of attention at just the critical moment when the study of literature has turned to historicism to enlarge the domain of both its authorized materials and its methodological procedures. Paradoxically, the *New Atlantis* and *The Blazing World* are recoverable as literary only at the moment that they are fully historicized. But if historicism's retextualization and allegorization of history brings these texts back into view, it has tended to absorb them within larger narrative structures of history for which they serve as illustrations or, conversely, to treat utopia as the inassimilable material of narrative history. Thus these texts continue to be read alternately as historically prophetic or unrealizable fantasies, destined in the bracing clarity of hindsight to produce the history they would describe (the *New Atlantis*), or to fail in the attempt (*The Blazing World*), rather than as allegories of history that engage and challenge contemporary rhetorical constructions of historical process. In other words, utopian fictions are read as historical effects of the allegoresis of history (that is, history as willful fiction as opposed to the "will to truth"), not as complex commentaries on historical method.

In this chapter I consider how More's *Utopia,* anomalous as it is, has come to be considered such an important and exemplary text for the theoretical elaboration of literature's relationship to history. Focusing on two classic studies of utopian discourse by Fredric Jameson and Stephen Greenblatt, I explore *Utopia's* historical location by and within theory. What I find most interesting about Jameson's Marxist and Greenblatt's new historicist readings of *Utopia* is, on the one hand, their mutual attraction to this text as a paradigm for reading history and, on the other, their diametrically opposed analyses of how utopia reveals or produces historical process. Yet despite the striking differences in their readings, both Jameson and Greenblatt rely on the feature of More's *Utopia least* relevant to other utopian texts of the early modern period, including those treated in this study; that is, *Utopia's* paradoxical frame that structures this text around lexical, semantical, and rhetorical contradictions; double negatives; and logical impasses. Nonetheless, *Utopia's* ability to make itself disappear, to annul its own arguments logically and rhetorically are taken as its most paradigmatic and symptomatic traits by these historicizing critics. Indeed, both Jameson's and Greenblatt's theoretical models rely on the way this text draws attention to and cancels out its very ficticity; it is *Utopia* as nowhere that allows the contours of history to stand in relief. Neither context nor subtext, *Utopia* becomes in such readings un-textual, a-textual, historicity's *anti*-text. But this is indeed to cancel out one of Tudor humanism's most profoundly and copiously intertextual documents, as I will argue in the chapters on More. The generic malleability and prodigious intertextuality of utopian discourse, its flexibility and numerous transformations with respect both to form and content, are features that continue to be overlooked both in accounts that deplore utopian fiction as static and fixed somewhere outside of history and in those readings that chart utopia's shifting course as the mirror of history. But it is history's emergence in the early modern period as a self-conscious and rhetorically inflected interpretive practice that can most illuminate the complex and shifting procedures of utopian discourse, whose origins share with history both a temporal and conceptual horizon.

I propose that we move beyond constructing utopian discourse as a necessarily negative hermeneutic to consider the generativity of utopian discourse, the way in which every reading of utopia inevitably participates in the genre by offering not simply an interpretation but a new utopian document produced out of and responsive to its own historical moment. I am asking not that we forget the history of utopia's situation as the antithesis of history but that we remember the history (and the philosophy of history) that produced that relation. My goal here, therefore, is not so much to argue against Jameson's and Greenblatt's brilliant, productive, and historically significant essays but, rather, to tease out their historical allegories as utopian exercises in and of themselves—an assessment I offer both as warning and as praise.

Louis Marin's *Utopiques: Jeux d'espace* (translated in English as *Utopics: Spatial Play*) has been one of the most important and influential contemporary theoretical investigations of utopian discourse.[1] Fredric Jameson's widely read review article of Marin's book, "Of Islands and Trenches: Neutralization and the Production of Utopian Discourse," extended as well as responded to Marin's argument that the utopian text be understood "as a determinate type of *praxis* rather than as a specific code of representation."² Marin's and Jameson's work offers a dynamic and transformative model for utopian studies; however, it is interesting to note that the transformative properties and ultimately positive value of *Utopia* are linked somewhat paradoxically to its "neutralization," a process described by Marin as "the empty—historically empty—place of the historical resolution of a contradiction" (xiii). Marin argues that because utopia is by necessity written and imagined within the very discourse it criticizes, it is able to point to a reconciliation of contradictions only somewhere beyond its own. Utopia is "seized and shot through with the category of time," but history is, finally, the absent term to which the utopian figure can only gesture (xxi). Marin will take pains, however, to distinguish "neutralized" utopic discourse from the fiction of neutrality, "the ideological trick played by institutions propped up by class rule," and from the fiction of a text "freed from society as it is historically and geographically positioned. . . . Rather, this neutral is the span between true and false, opening within discourse a space discourse cannot receive. It is a third term but a supplementary third term, not synthetic" (7). Jameson's review articulates Marin's poststructuralist model of utopia within an explicitly Marxist frame, and he points both to the period of nascent capitalism that situates More's text and to Marin's Nanterre seminar in May of 1968, which provided both an occasion and a content for Marin's reconsideration of the utopian impulse.³

For Jameson, however, the ultimate value of Marin's model is not in understanding it as a historically articulated or situated reading of *Utopia,* but rather in seizing it as a method for producing history. In elaborating Marin's notion of neutralization Jameson declares that "to understand Utopian discourse in terms of neutralization is indeed precisely to propose to grasp it as a process, as energeia, enunciation, productivity, and implicitly or explicitly to repudiate that more traditional and conventional view of Utopia as sheer representation, as the 'realized' vision of this or that ideal society or social ideal" (6). Such corrections of idealist readings of *Utopia* open the possibility for a critical study of utopian method or process and very much link the projects of Marin and Jameson. But Jameson will most depart from More's method when he seems most to embrace it, particularly at the point at which he severs Marin's model from its point of departure and its principal point of reference: "So far we have been content to grasp neutralization as something like an objective process in its own right, as an 'event' that happens to a preexisting structure, or better still, as a restructuration that

takes place through the text itself. But of course this is itself only a figure of speech, and looked at more rigorously what we have been calling
'neutralization' is a feature not of the text itself, but rather of our
(Marin's) model of the text" (87).

Understanding neutralization finally as "only a figure of speech,"
when applied *to Utopia,* but as a real feature discovered in Marin's theoretical elaboration suggests a paradoxical relation between the rhetoric
and the semiology of the utopian model, for it allows Jameson to trace a
movement from reified structure now associated with "the text itself" to
a kind of rhetorical openness found in the utopian model, existing
somewhere beyond the limits and structure of the text it analyzes and
productive of a new set of figurative relations.[4] Jameson's figure/feature
distinction cannot be stable, however, because, according to the model,
the full scope and range of praxis can be present only in a figurative
sense. The notion of utopian practice remains, in Jameson's account,
suspended in a kind of limbo between fiction and function. Thus, despite the paradigm function of More's *Utopia,* understanding "Utopian
method" will, in the end, become identified as the ability "to grasp the
spirit of Marin's method" (98). And it would seem that the method for
writing and for reading utopia are confused at precisely the moment
when the neutralized and untheorized Utopia threatens to remerge with
ideology: "This absence of a theoretical discourse yet to be developed,
this figural anticipation, in the form of a blank or gap, of what could not
in the very nature of things be conceptualized, is for Marin the very
place of origin and inauguratory impulse of the genre itself" (97). Or, as
Marin puts it in a passage translated and quoted by Jameson, "Utopian
discourse is the one form of ideological discourse that has anticipatory
value of a theoretical kind: but it is a value which can only appear as
such after theory itself has been elaborated, that is to say, subsequent to
the emergence of the material conditions for the new productive forces"
(97). Here, working out of the blank space of utopian figuration, the
true utopian is discovered to be the critic, the one who can articulate a
theory for the historically prophetic (hence premature) text.[5] What is described as "praxis" quickly reconfigures itself into a new kind of graphic,
textually productive model (designed by Marx, Greimas, Marin, Jameson
et al.), suggesting the intimate connections between reading and "mapping" models for social transformation.

Yet it is clear that such substitutions are neither illegible nor irrelevant,
for as Mannheim suggests in his manifesto for a sociology of knowl-

edge, *Ideology and Utopia,* the dialectical relation of utopia to ideology inheres not only in texts but also in readers:

> The very attempt to determine the meaning of the concept "utopia" shows to what extent every definition in historical thinking depends necessarily upon one's perspective, i.e. it contains within itself the whole system of thought representing the position of the thinker in question and especially the political evaluations which lie behind this system of thought. . . . It is no accident that an observer who consciously or unconsciously has taken a stand in favor of the existing and prevailing social order should have such a broad and undifferentiated concept of the utopian; i.e. one which blurs the distinction between absolute and relative unrealizability.[6]

The role of perspective—political and historical—in the construction of utopia clearly pertains both to the conception of the utopian thinker and to its reception by any particular reader, although arguably this is true of the construction of every text and every reading. Nevertheless, despite Mannheim's assumption that there is a proper perspective from which the difference between "absolute and relative unrealizability" becomes clear, utopia has, historically, remained an unstable and ambiguous genre not only for those who endorse "the prevailing social order" but also for those vitally interested in imagining a method of cultural critique, political reform, or social transformation.

The Marxist rejection of utopian socialism and its differentiation from true scientific socialism, articulated by Engels in "Socialism: Utopian and Scientific" (1880), offers the preeminent example of utopia's historical reversibility. It is of particular interest, as Ernst Bloch's Marxist redemption of the utopian in *The Spirit of Utopia* (1918) and also in his masterwork, *The Principle of Hope* (written 1938–47), has made Marxist criticism one of the few places that utopian thought is defended in modern or contemporary critical practice.[7]

It is interesting to note, however, that some of utopia's most suspicious contemporary readers tend also to be identified with the left end of the politico-critical spectrum.[8] In general, the new historicism's emphasis on the ability of the dominant ideology to subsume, co-opt, or contain almost every attempt at revision or subversion would necessarily make of most utopian authors ideological apologists or unwitting collaborators. As Stephen Greenblatt puts it in an inverted paraphrase of

Kafka's remarks to Max Brod on the possibility of hope, "There is sub-version, no end of subversion, only not for us."[9]

The term "utopian" takes on an unambiguously negative value in Greenblatt's essay "Towards a Poetics of Culture," in which he outlines his own historical method.[10] In this essay, Greenblatt offers a critique of both Jameson's Marxist and Jean-François Lyotard's poststructuralist analysis of the relation between art and society. Greenblatt argues that, for Jameson, capitalism serves as the origin of "repressive differentia-tion," whereas for Lyotard it serves as the source of "monological total-ization." Nonetheless, he concludes that for both critics "theoretical satisfaction here seems to depend upon a utopian vision that collapses the contradictions of history into a moral imperative" (5). The charge "utopian" thus carries with it the familiar polarities of the failed utopia: both the frivolously impractical (the inability to reckon with "complex historical movement in a world without paradisal origins or chiliastic ex-pectations" [6]) and the dangerously dictatorial (the moral imperatives of totalizing accounts of history).[11]

Yet despite the suspicion with which Greenblatt treats the utopian in-flections of these theoretical positions, More's *Utopia* serves for him, as for Jameson, as a kind of foundation text. Both admire this text, and both base their admiration, in large part, on its paradoxical and self-contradictory structure—features of the Utopia that, as I suggested in the beginning of this chapter, most limit its use as a model text for other unironical Renaissance utopian texts (such as Bacon's and Cavendish's).

As the subject of the first chapter of his seminal study *Renaissance Self-Fashioning,* More serves as a paradigm for Greenblatt's influential notion of Renaissance self-fashioning.[12] Despite his position as an am-bitious and worldly servant of Henry VIII, More escapes the role of ideological apologist only by a painful and self-conscious act of "self-cancellation," the existential inversion of Marin's notion of neutralization that can offer no similar historical redemption. Yet More is potent as a subject for Greenblatt, just as his *Utopia* is for Jameson, precisely for being situated in an underdetermined historical moment. "There are pe-riods," argues Greenblatt, "in which the relation between intellectuals and power is redefined, in which the old forms have decayed and new forms have yet to be developed" (36). *Utopia*'s author, if not the text it-self, is set in this temporal blank space at the vortex of historical crisis.[13]

For an illustration of the complex procedures of self-fashioning/self-cancellation and More's "profound alienation from his society, from the greater part of his acquaintance, from himself" (16), Greenblatt turns to Hans Holbein's painting *The Ambassadors*. The juxtaposition of text and painting is introduced by a singularly slippery passage: "To grasp the precise character of what I have called More's estrangement, we might compare it with the mood evoked by Holbein's famous work 'The Ambassadors,' . . . painted in London two years before More's execution" (17). Leave aside, for the moment, that these two works date to extremely different points in More's career, that they are separated by the birth of the Protestant Reformation, and that they belong to different artists working in distinct media, Greenblatt leaves quite ambiguous even the figurative relation he is trying to establish between the two. How are we in fact to "grasp the precise character" from an evocation of a "mood"? After his elegant reading of the irreconcilable rift between the symbolic poise represented by the French ambassadors, Jean de Dinteville and Georges de Selve, and the disruptive force of the anamorphic death's head, Greenblatt explains his juxtaposition as follows, "I justify this long discussion of 'The Ambassadors' on the ground that it plunges us, with the sensuous immediacy and simultaneity that only a painting can achieve, into the full complexity of More's estrangement and the richness of his art. The world of Dinteville and Selve was More's world" (21). But the sensuous immediacy of painting is precisely what most separates the two works. The painting offers two perspectives only— one established by the ambassadors and their array of worldly instruments and the other by the anamorphic skull that slashes across the patterned floor. For one image to be legible, the other must be annulled. Indeed, the poignancy of the image depends on the choice that this fact of perception forces, as the viewer is "moved"—in a very literal sense— to choose between the two views. It is precisely the function of the painting's anamorphism that requires these perspectives to be either/or; they cannot be both/and. More's *Utopia*, however, has a much more complexly modulated surface. All perspectives are partial and simultaneous; none predominates, and none is entirely consistent.

Greenblatt nicely observes of the Holbein painting that the French ambassadors have in their possession "the instruments—both literal and symbolic—by which men bring the world into focus, represent it in proper perspective." He contextualizes this observation by noting that the Renaissance in general and Neoplatonism in particular invested perspective with more than technical significance: "the power to map, mirror, or represent the world bore witness to the spark of the divine in man" (18). But such technical ability suggests no less the power to meditate on the differences between the operations of abstraction, reversal or mimesis inherent in these triple powers to map, to mirror, and to represent the world. The composite Utopia, by including all three activities and yet exposing any number of discrepancies between them, suggests that what is at stake in the choice of the tools for representation is nothing less than the shape of the world produced. Technique is much more than an issue of style, and comparisons between techniques may point out the limitations of analogy by the very ingenuity that enables them. The entire "system" of *Utopia* is built on the principle of analogy and the complex process of discrimination, which renders comparison both useful and suspect. Utopia is and is not like Europe. It takes a slanted but not a monocular view. Utopian perspective offers neither a consistently inverted nor a coherently corrected view. Every point of comparison requires a sequence of subtle adjustments. The differences cannot be defined as true vs. false, literal vs. figurative, letter vs. spirit, material vs. spiritual, reality vs. appearance, or sense vs. nonsense, although the act of discrimination requires an assessment of the claims of any number of such oppositions.

In *The Art of Describing,* art historian Svetlana Alpers makes some useful distinctions between the perspective techniques employed by southern and northern visual artists, which can shed light on such interdisciplinary cultural connections.[14] She identifies as peculiarly northern the treatment of perspective as a "sum of representations" and "an aggregate of aspects," which she contrasts with the authority of the coherent singular view constructed by the Italian perspective arts (59). Northern Renaissance artists, as she demonstrates, were more preoccupied with the science of optical illusion than with the scientific illusion of perspective.[15] Alpers's distinction between "the northern mode (the world prior to us made visible) and the southern mode (we prior to the world and commanding its presence)" (70) suggests, perhaps, a more useful context than Greenblatt's Neoplatonic connection when considering the perspective tricks of *Utopia,* whose reforming view is characterized more by what is exposed than by what is commanded or proposed.

Greenblatt's reading of the Holbein painting is compelling, but if history is the justification for the juxtaposition, the gap of seventeen years makes it the product of a very different historical moment from that of More's *Utopia.* Finally, he pulls back from theorizing the nature of the connection of text and painting, although making such connections between different modes of cultural production is the trademark of the new historicism. The topos of *ut pictura poesis* displayed in the example of Hans Holbein's *Ambassadors* belongs, of course, as a figurative gesture to Greenblatt rather than More, and it suspends, for the moment, the heuristic crisis it provokes.[16] Furthermore, despite Greenblatt's later expressions of suspicion about the relevance of psychoanalysis as a model for studies of Renaissance subject formation, his study of *Utopia* tends to be more interested in More's individual pathology than in a normative, anthropological paradigm to describe the circulation of self and society, further complicating the domain and function of analogies drawn from such distinct sources.[17] Michel Foucault, for example, discusses psychoanalysis and ethnology together as "sciences of the unconscious"; in concluding his analysis of the human sciences, however, he argues that they have an inverse relation to "historicity."[18]

The modus operandi of history in, on, or through literature is suspended here, as in Jameson's account, somewhere between syntactical juxtapositions and figurative transformations.[19] While both Marxist and new historicist methodologies rely on the interconnectedness of literary and nonliterary cultural productions, the nature and direction of that connection remain a matter of intense debate.[20] From the examples of Jameson and Greenblatt, it becomes clear that an anti-idealist, anti-formalist, ideologically self-suspicious, and historicizing orientation alone does not seem to offer a more unified concept of "the utopian principle," any more than it can guarantee that readings generated under such a banner will escape their own idealizing, ideological, and formalist pitfalls.[21]

The question of utopian praxis and its relation to ideological discourse might, therefore, be more usefully taken as a point of departure than as a critically inflected foregone conclusion. Mannheim has argued that the fictions of utopia (which seek to transform society) and the fictions of ideology (which seek to obscure and therefore stabilize the real conditions of society) are antithetical in nature. His description of their operations suggests, however, that the two impulses are distinguished more by their goals and their immediate relation to authority than by their methods, which mutually depend on the construction and control of social fictions to do their work as well as a willful denial of the limitations of the actual conditions of society. A quick review of the sixteen definitions of ideology collated by Terry Eagleton can further outline the nature of the difficulty in asserting any simple opposition between utopian and ideological thinking, particularly if ideology is alternatively or at once:

> a) the process of production of meanings, signs and values in social life; b) a body of ideas characteristic of a particular social group or class; c) ideas which help to legitimate a dominant political power; d) false ideas which help to legitimate a dominant political power; e) systematically distorted communication; f) that which offers a position for the subject; g) forms of thought motivated by social interests; h) identity thinking; i) socially necessary illusion; j) the conjunction of discourse and power; k) the medium in which conscious social actors make sense of their world; l) action-oriented sets of beliefs; m) the confusion of linguistic and phenomenal reality; n) semiotic closure; o) the indispensable medium in which individuals live out their relationships to a social structure; p) the process whereby social life is converted to a natural reality.[22]

As this list of widely diverging but necessarily incomplete definitions makes clear, ideology does not offer utopia's opposite any more clearly than does dystopia. Like ideology, utopia is susceptible to a number of irreconcilable definitions, some framed in terms of epistemology, some in terms of sociohistorical analysis. The very terms of the debate about the nature of ideology—whether it deals with "ideas of true and false cognition" or "the function of ideas within social life" without respect to their "reality or unreality"—mirrors, rather than inverts, the history of utopian thought.[23]

In his conclusion to *The Political Unconscious,* Jameson argues that "all ideology in the strongest sense, including the most exclusive forms of ruling-class consciousness just as much as that of oppositional or oppressed classes—is in its very nature Utopian" (289). This is an important observation if only because it is the reverse proposition that has come to be regarded as axiomatic. But even if there is a formal and logical symmetry to the assertion that all ideologies are utopian and all utopias are ideological, it would be brutally syllogistic to collapse this into a proposition of identity. For while the similarities in the discursive operations of utopia and ideology suggest why such categories perpetually reverse themselves under the scrutiny of different readers, most readings of utopian fiction (and especially those most committed to showing the mutual implication of utopia and ideology) are built around the principle that one can tell the difference, and that it is worth remarking on.

The new historicist attempt to reckon with the inescapable nature of ideological thinking—the impossibility of an Archimedean point from which to move, or even to judge, one's own historical situation—informs both the new historicism's polemical and its paranoid tendencies. Louis Montrose, in his essay "Renaissance Literary Studies and the Subject of History," declares that as "teachers of a new historical criticism, our first task must be to disabuse students of the notion that history is what's over and done with; to convince them that, on the contrary, history is always now."[24] But the urgency of this self-improving history lesson is haunted by its shadow: the suspicion that one's critical preoccupations are merely academic—produced by and limited to an ephemeral (rather than enduring) institutional authority. Consequently, Montrose suggests in the same essay that the "emergent social/political/historical orientation in literary studies," with its concern about "writing as a mode of *action*," may be "impelled by a questioning of our very capacity for action—by a nagging sense of professional, institutional, and political impotence" (11–12). Alan Liu, noting the frequent appearances of this topos of embarrassed marginality in new historicist criticism, wryly observes that " 'power' is the interpreter's figure for powerlessness" (746).

The difficulty in approaching *Utopia,* the *New Atlantis,* or *The Blazing World* is precisely, however, in locating the relation of these literary artifacts to power. In their figurative strategies, these texts do not obviously enact either carnivalesque contestations of power or ceremonial ratifications of the reigning monarch's sovereignty—the alternatives that serve as the new historicism's governing paradigms. Utopian fiction instead relocates power to a discursive nowhere, where its mechanisms are both reified and revised. Neither the inverted gold standard of the Utopians nor the unabashed absolutism of Cavendish's empress of the Blazing World situates these utopian fictions in any obvious way within the controversies about how literature alternately effects or performs acts of subversion or containment—although they invite, and provide evidence for, both conclusions.

Those who have followed Foucault's analysis of power/knowledge in readings of utopian fiction have often ignored or deliberately modified his historical argument to discover in sixteenth- and seventeenth-century utopian texts a disciplinary regime, a system of surveillance or constraint whose development Foucault himself locates in the eighteenth and nineteenth centuries.[25] But this construction of utopia as anticipatory is in many respects to return utopia to its traditional (if nonetheless anachronistic) "historical" location in the future. And it returns us as well to the problem of deciding whether the significance of utopian discourse is in its ability to anticipate and produce history, or its ability to anticipate and confirm theory.

Of course it would be utopian indeed to argue that the operations of utopia could be assessed somewhere outside of theory. The readings that follow are as much *formed by* as informed by the theoretical concerns I critique here. In this respect, even my critical posture is one entirely provided for by the self-critical imperative of all historical and political criticism interested in interrogating its own ideological underpinnings. Indeed, this study does not offer a retreat from theory but a theoretical interrogtion of what we mean when we talk about history in readings of early modern utopian fiction.

In order to begin, however, it seems necessary to acknowledge the early modern utopias themselves as among the first and most profound theoretical articulations of the problems posed by history—both as an emerging and transforming field of study and as the object of that study. It is particularly the gap between the two opened up by humanist theory and practice that will concern the following chapter on More's originary *Utopia*.

Chapter Two

Mapping Out History
in More's *Utopia*

Methinks it would please any man to look upon a geographical map, *suavi animum delectatione allicere, ob incredibilem rerum varietatem et jucunditatem, et ad pleniorem sui cognitionem excitare* (which insensibly charms the mind with the great and pleasing variety of objects that it offers, and incites it to further study), chorographical, topographical delineations, to behold, as it were, all the remote provinces, towns, cities of the world, and never to go forth of the limits of his study, to measure by the scale and compass their extent, distance, examine their site.

—ROBERT BURTON, *The Anatomy of Meloncholy*

GUIL (leaping up): What a shambles! We're just not getting anywhere.
Ros (mournfully): Not even England. I don't believe in it anyway.
GUIL: What?
Ros: England.
GUIL: Just a conspiracy of cartographers, you mean?

—TOM STOPPARD, *Rosencrantz and Guildenstern Are Dead*

Method and Reform

The controversies surrounding interpretations of *Utopia* from the sixteenth century to the present suggest that Utopia has never been located twice in the same place, nor has there been any kind of consensus as to the grounding of its social, political, moral, or spiritual precepts. Yet consensus is precisely what the insular world of Utopia seems to require as a precondition of its existence, or at least as a condition of its continued existence. The productive ironies generated by the divide between the unresolved debates of Book 1 and the Utopian consensus of Book 2 find their most interesting sources, I argue, in a fundamental ambivalence about the methodological procedures of reform at the heart of the humanist program. The historical situation of *Utopia* captures, without resolving, the divide between the humanists' recovery of history as coherent and verifiable, traceable to its universal origins, and their reinvention of history as a rhetorically open form, drawing on the copia of language arts.[1] That is, *Utopia* does not attempt (or fail) to escape history, but instead offers a map of the uneven topography of humanist historicism.

The analysis of More's utopian method has been variously approached, through close philological and rhetorical analysis,[2] analogues taken from other media,[3] the comparison of *Utopia* to various classical literary and historical models,[4] or, in those examples of greatest interest to this study, through pursuit of the history that produces Utopia as text or genre.[5] Even when they share nothing else, methodological investigations that propose to examine not just what the text means, but how it works, often have in common an analysis dependent on negation (or double negation)—whether in the form of satiric inversion or dialectical "neutralization"—to make sense of this perplexing and self-contradictory text.[6] But strategies of negation, dialectical or not, often end with the same questions with which they begin and do not always help us decipher the local textual paradoxes they point out. The status of such reversals (and reversals of reversals) remains notoriously difficult to map out. The problems become all the more intractable when we must deal with the relation of structure to character in the inclusion of More's voice as the skeptical antiphony to his principal narrator. In the end, to catalog the various textual levels of More's strategy of negation is to illuminate the *effect* of More's method rather than to analyze the nature or ambivalences of a method that generates any number of contradictions.

While I cannot offer any direct path out of this labyrinth, I would like to suggest another way in by consulting as a guide or user's manual perhaps the most intriguing and original contributions by More's humanist collaborators to *Utopia's parerga,* the Utopian map and the Utopian alphabet. Both allow for a useful discussion of the *Utopia's* intertextual method of collaboration as well as a way of charting a functional ambivalence of method both prior to and productive of this text's antipodal inversions. The Utopian map and alphabet are both opposed and complementary. The map represents in miniature the material, concrete shape of the island. It asserts the presence that the punning, oxymoronic utopian names deny. And yet the very shape of Utopia is a cipher formed around its central harbor—a place so dangerous to enter that only native Utopians can negotiate the treacherous rocks at its mouth. It is a place, it would seem, you must be from to be able to get to.

The difficulty in entering Utopia is exacerbated by the fact that we have no utopian guide, but only Raphael Hythlodaeus, the Portuguese philosopher-sailor who acts as the anything-but-transparent mediator between European values and utopian customs. Because any attempt to get to Utopia is possible only through Hythlodaeus—or, more specifically, through More's ability to remember and re-create Hythlodaeus's speech—a fundamental contention between the claims of documentation and the claims of performance, between the historical "facts" and the rhetorically persuasive subject, is built into the very structure of the narrative. When we discover the same tug-of-war writ small in even the most abstracted and impersonal representations of Utopia offered by the map and alphabet, it becomes clear that there is no simple way of dividing the text between these seeming antitheses or privileging one above the other, although this in no way neutralizes the conditions of the contest. The domain of Utopia is, in this respect, peculiarly double in aspect.

It is important to point out from the beginning that whether it is ultimately (or alternately) satiric or earnest in its reforming spirit, More's antipodal *Utopia* is not simply a world turned upside down. All familiar hierarchies and hegemonies remain intact, even where they are most severely challenged. Whereas Erasmus's *Praise of Folly,* the humanist paradoxical encomium with which *Utopia* is most often compared, features a topsy-turvy world ruled by Folly and her inane entourage, *Utopia*'s characters are literally (and figuratively) "men of the world": Peter Giles and Cardinal Morton, two men with whom More had intimate connections; More himself; his pupil, John Clement; and the well-traveled (if fictional) stranger, Raphael Hythlodaeus, who is introduced as a participant in the last three of Amerigo Vespucci's four renowned expeditions to the New World.[7]

Although Hythlodaeus has been to the antipodes and back, his most cutting remarks in Book 1 are quite straightforwardly, and without satiric indirection, heaped upon bad European princes and those who serve them, establishing the business of rule and of service as central preoccupations of the text. And, indeed, such concerns were very preoccupying for More and his fellow humanists, particularly at a point in Henry VIII's reign when men devoted to the new learning enjoyed great prominence, and More himself was off doing the king's business. When Henry VIII first took the throne in 1509, expectations of the young king were distinctly utopian. William Blount, Lord Mountjoy, wrote Erasmus in that year, "Heaven smiles, earth rejoices; all is milk and honey and nectar. Tight-fistedness is well and truly banished. Generosity scatters wealth with unstinting hand. Our king's heart is set not upon gold or jewels or mines of ore, but upon virtue, reputation, and eternal renown."[8] By 1515 the mood was considerably less euphoric, however, and Erasmus would write to Cardinal Raffaele Riario of his disappointed hopes for a Golden Age in England: "I dreamt of an age truly golden and [of] fortunate isles—and then, to quote Aristophanes, 'up I woke.'. . . My other friends, and even the king himself, the parent of the golden age, were soon overtaken by the storms of war and torn from commerce with the Muses."[9]

Yet despite its implicit criticism of Henry's foreign and domestic policy, Book 1's Counsel of Service establishes a more inclusive and self-reflexive diagnostic critique in *Utopia* than, for example, the attack on tyranny offered by More's contemporaneous work, *The History of Richard III*. The very real questions of service lend to the debates of Book 1 a pervasive tenor of humanistic self-evaluation and self-criticism. It is not insignificant (to indulge in More's characteristic litotes) that one of the most prominent scapegoats of Book 1 is a lawyer at Morton's table, as his professional lampooning implicitly indicts More as well.[10] John M. Perlette has pointed out More's double identification with the hanger-on in the digression in Book 1, glossed *"festivus dialogus fratris and morionis,"* in which More is identified linguistically with the "morionus," just as he is identified historically as another "parasitus," who fed at Cardinal Morton's table.[11]

But the self-critical posture suggested by both the structure and diction of More's fabulous *historia* goes further than either hagiographic invocations of More's hair shirt or critical reappraisals of More's deep ambivalence toward his worldly ambitions would immediately suggest. The ethical challenge *Utopia* constitutes need not be considered as principally personal. The text's confident ludic spirit tolerates many more undecidable paradoxes than a work generated by a deep spiritual crisis might reasonably be expected to sustain.

Nonetheless, biographical reconstructions of More's personality and the drama of his late career and martyrdom have cast a long shadow over interpretations of his early work. Christopher Kendrick has described the liberal humanist bias toward "biographism" that privileges More not only as the author but also as the principal subject of *Utopia*. Kendrick represents (and scrutinizes) the presumption of the humanist reader of More with a rhetorical question: "What else could utopia figure but More's quintessential humanity?"[12] The question, however rhetorical, remains: What else indeed? If history is the answer for contemporary criticism, it must be noted that the narrative of More's humanity (whether treated as an encomiastic subject or as an object of hermeneutic suspicion) has never been disentangled from the narrative(s) of history. Kendrick's avowed interest in "marginalizing biography" nonetheless stresses the importance of "situating the biographical object historically," and Greenblatt's study of More's "self-fashioning" is another exemplary study in this mode. But what such corrective, "historicizing" readings sometimes underplay is the remarkable degree to which utopian criticism has *historically* taken history as its principal hermeneutic paradigm. Indeed, even the most romantic accounts of More's life and work, which understand More as the "man for all seasons," substitute "history" (whether hagiographic, universal, or national, the rational expression of Absolute Spirit, or the nightmare from which we hope to awake) for the coherent narrative that *Utopia* so conspicuously fails to supply. History, it must be remembered, is not simply the record of what time has erased; history has often been the instrument of erasure, with its own utopian or dystopian agendas. To measure what has changed in the wake of recent historicist attention to utopia it must be determined what counts as utopian and what counts as historical, even if the ultimate intersection of these two coordinates can only be approached asymptotically.

By arguing that utopian criticism has always been preoccupied with and characterized by historical thinking, I do not simply mean to assert that, like all textual or cultural productions, it cannot but be marked by history. I mean, rather, to point out that utopia has been peculiarly susceptible to symptomatic historical readings precisely because it is structured by the formative yet divided preoccupations of early modern humanist historical thought. If *Utopia* fails to disclose a coherent story in the outline of its 1,760-year history, it is perhaps more useful to attend to the methodological emphasis of the Greek etymology of *historia* as a means of knowing by inquiry as well as an account of one's inquiries. To illuminate *Utopia*'s profound engagement with the humanist historical project, let us turn to the figures from the text's *parerga:* the map and the alphabet.

Figuring Out Utopia

In its first edition, published in Louvain in 1516, and in the third, somewhat revised Basel edition of 1518, More's *De Optimo Reipublicae Statu* or *Utopia* is accompanied by both an alphabet and a map. Fredric Jameson has discussed the dual registers of image and text, description and narration set forth in "the relationship between, and the gap that separates, the map of the imaginary non-place and the verbal *discourse* in which the place and its institutions are recounted" (94). Jameson rightly assimilates both these functions of utopian figuration—description and narration—to the verbal discourse, although he mistakenly makes of this move a kind of default because, he says, "the map is not given as an accompanying plate or illustration bound within the volume, but must rather be reconstructed from the data furnished by Hythloday's account".[13] There is indeed a map, however, as well as an alphabet, provided among the *parerga,* and it is in these graphic representations of Utopia and its language that the tensions Jameson describes are most heightened, and the method for—and relation between—reading and reaching utopia is most brought into question.[14] Neither of these supplementary "texts" is attributed to More, yet between them lies an often overlooked point of entry to the text.[15]

The map, by Ambrosius Holbein, and the alphabet, attributed to Peter Giles—along with the prefatory letters by some of the most renowned humanists of the era—serve as documentary evidence of the existence of Utopia, providing a veritable "romance of fact."[16] But these "documents" raise in turn the question of the best way in which Utopia is to be represented, and whether that representation is best understood as translation and the recovery of original meaning, or as exposition and exploration—that is, as a recovered history or as one that remains to be charted out. These alternate representational strategies have direct bearing on our understanding of More's historical method, which both features and fractures the sometimes uneasy partnership between the philological and rhetorical aspects of the humanist program—that is, between reading backward against origin or forward against performance. Curiously enough, where one might expect the alphabet and the map of Utopia to divide between the domain of grammar and the arena of persuasion and performance, respectively, a dialectic between these modes of representation is very much in play within each utopian figure, as the following readings suggest.

By using the map and the alphabet to trace the intersection of the fiction of self and the fiction of history, I hope to show how the fundamental dilemma in the text's humanist method and utopian procedure comes out of the vexed and yet inextricable relation between these two models for reform and perfection. This reflection on the contradictions implicit in *Utopia*'s method of reform is, I believe, a more fruitful way of approaching the paradox of utopian representation for More and his collaborators than the customary oscillation between oppositions of tone (earnest and satiric) or mode (utopian and dystopian)—oppositions that tend to mask some of the most important motives for the radical unlocatability (dislocation, reallocation) of this particular "Nowhere."

The structure of More's text as a type of paradoxical encomium has allowed readers to establish any number of dualisms between Europe and Utopia, More and Hythlodaeus, fact and fancy, satiric commentary and passionate proposals for reform. But the constitutive dilemma that underlies, underwrites, and ultimately undermines each of these oppositions can be found in the nature of the humanist project that must negotiate that dangerous gap between the historical subject and the affective goals of humanist reform.

Those scholars devoted to the study of *grammatica, rhetorica, poetica, historia,* and *philosophia moralis* and now known collectively as humanists were cursed and blessed with a kind of double vision. This double vision allowed for the great diversity of views among the Italian humanists, and between them and their northern followers, but united them in certain interpretive problems. Their training in and attention to language allowed them to recover history as the gap between cultures, and yet some of the most important of the texts they so painstakingly recovered were used in many cases to authorize a fundamentally ahistorical, rhetorical, and poetical re-presentation of the world. Cicero and

Quintillian would stand as the towering giants in the defense of eloquence and a rhetorically derived vision of composition and reform; but
even the avowed anti-sophist, Plato, became in the hands of the humanists a model for fictionalized dramatic dialogues, both as poetic defenses
and as rhetorical showpieces. Thus Erasmus's eloquent attack on eloquence in Book 2 of *The Antibarbarians* is implicitly an artful platform
for the defense, which, ironically, he never finished.[17]

Despite the compelling motives of eloquence, however, the philological direction of humanist scholarship had, in turn, a measured anti-
rhetorical impact. For although the humanists gave rhetoric pride of
place before logic in the trivium, the debate on the relative merits of
wisdom and eloquence never divided neatly between scholastic
philosophers and humanists, as the famous exchange between Pico
and Ermolao Barbaro makes clear.[18] The humanists' celebrated (or no-
torious) exposures of literary forgeries, of fraudulent attributions and
erroneous dating, were achieved only by resisting the intrinsic persua-
siveness, or ostensible ethical merit, of individual texts and investigating
analytically their linguistic and historical development and transmission.
Petrarch's discovery of the forgery of an Austrian donation, allegedly
made by Caesar to the Hapsburgs; Lorenzo Valla's exposure of the Donation of Constantine, a document on which the papacy grounded its
claims for temporal power (in *Declamatio de falsa credita donatione
Constantini* [1440]); and the scholarship that led Grocyn to maintain in
lectures at St. Paul's that the author of the widely influential *Celestial Hierarchies* could not have been Dionysius the Areopagite were predicated on whole new criteria for assessing the authority of texts that had
been honored for centuries.[19]

While it is important not to confuse the humanists' new sense of the
historical contingencies of the texts they were rereading or recovering
with the philological sciences developed in nineteenth-century Ger-
many, the role of grammar was never easily or entirely assimilated to
rhetoric.[20] Indeed, the frequent role of rhetoric was to efface the historical gaps that philological inquiry uncovered to view. *Utopia* can be
charted as a fictive field in which the encounter between two rival con-
ceptions of history and reform is staged, where the long look back is
conditioned and enabled by its present revision, and the good and
the true must be reckoned with separately to allow for their ultimate
integration.

Mapping Out Utopia

The parerga of the first edition of *Utopia* (Louvain, 1516) includes an anonymously authored woodcut map of the island (Figure 1). This rather crude depiction is replaced in the third edition (Basel, March 1518) by Ambrosius Holbein's more elaborate and decorative version of what is essentially the same map (Figure 2).[21] The choice to include (and improve) the Utopian map situates *Utopia* at an important intersection of new textual and cartographic sources that inspired humanist scholarship across Europe while exciting nationalist designs on the new learning.

Utopia's most obvious contemporary cartographic model is Martin Waldseemüller's *Cosmographiae introductio* published in Saint-Dié in Lorraine in May and September 1507.[22] Waldseemüller's text not only offered the first *mappamundi* (or world map) to depict—however crudely—the New World as such, but it also included the letters of Amerigo Vespucci, whose voyages of discovery serve as the imaginative point of departure for his fictional compatriot and fellow traveler, Raphael Hythlodaeus.[23] Waldseemüller is credited with first naming America for Vespucci, and he pairs a portrait of Vespucci with one of Claudius Ptolemy in the map's margins to illustrate the two greatest influences, ancient and modern, on cosmography.[24] The map's full title makes the two directions of this debt explicit: *Universalis cosmographia secundum Ptholomaei traditionem et Americi Vespucci aliorumque lustrationes* (A Map of the World According to the Tradition of Ptolemy and the Voyages of Americus Vespucius and Others).

More and Holbein were also likely to have been aware of contemporary Italian portolan charts, whose detailed navigational routes included up-to-date information based on firsthand accounts, as well as such geographical speculations as the Islands of the Blessed, Antillia (the seven cities fabled to lie to the west of Ireland), St. Brendan's Island (named for a sixth-century Irish monk who was promised by an angel he would voyage to the earthly paradise), and the mythical Isle of Brazil.[25] For all their impressive accuracy and practical use, the portolan charts, no less than the *mappaemundi,* displayed their reliance on classical and medieval textual authorities (including, among others, Herodotus, Strabo, Pliny, Ptolemy, Isidore of Seville, Mandeville, and Marco Polo) when faced with the uncharted western expanses. The authority conferred by

VTOPIAE INSVLAE FIGVRA

Figure 1. VTOPIAE INSVLAE FIGVRA. Map of *Utopia*. From Thomas More, Utopia (Louvain, 1516). By permission of the Beinecke Rare Book and Manuscript Library, Yale University.

Figure 2. Ambrosius Holbein. *VTOPIAE INSVLAE TABVLA*. Map of Utopia. From Thomas More, *Utopia* (Basel, 1518). By permission of the Beinecke Rare Book and Manuscript Library, Yale University.

tradition, history, and religion, augmented by the empirical evidence supplied by navigators, made the portolan charts powerful rhetorical tools in the hands of explorers seeking patrons. John Cabot was said to have persuaded Henry VII with just such a "caart & othir demonstrations reasonable" to provision a ship in 1498 to search for a Northwest Passage and, en route, "to seeke out, discover, and finde" all land unknown to Christians and to "subdue, occupy and possess . . . the same villages, townes, castles, and firme land so found."[26]

If Hythlodaeus's course to Utopia is difficult to trace on any map, his claim to have traveled with Vespucci on the last three of his four voyages grounds his previous travels in Brazil. The interesting double etymology of Brazil and its dramatic cartographic migrations may have had particular resonance for *Utopia,* for it draws (like the Utopians themselves) on two independent languages and traditions.[27] Long before Cabral claimed Brazil for the Portuguese in 1500, an island called Brazile appears on the Angelino Dulcert map of 1325 in the Atlantic at the latitude of Southern Ireland. The island appeared with the other mythical Atlantic Islands on numerous maps over the next two hundred years, including the influential woodcut map of the New World added by Waldseemüller to the edition of Ptolemy printed at Strassburg in 1513.[28] John Cabot sailed out of Bristol in 1480, hoping to discover the elusive island as a stepping-stone to the orient, but was forced to abandon his quest after nine months because of storms. It has been suggested that the etymology of the insula de Brazile (alternately spelled Breasail, Brasil, Hy-Brazil, or, most commonly, Brazil) originally derives from two Gaelic words, *breas* and *ail,* which Raymond Ramsey has translated as "superbly fine," or "grand and wonderful," to yield, in his whimsical turn of phrase, "Most-Best Island."[29]

In the Romance languages, however, Brazil is linked etymologically to dye production, and it was the discovery of a red-dye wood in South America led to its being named "terra de brazil." This association may help to explain the otherwise surprising Utopian production of "scarlet and purple dye-stuffs" that were not required for their own simple dress of undyed wool and bleached linen.[30] This unresolved contradiction between Utopian practice and Utopian trade might perhaps be measured as the distance between Braesail and Brazil; that is, the distance between the land that fulfills desires and the land that generates them.[31] The ironies of this discrepancy only deepen when mapped against England's shifting trade practices in the export of unfinished woolen cloths, which fed the insatiable desires of a European luxury market abroad but only by starving the local peasantry through enclosure laws.

Although Waldseemüller's map provides a clear source of inspiration in conjoining a map of the New World with Vespucci's travel narrative, and contemporary portolan maps offer additional provocative speculations about the New World, the modest woodcut map of the insular Utopia may owe as great a debt to the sketch plans increasingly introduced as evidence in legal disputes over rights, ownership, and jurisdiction.[32] As Peter Barber notes, such maps "would have been relatively familiar to younger lawyers who were to become ministers under Henry VIII, such as Thomas More and Thomas Cromwell" (27). The use of plans of this type as a model for Utopian geography relies, of course, on an ironic vision that figures "nowhere" as the propertyless place or, quite literally, no man's land. Thus the Utopian maps are situated between the *mappamundi*'s attempt to figure the world as a coherent whole, the sum of its representations, and the chorographical intentions of property maps to apportion the world into clearly divisible and historically demarcated plots.

It must be remembered that when the *Utopia* was published, maps were still rare and occult objects.[33] England was not a center for the new geography, and maps during Henry VIII's reign were more potent as symbols for display than as tools for government or administration.[34] It would not be until the publication of Christopher Saxton's great atlas of county maps in 1579 that British subjects could imagine in any detail the land to which they belonged.[35] Topographically speaking, Utopia graphically locates the discovery of the other as the discovery of self at the very border shared by geographical and chorographical traditions.

An important cartographic reader of *Utopia,* Abraham Ortelius, explores precisely this double location of Utopia in his own version of the Utopian map produced circa 1595 (Figure 3).[36] Ortelius depicts a completely revised topography and dozens of new place names, some of Utopian extraction and others in a variety of ancient and modern languages, "whereby each nation may recognize something of its own in this Utopia."[37] The title cartouche of this map declares its collaborative, international, and transhistorical authorship: "VTOPIE, TYPVS EX, Narratione Raphaelis Hythlodaei, Descriptione D. Thomae More, Delineatione Abrahami Ortelij." Foregrounding the transmission of Utopia's charter and addressing the viewer directly ("ad spectatorum"), Ortelius offers not just a rendition of Utopia but a reading. His map of Utopia graphically argues that the distance between here and there must be measured both temporally and ethically.

Whatever Utopia's topicality, it must be admitted that it is deliberately disorienting to put Noplace on the map at all, and it is clear that the Utopian map is not best understood as the technical expression of contemporary cartographic thinking. Getting to Utopia will require more than a compass; indeed, the danger of directing one's course by mechanical guides alone is the subject of one of Hythlodaeus's first anecdotes. Passing through a savage equatorial zone, Hythlodaeus and his company travel from the *oikoumene* (or known world) to the *antipodes* (literally the world "on the opposite foot") in a journey that overlays geographical and historical progression.[38] They first encounter ships of a primitive sort, flat-bottomed with "sails made of papyrus or osier stitched together and sometimes under sails made of leather," then eventually ships with pointed keels and canvas sails "like our own in all respects" (52/53).[39] Hythlodaeus wins great favor with these mariners by making them a gift of the magnetic needle.[40] Unfortunately, this knowledge proves an ambiguous boon, for since the introduction of the magnet, these people who once set sail only in fair weather have recklessly abandoned all caution: "Now trusting to the magnet, they do not fear wintry weather, being dangerously confident. Thus, there is a risk that what was thought likely to be a great benefit to them may, through their imprudence, cause them great mischief" (52/53). This little fable contains a thoroughly humanist moral: the value of technical knowledge must be measured against experience and common sense. It also demonstrates quite forcefully that literal readings out of context and without sufficient training can have devastating consequences.

The Utopian map provides no compass points or graphic indications of the distance between Utopia and recognizable lands or waters by which to guide our path. A closer reading of the two versions of the map, however, can lead us back to the principal preoccupations of humanist method. The original 1516 map is given the title VTOPIAE INSVLAE FIGVRA, which Holbein replaces with the heading VTOPIAE INSVLAE TABVLA, adding (or, perhaps more properly, restoring) to the "figure" of *figura*[41] the more artifactual properties of "painting," "map," "plan," or "document" suggested by *tabula*. The Holbein woodcut retains many of the features of the original (which it clearly takes as its model), but by reversing the direction of the ships in the middle foreground, this map seems to invite at first glance the speculation that ei-

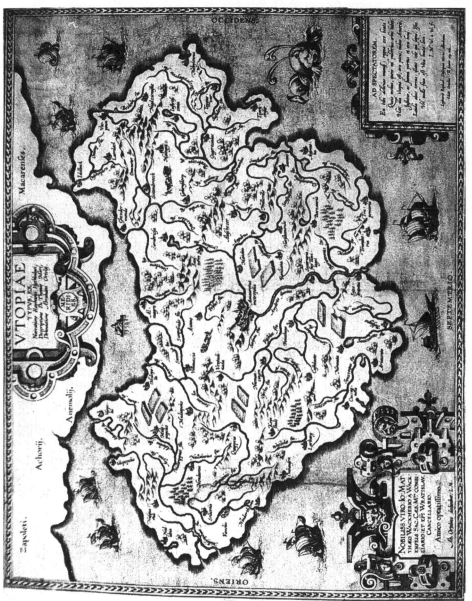

Figure 3. Abraham Ortelius. Map of Utopia. Reproduced by permission from Marcel P. R. van den Broecke, *Ortelius Atlas Maps: An Illustrated Guide* (Goy: The Netherlands, HES Publications, 1996; ISBN 90-6194-308-6).

ther the prototype or Holbein's *tabula* is reversed, turned inside out. On closer examination, other parallels and discrepancies become manifest. Holbein retains the graphic relationship between the captions declaring the source and mouth of the Anydrus River from left to right, respectively, but then reverses their relation pictorially. The spouting waterfall appears now at the river's mouth, instead of its source.

Such discrepancies would seem to pit the two versions against each other. If one is correct, then certainly the other must be wrong. And yet, the very symmetry of the island raises the not entirely innocent question of whether such reversals would make any difference. Referring to the text confounds rather than clarifies the question of orientation raised by the two maps. Book 2 describes how the ebb and flow of the Anydrus reverses direction every six hours, and the black-letter gloss points out explicitly the similarity of the Anydrus's shifting course to that of the Thames (118/119). Holbein's map, the narrative description, and its gloss all participate in the fusion and confusion of source and outlet, of paradigm and analog. And it is this conflation that lends to Holbein's revision the authority of the original, even as it casts it in doubt.

In a text full of punning inversions, reversals can be of different kinds and have different consequences. To have turned something inside out, or to point out a parallel, is not to have defined the nature of the difference, or the relation or priority between its component parts. The additive yet inconsistent inversions from map to map, or from text to map, can be understood alternately as corrections or corruptions; but in either case, the anxiety of authenticity that this inspires leads the careful reader to reconsider what an authentic vision of Utopia should look like—in what ways familiar, in what ways strange.

In the final analysis, the map's failure to add up to a definitive picture of Utopia will serve more reliably as a methodological than as a topographical illustration. The map's discrepancies, adjustments, and lacunae may not entirely match up with More's textual description of Utopia, but they will have numerous procedural parallels in a text whose authority is continually called into doubt by the most trivial questions of detail and subtle shifts in terms, by the length of a bridge disputed by More and his student Clement, or by the textual drift from the similar to the simulacrum. Such doubts are more than playful clues that Utopia is only a fiction. Again and again we are asked to reconsider the source, and the relationship of origin to version. The perpetual confusion of these is, in fact, what allows Utopia to be a "model" commonwealth in all senses of the word: a representation, a plan, an epitome, an archetypal pattern, an object of imitation, a draft or version, but in any case not the thing itself. Jean Baudrillard opens *Simulations* with the figure of a map drawn from a Borges story where the cartographers of a fabulous empire "draw up a map so detailed that it ends up exactly covering the territory."[42] This fable in which the map becomes confused with the very geography it describes reminds us that to succeed as an abstraction, the map is destined—indeed, required—to fail as a mimetic exercise or simulation. In contrast to Borges's allegory, or Baudrillard's articulation of its postmodern moral, the design and the allegory of Holbein's map are oriented in the opposite direction to highlight the distance, rather than the coextensivity, between the model commonwealth and its representation, even as it purports to offer the graphic link between source and version.[43]

Whatever peculiar discrepancies exist between the anonymous "original" map of 1516 and the Holbein "copy," both versions vary from the text in noteworthy ways. The utopian cities, for example, are not depicted on either map as identical, one of the "distinctive" features of More's urban planning. Although these cities are symmetrically disposed and roughly comparable in size, they provide no principle for generalization. The buildings are stubbornly individual (as well as very European in aspect), and Amaurotum is notably larger and more central. It is, in Orwellian terms, "more equal" than the cities for which it is the paradigm, or rather the paragon. But this seems less a departure from the text when we note that Hythlodaeus's description of Amaurotum in Book 2 similarly vacillates between the representative and the exemplary: "The person who knows one of the cities will know them all, since they are exactly alike insofar as the terrain permits. I shall therefore picture one or other (nor does it matter which), but which should I describe rather than Amaurotum? First, none is worthier, the rest deferring to it as the meeting place of the national senate; and, secondly, none is better known to me, as being one in which I had lived for five whole years" (116/117). This civic approbation suggests a paradox of praise. According to utopian normative values, it is quite literally true that no city is worthier than Amaurotum (*nec ulla dignior est*), for all utopian cities should be precisely the same. For descriptive purposes, being "more representative" in a uniformly representational system is no more meaningful than being "more unique," and yet More will press both these apparent redundancies to their limits as Utopia's principal defining properties. Consequently, the best reason for singling out

Amaurotum is that it is the city Hythlodaeus knows best and where he lived for five years. The situation of the viewer or speaker is both arbitrary and relevant—locus will be defined in the text, as on the map, by more than geography. The highly self-conscious rhetorical construction of Utopia provides another dimension to our voyage there and back. The utopian topos is both a literalized and self-authorizing "commonplace" and the singular epedeictic performance of Raphael Hythlodaeus. More places in doubt, by placing in tension, the relationship between the ethos reflected by and contained in his *"optimo reipublicae statu"* and the ethos of its European defender. The full title of Book 1 registers the problem in its very attempt to declare its proper subject: "THE DISCOURSE OF THE EXTRAORDINARY CHARACTER, RAPHAEL HYTHLODAEUS, ON THE BEST STATE OF A COMMONWEALTH, BOOK ONE, AS REPORTED BY THE RENOWNED FIGURE, THOMAS MORE, CITIZEN AND SHERIFF OF THE FAMOUS CITY OF GREAT BRITAIN, LONDON" (46/47). The discourse owes its excellence, as well as its authority, to the extraordinariness of Hythlodaeus, the renown of More, and even the fame of London, for the *laus* of Utopia relies for both its credibility and its moral authority on the praiseworthiness of the praisers, as well as the circumstances of the praise-giving.[44]

In the Holbein woodcut, the problem of representation and the incalculable distance between the reporters and the report is represented emblematically by the introduction of the figure of Hythlodaeus, absent in the 1516 prototype. On Holbein's map, Hythlodaeus (labeled with caption) speaks with another man (not labeled, but presumably More) on a bit of turf in the foreground, where the act of viewing is situated and distinguished from the view. Hythlodaeus gestures to the ship and the island beyond, while his rapt auditor gazes at the gesture and away from the island itself. A few paces apart an unidentified third figure, wearing a sword (military rather than humanist dress)[45] stands facing the island with his head tipped toward the other two. The two ships heading away from Utopia converge in their course toward the two interlocutors at the left; and on the larger ship a tiny figure with his back to Utopia also leans forward in a pose of attention toward the speaking Hythlodaeus—a reversal of the posture of the tiny schematic sailor who faces the island in the anonymous map of 1516. It is immediately apparent that the most remarkable difference between Holbein's *tabula* and the anonymous 1516 *figura* is that the real drama of Holbein's map is entirely centered on Hythlodaeus and the staging of the rhetorical moment in which Utopia is described. Rather than ground the fantasy of Utopia, this map displays its own creation myth by drawing attention to Hythlodaeus's performance in an unlocated setting no less imaginary than Utopia. Thus the gulf between Utopia and Hythlodaeus spans the divide—as well as the necessary relationship—between Utopia's entry into history and the rhetorical construction of self.

Holbein's *tabula* is remarkable not so much for signaling the power of the map as a rhetorical device but for featuring its rhetorical method as its explicit subject. While the whirl of human activity centered on the figure of Hythlodaeus seems entirely at odds with the studied, symmetrical, and ordered calm of the 1516 Utopian map, it provides a much fuller portrait of how New World construction, in fact, proceeds. A glance at the neutral, schematic map of 1516 provides an interesting measure of the difference that Holbein's humanist portraiture makes. Holbein's map is poised at such a particular, dramatically defined moment that its cartographic qualities of abstraction and generalization are correspondingly diminished. This does not, however, make the map a group portrait arranged against a landscape, although, conveniently enough for purposes of comparison, such an illustration does accompany the 1518 editions in a woodcut attributed to Hans Holbein (Figure 4).[46] Here Hythlodaeus, More, and Giles, attended by John Clement, are each designated by caption and shown engaged in conversation in the Antwerp garden setting recognizable from and traceable to its description at the end of Book 1.

Gardens, like maps, rely on both nature and convention for definition, but where the garden scene described in Figure 4 absorbs nature into an entirely conventional *hortus conclusus,* the very novelty of Utopia—both as a place (map) and as a genre (narrative)—makes the relation of nature and convention a far more ambiguous affair. In English that ambiguity is in part expressed by the prepositional confusion about whether what we see is "in" the map or "on" it. The garden woodcut represents a conversation inscribed in its *locus amoenus.* But on (or in) the map, Hythlodaeus's rhetorical performance, insofar as it captures the attention of his auditors, is shown in a kind of competition with his ostensible subject—the island of Utopia. In Book 2, the utopian gardens themselves are transformed from places apart from the world to sites of competition directly connected to the original urban plan. In fact, the utopian gardens provide the bridge to the account of Utopian history that immediately follows their description. As such, the Utopian garden

Io. Clemens.   Hythlodæus.   Tho. Morus. Pet. Aegid.

Figure 4. Hans Holbein. Hortus Conclusus. Title page illustration. From Thomas More, *Utopia* (Basel, 1518). By permission of the Beinecke Rare Book and Manuscript Library, Yale University.

offers not a fall into history as loss but the historical grounds for an improved culture and nature, for if "they have not a very fertile soil or a very wholesome climate," "the naturally barren soil is improved by art and industry" (178/179).

As with the Utopian gardens, the competition exemplified by the Utopian map does not produce an easy division between foreground and background, culture and nature. The naturalistic details of the wood-cut map, including the figures and the tufted foliage in the foreground, are countered and at the same time heightened by the unnaturalistic sense of scale, with the overlarge utopian cities cropping out of the consequently miniaturized landscape. Of course, most maps in the early sixteenth century did not follow an absolutely scrupulous or consistent sense of scale, and topographical details in particular were more often ornamental—representative of typical features of the areas they illustrated—than they were illusionistic or internally consistent views, following the innovations of geometrically derived focused perspective. But it is precisely the tensions between the exemplary uniqueness of Utopia and the conventions of Tudor cartography that are of interest here, for

Holbein's *tabula* seems to intensify play between utopia as map and landscape, emblem and portrait, general idea and particular reality.

The cartographic historian J. B. Harley describes the complex function of Tudor maps as follows: "Many of the maps of Tudor and early Stuart England depended on written captions—to say nothing of place names—for part of the meaning to be triggered in the mind of their users. They present an intractable problem of duality. In several respects—such as those of written language and graphic image of mimetic and abstract sign, of art and science, and of reality and deliberate idealization—the map image is a hybrid." [47]

The figurative contradictions inherent in the Holbein map's pictorial and graphic components, its mimetic versus idealizing functions are best exemplified by the decorative lanyards that hang from its upper corners. These twining, floral garlands support banners with captions identifying the city of Amaurotum (Amaurotus Urbs), the source of the River Anydrus (Fons Anydri), and its mouth (Ostium Anydri). The presence of the lettered captions determines the legibility of the island and assures us of the map's correspondence to the text it accompanies. Visually, the garlands contribute to a surface pattern that ties the island to the background mainland landscape, while spatially, they form a *repoussoir* device, emphasizing the distance between foreground and background. The garlands both flatten and define space in the *tabula,* providing a pictorial demonstration of the dynamics of distance and proximity featured by the text, whereby the relation of Utopia to Europe is simultaneously discovered to be so very far and yet so strangely near.

The decorative banners also serve to fix the vantage point for the view they announce, and in so doing they fix the position (and even impede the approach) of the viewer. Whereas the captions of the original *figura* seem to be inscribed directly on the face of the island, those of the *tabula* hang suspended in a plane parallel to the European foreground occupied by the gesturing Hythlodaeus and his unlabeled companions. If the viewer advances beyond the markers, Utopia ceases to be a map and becomes once again an enigma. In this fashion, the view's perspective is fixed both by the inclusion of the European viewers and the plane of legibility established by the hanging captions. But these two perspectives—even though they are established by the same plane—are fundamentally different. Here in Holbein's *tabula,* it is not those who stand within view of the map but the viewers of the island-as-map who have the most complete view. The map registers both the gap (between here and there, then and now) and the critical distance that makes that gap legible, comprehensible—in short, meaningful. As Claudio Guillen puts it, "A perspective, then, is a changing relation between the level of judgment and the level of existence."[48] It is, I believe, this distinction that illustrates precisely the critical juncture—emblematized by this map—between reading and reaching Utopia.

A very different dramatization of the distance between Old World and New World figured on a largely fictive map can be found by turning to a play by More's brother-in-law, John Rastell: "A new interlude and a mery of the nature of the four elements" (ca. 1510–20).[49] In this figure can be traced a more direct, if no less problematic, connection between Tudor geographic fantasies and the promise of colonial expansion. Like Holbein and his anonymous predecessor, Rastell exploits the novelty of maps as a focus of interest and a tool for persuasion. But Rastell's "scientific" morality play disguises (even as it exploits) his map's purely rhetorical base by making it an illustration of and an instrument for nature.

As the play opens Nature, Humanity, and Studious Desire enter with a map ("Hic intrat Natura naturata,[50] Humanyte and Studyous Desire portans figuram") to which Nature refers throughout his lecture to Humanity:[51]

> What I have shown, man, print well in thine heart,
> And mark well this figure that here shall remain,
> Whereby thou mayest perceive many things more plain
> Concerning the matter I spoke of before;
> And when that I shall resort here again
> Of high points of cunning I shall show thee more.
> (A₈r; 12)

In a later bit of dialogue, Experience and Studious Desire will point again to the figure of the map, and after using it to chart Experience's voyages, the map is once more connected to Nature's higher purpose and design:

> Experience. Sir, as for all such questions
>   Of towns to know the situation.
>   How far they be asunder,
>   And other points of cosmography,
>   Ye shall never learn them more surely

Than by that figure yonder;
For who that figure did first devise,
It seemeth well he was wise;
And perfect in this science;
For both the sea and land also
Lie true and just as they should do,
I know by experience.
Stud. Desire. Who think you brought here this figure?
Experience. I wot not.
Stud. Desire. Certes, Lord Nature
Himself not long agone,
Which was here personally
Declaring his high philosophy
And left this figure purposely
For Humanity's instruction.

(B₈r-B₈v; 23–24)

The putative transparency of this "Natural" map achieves a kind of historical—if not intentional—irony when regarded in view of Rastell's career. John Rastell's personal ambition to travel to the New Found Lands was, in fact, stymied by his failure in 1517 to persuade a mutinous crew to continue with the voyage farther than Waterford, Ireland.[52] This may also suggest why Rastell did not place ultimate reliance on the force of rhetoric to persuade his audience to a new cosmography, even in his own highly rhetorical defense of the map's near-occult scope and powers.

The map stays on stage throughout the play and is central to the demonstrations of a variety of the play's allegorical characters. Nature uses it to distinguish between the "ethereal region" of heaven and the "lower region, called the elemental," and to elaborate the qualities of the elements. Studious Desire uses it to prove the Earth is round and hangs in the midst of the firmament. Experience uses it to point out England and its relation to the known world, and then to define England's moral and material relation to the New World as, alternately, bestower of civilization and reaper of "great riches." For the audience, the map serves as natural philosophy lesson, a guide by which to steer clear of Sensual Appetite (the only important interlocutor in the drama who ignores the map), and a promise of both the enlargement of Christendom and of substantial financial gain—presumably, albeit ironically, the compensatory material rewards for avoiding the grosser appetites.[53]

On the one hand, the map serves as a visual emblem of the rational order and harmonic congruence of the universe; on the other, it performs a central role in the morality structure of catechism and initiation, suggesting a discrimination, yet ultimate connection, between inclusive and exclusive spheres. Humanity must undergo a personal conversion so that he can "print" the figure of the map in his heart and thus internalize its message about his proper place in the cosmography it outlines. Global expansion is but an organic incorporation into the little world of man.

However expansively universal in scope, this map is decidedly national in orientation. The delineation of the elemental world gives way to a declamation of the relationship that England could or should have to the New World, transforming it in the process from a purely descriptive to an aggressively prescriptive chart. Nevertheless, it would be extremely reductive to assert anything like a simple correlation between this cartographic prop in Rastell's play and the unfolding map of English colonial history. The uncertain dates of the play (1510–20) situate it ambiguously on one side or the other of Rastell's own failed exploit, but it seems inevitable to me to read this as Rastell's compensatory literary response to his literal failure as a New World explorer rather than an untroubled call to set sail. The drama's struggle with Sensual Appetite as arguably the principal goad to travel and yet represented here as its chief obstacle seems to me a clear representation of and response to Rastell's own experience with those mutinous sailors. Viewed in such a light, however, it becomes even more ironic to read this play as historically prophetic of, or productive of, colonial expansion. It represents the desire, to be sure, and it represents the (now familiar) rationalizations of colonialism, but this is a fantasy forged out of and framed by its failure.

Despite Rastell's reliance on this map to serve as a clear illustration, delineating its dimensions as prop or figure is not at all a simple prospect. The features of the map as described during the play surpass both in detail and abstractness what might be plausibly represented on its face. Indeed, Rastell's map, like the map of Borges's fable, offers itself as identical to the world it would describe. This is, in Baudrillard's terms, the "representational imaginary, which both culminates in and is engulfed by the cartographer's mad project of an ideal coextensivity between the map and the territory" (3). This map is also imaginary in the more purely Lacanian meaning, providing an illusory sense of presence and identity, a fictional coextension with the world based on a fundamental misrecognition of the self.

The historical situation of Rastell's map can be regarded as the temporal counterpart to its fantastic geographical extension. The map's historicity, as it is worked out in this drama, is cognitive rather than actual. This map constitutes the real neither in fact (as Rastell's own thwarted ambitions suggest) nor in history (which this essentially medieval morality play can hardly anticipate) but in the imaginary. If Rastell's map is the repository of his play's utopian content as the fantasy of resolution between the historical subject (Humanity) and his destiny (as possessor of the plenitude of the world), then it is here that Holbein's and More's utopian representations most depart from it. Those features that indicate the utopian design of Rastell's cartographic drama (its dialogic setting, its fantastic dimensions, and its visionary plan) seem to be entirely subsumed by its ideological base precisely because the play does not engage in utopian discourse as critical practice, but only as wish-fulfillment.

Nonetheless, for all their differences, Rastell's drama, like his brother-in-law's *Utopia,* relies for its force on the tension between viewing its imaginary heterocosm as metonymy and viewing it as metaphor. These alternatives connect us again to the humanist dilemma of viewing utopia either as a figure of historical substitution and transference or as a locus of historical and personal transformation. In the end, however, I would argue that More, in his refusal to idealize Utopian colonial practice, its mechanisms, its motives, and its consequences, offers a critique of the very project of colonial wishful thinking embodied by Rastell's play and in his attempts at New World exploration.[54] More's critique, it is clear, cannot be read through liberal individualism; it is neither an attack on nor a defense of indigenous populations or principles of self-determination. *Utopia,* rather, represents a working out of the internal logic of and relationship between Tudor expansionism, land management, and national identity.

In the section of *Utopia* entitled "Social Relations" (*De Commerciis Mutuis*) and nestled between the discussion of the disposition of children within and between households and the organization of Utopian markets, More desribes Utopian colonial practices: "And if the population throughout the island should happen to swell above the fixed quotas, they enroll citizens out of every city and, on the mainland nearest them, wherever the natives have much unoccupied and uncultivated land, they found a colony under their own laws" (136/137). If the natives do not choose to assimilate and abide by Utopian law, the generally pacifist Utopians drive them out or conquer them by force. The Utopians justify their invasion and enforcement of law by "rule of nature" (ex naturae praescripto), as "they consider it a most just cause for war when a people which does not use its soil but keeps it idle and waste (inane ac uacuum) nevertheless forbids the use and possession of it to others" (136/137).

Unlike Rastell's personification of Nature as Natura Naturata, More points immediately to the waste of nature that requires the transformations of human industry. This is not a romance of garden worlds that deliver up their treasures willingly, nor even an invitation to lay waste to a richly fertile and exotic world; this is, rather, a quest for the empty space on the map that has yet to be inscribed. But where is this empty space? The Yale editors rehearse the various possibilities:

> Precisely what relevance has this whole passage to the contemporary scene? It is difficult to determine. In one sense, dispossessed farmers, unemployed weavers, etc. are surplus population, whom More would transfer to the deserted tracts of the New World. Oncken mentions a document dated October 7, 1515, directed at settlements in Ireland . . . but the latter is hardly a continent. The continent adjacent to Utopia (i.e. England) was Europe, but where were the waste places? Only the New World remains for More and England. (416)

Because the editors identify Utopia with England as a coterminous body on the same world map, the only possibility they seem unable to consider is that one of the waste spaces may be England itself. But certainly the attack on enclosure laws of Book 1 and Hythlodaeus's description of the overextended Achorians invite us to consider Utopian colonial practice as both or alternately an expansion and a retraction. In fact, Utopia's colonial justification draws from and replicates its own origin story:

> As the report goes and as the appearance of the ground shows, the island once was not surrounded by sea. But Utopus, who as conqueror gave the island its name (up to then it had been called Abraxa) and who brought the rude and rustic (rudem atque agrestem) people to such a perfection of culture and humanity as makes them now superior to almost all other mortals, gained a victory at his very first landing. He then ordered the excavation of fifteen miles on the side where the land

was connected to the continent and caused the sea to flow around the land (112/113).

Hytholdaeus describes a land not discovered, but rather invented from nothing. The "uncultivated" (rudem) rustics, who labor alongside the soldiers, yield the new Utopia from whose gifts they also benefit.

If this suggests for Tudor readers an invitation to, model for, or rationalization of future colonial exploitation (and I preclude none of these readings), it is based on historical self-exploration. Utopus's relation to the native, colonized Abraxans suggests a palimpsestic text through which we might read the mytho-historical Brutus, conquerer of British barbarians and the deliverer of Roman culture.

The intersection of the Utopian historical trajectory and that of Britain and Rome is further suggested in the shipwreck that stranded a company of Romans and Egyptians on Utopian shores some 1,200 years before Hythlodeaus himself landed there. This important cultural transplantation thus dates around 300–315 C.E., just when Constantine I (Constantine the Great) claimed title to the imperial throne from Britain after his father's death in York (306 C.E.). Pointing thus to the consolidation of Roman empire under Constantine, More suggests both a political and a religious allegory. It was in good part Constantine's patience, his willingness to bide his time in the provinces, that gained him the much-contested imperial throne as he turned his rivals against one another.[55] Britain's peripheral setting turned out to be central to Constantine's success. When he finally moved into Italy with his enormous force of Briton, Gallic, and German soldiers against Maxentius in 312 C.E., they met at the Milvian Bridge on the Tiber, where Constantine was reported to have seen a flaming cross in the sky inscribed with the words "In this conquer."[56] Eusebias writes of the pagan Constantine as an instrument of God in his *Vita Constantini:* "Starting from the British sea and the lands where the sun is ordained to set, He repulsed and scattered by His divine might the encompassing powers of evil, to the end that the human race might be recalled to the worship of the supreme law. . . . and that the most blessed faith might be increased with the Almighty as guide."[57]

Constantine's policy of religious toleration was a period of great gain for the early Christian church. His Edict of Milan (313 C.E.) granted universal religious tolerance, offering a historical context for the Utopians' parallel policy, one of the few regulations explicitly attributed directly to Utopia's founder, who had "especially ordained that it should be lawful for every man to follow the religion of his choice" (220/221). Hythlodaeus goes on to say that "Utopus laid down these regulations not merely from regard for peace, which he saw to be utterly destroyed by constant wrangling and implacable hatred, but because he thought that this method of settlement was in the interest of religion itself" (220/221).

More's description of the Utopian incorporation of Roman culture occurs at the very end of Book 1 and, in fact, offers a significant bridge between Utopian cultural geography and the physical geography of the island that opens the second book, even as it provides a bridge between the garden conversation in the Old World and the New World island described in Book 2. More explicitly, if elliptically, links Roman lessons with British soil when Hythlodaeus concludes his comments on the remarkable ability of the Utopians to assimilate all the shipwrecked sailors brought them: "The Roman empire possessed no art capable of any use which they did not either learn from the shipwrecked strangers or discover for themselves after receiving hints for investigation—so great a gain was it to them that on a single occasion some persons were carried to their shores from ours" (tanto bono fuit illis aliquos hinc semel illuc esse delatos) (109/110). The seeming slippage of location in this passage from the arts of Rome learned from Romans and the benefits "from this place" ("hinc"), (or what the Yale editors translate as "carried to their shores *from ours*" [emphasis added]) can be resolved if we fully consider the Roman context of Constantine. That is, what the Utopians seem to receive circa 300 C.E. from "our" shores is a history of Roman arts in the context of Christian consolidation, and both, it would seem, "from this place"—not the Roman capital, not Antwerp, but Britain, the far-off outpost of an empire whose overextension will ultimately destine it for collapse while the Utopians thrive and prosper.

If the historical location of this gift of Roman learning allows us to read it as alternately productive of empire or prophetic of its demise, it is just this ambiguity that allows the history of Utopia to rival England's. When Peter Giles protests Hythlodaeus's favorable comparison of Utopia to Europe in Book 1, saying "it would be hard for you to convince me that a better-ordered people is to be found in that new world than in the one known to us," Hythlodeaus responds, "you could give a sounder opinion if you had read the historical accounts of that world. If we must believe them, there were cities among them before there were men among us" (106/107). Utopia's claim to authority is clearly not its novelty but the history that situates it as anterior to, yet derived from the same history as Britain's. These historical accounts of Utopia do not chart England's future as much as its past, tracked along an alternate rather than actual destiny.

The intimate connection between mapping Utopia and charting its history is suggested quite clearly in the text. More's allusion to the Utopian annals that record its 1,760 years of existence directly follows (and follows from) the plan of Utopia (*urbis figuram*) sketched by Utopus himself but left to posterity for improvement: "He left to posterity, however to add the adornment and other improvements for which he saw one lifetime would hardly suffice" (120/121).

It has been a commonplace to regard Utopia as a repository of classical virtues (principally Stoic or Epicurean), or a Golden Age commonwealth.[58] If, however, Hythlodaeus's *laus* of *Utopia* provides an analog to the humanist reassessment and privileging of the classical past, Utopia provides an equally compelling and far more challenging analog as a society, *like* Europe, faced with the prospect (or problem) of assimilating whole new bodies of knowledge (like the arts brought to Utopia by the Romans and Egyptians twelve hundred years before, and the "literis et disciplina Graecorum" and Christian moral philosophy imported by Hythlodaeus) and whole new technologies (like the printing press) made possible by the commerce of ideas. According to one analogy, Utopia is like the past that Europe encounters; according to the other, Utopia is like Europe encountering the past. Such shifts of temporal and spatial perspective radically challenge both the notion of a fixed and separate Utopia and the idea that one must, or even can, leave it behind.

From Utopia to History and Back

The recursive nature of Utopia's geographic and historical dislocations suggests the inadequacy of the customary characterization of the division between Book 1's European foreground and Book 2's Utopian background as the distance between reality and fantasy, history and myth. Even those critics most invested in understanding these realms as intimately interconnected, offering representational rather than ontological polarities, often slip into treating Book 1 as reality principle or realpolitik and Book 2 as escapist fantasy. But to do so is to fall into the kind of literal reading that *Utopia* takes pains to compromise through conspicuous overdetermination. The relation between the text's intimations of pastoral and its analysis of the devastating effects of England's suddenly enlarged pasturage can serve as an illustrative example.

Harry Berger, Jr., dividing Utopia between the "second world" of Book 1 and the "green world" of Book 2, has described Utopia as a place of premature pastoral retirement: a "Platonic Garden of Adonis, a place without pain where everyone learns everything the short smooth way"[59] Despite the intimate connections Berger outlines between the levels of representations suggested by green world and second world, Utopia's green world is ultimately described as utterly removed and utterly fixed. Indeed, these represent precisely the qualities to which it owes both its initial pastoral attraction and its ultimate moral failings.

More recently, John Freeman has distinguished between "the sense of urgency and historical contingency" of Book 1 and the mythic and artificially insular Book 2.[60] Freeman describes the relation between these books with the analogy of large-scale enclosure: "As a form of 'expropriation' and consolidation, enclosure governs not only the discourse between text and historical contingency but also the discourse between its two books" (290). Unfortunately, Freeman's reading of *Utopia* as an "alibi for enclosure" (294) requires that he read Book 2 first (justified on the grounds that it was the first book *historically,* that is, in order of composition). It is only proceeding through Utopia backward that it can emerge, in Freeman's terms, as "an ideal case study for the New Historicist enterprise" (289), following a movement from consolidation to subversion, and ultimately to containment.[61]

I would like to suggest, however, that the relation between the dreams of pastoral escape and the nightmare of history represented by enclosure neither divides between Books 1 and 2 nor contains them in a single inverted narrative. Despite the inevitable association of Book 2 with the mythic or pastoral, the most clearly pastoral passage in the text is presented not in Book 2, but in Book 1, in the image of the world overrun with sheep. More envisions England after the enclosure laws have run their course, as requiring only "a single shepherd or herdsman" to sustain it, where all that was once cultivated has been turned into a "solitudinem." It is, unmistakably, a frightening image of an entire population displaced and devoured, as well as a perverse literalization of the king's role as a shepherd to his people. It is no less unmistakably the realization of a pastoral England, run by high-born "shepherds."

Consequently the deficiencies or "myths" of the fictional Utopia are conspicuously measured against the false perceptions, the fictions of the Old World. In *The History of Richard III*, the expression "grene world" conjures an England rife with ugly, willful fictions and deep dissimulations, with no less the power to affect the course of history for their being false.[62]

For Renaissance humanists, metaphor provided entry into and connection between both the known and the unknown world, the real and the possible, and this connection or extension allowed fiction to be something other or more than feigning.[63] But if More realized that the similitudes offered by metaphor had the potential to inspire the imagination to reform, he seemed equally at pains to point out that such analogies were also susceptible to corruption. This would distinguish the function of More's *Utopia* sharply from Sidney's claims for the autonomy of poetry (a separate and therefore better world), and it would explain why Sidney would invoke More's model commonwealth and then express his great discomfort with it in his *Defense of Poetry*. More's *Utopia* was, doubtless, neither separate nor perfected enough for Sidney's taste. On the other hand, contemporary criticism seems frequently to generate the reverse complaint—that Utopia is too perfect, too separate, arguing that it is only when Utopia's design fails that history rushes in.[64]

Utopia very explicitly and persistently engages the problem of history, however: the problem of encountering history and the problem of inserting oneself into a history whose landmarks have suddenly shifted. The composition of *Utopia* interrupts More's *History of Richard III*, a work that was to have been the complete history of More's own time.[65] *Utopia* is not so much a fantastic departure from that project as a fanciful intervention. It belongs not to the world of "might have been" or "could be," so much as to the excesses of the historic present and the pressing humanist problem of what was to be done *now* with the lessons of history.

If the map of Utopia can be used as a guide, contact between Europe and Utopia is not only inevitable, but has already happened. One tiny graphic detail introduced by Holbein indicates a profound and total religious, social, and symbolic transformation. The tiny crosses on the tallest steeples indicate that the island has already been Christianized. Amaurotum is the ghostly double of London, but whether one considers the Utopian map as obliterated by its double, England, or as built on its foundations colors or even reverses the direction of "the plan." As with the "Waterless" River, source and outcome are finally reversible, allowing Utopia to be at once admonishing and hortatory, visionary and pessimistic—although, significantly, the pagan or Christian features to which such oppositional attributes adhere become increasingly unmoored in the process of their suspension and potential reversal. This tension is only heightened when we consider how the appearance of these Christian symbols is attended by and anticipates a darker sort of doubling, for between these two woodcuts—the churchless image of the original 1516 map and the two churches of 1518—is, of course, the church door at Wittenberg, which served symbolically to open the Protestant Reformation and the possibility of a church irrevocably divided.[66]

A textual analog to the cartographic image of a reformed Christian Utopia can be found suspended in the unanswered question about Utopia's location that More puts to Giles. Indeed, it does not seem to occur to More that he does not know precisely where Utopia is until a theologian of his acquaintance expresses the desire to be the first Utopian bishop and bring about the conversion of the island. This mission takes on a whole new value when read against what we later learn of the Utopian strictures regarding zealots: "If a person contends too vehemently in expressing his views, he is punished with exile or enslavement" (220/221). The association of zealousness with crime is first made in the pun on zelus/scelus in Book I, where, as the gloss notes, "the Friar, because of His Ignorance of Latin, Misuses 'Zelus' (Zeal) as if it were Neuter like 'Hoc Scelus' (This Crime)." Thus, misquoting Scripture, the Friar declares inadvertently, "The 'crime' of Thy house has eaten me up" (84/85). Mapping the vision of a Christian Utopia against such moments in the text only raises the unanswered question of whether Utopia's meliorist credo and Christian zeal can be served at the same time, and in the event of failure, whose house will be "eaten up." This is precisely the question that places the greatest strain on the relation between the authority of origin and the efficacy of action—a question More is willing to suspend here in order that it be addressed in another setting altogether. But history intervenes with its own narratives, and, retrospectively, this self-critical question can only seem what it could not have been intended to be—darkly prophetic for both New World and Old.

Chapter Three

Utopia Spelled Out

The grammar of utopian language is by definition an ideal grammar. It guides the mind to its ends by the most natural and perfect paths. It is a code of intelligence, containing *in potentia* many other codes. . . . One could almost say that everything within the pagan utopia, as within the Christian universe, proceeds from the verb. The verb is the source and the end. And at times it constitutes for us, the readers, the key to its doctrine.

—ÉMILE PONS, "Les Langues imaginaires dans le voyage utopique"

The city is redundant: it repeats itself so that something will stick in the mind. . . . Memory is redundant: it repeats signs so that the city can begin to exist.

—ITALO CALVINO, *Invisible Cities*

The invention and inclusion of the Utopian alphabet and verse, no less than the Utopian map, challenge the reader to determine Utopia's cultural location and historical situation (Figure 5).[1] These prefatory materials offer a bridge between Utopian and Latin European letters, but the dimensions of this bridge are as dubious (and as tensile) as the bridge over the river Anydrus, whose length is disputed by More and John Clement, giving rather mixed evidence about Utopia's accessibility or inaccessibility.[2] The manifold linguistic paradoxes of the Utopian language rely on the reader's ability to break down facile correspondences (or facile inversions) to construct sense out of nonsense and nonsense out of (merely apparent) sense. In utopian translation, the fragile relationship of words (*verba*) to things (*res*) is shown to be not exclusively a problem of grammar, or even epistemology, but a question of the moral gulf between language and action. The humanist reformer faces that divide with particular poignancy, as it corresponds to the most profound ambivalences of the humanist vocation: between the contemplative and active life, between the past and the present. And yet the act of translation can also be seen as the bridge between these divides. Thomas More was twenty-six when he translated *The Life of Pico,* and, as R. J. Schoeck points out, "the act of translating seems to have coincided with his decision not to remain in the Charterhouse and to live instead a secular life."[3]

The importance of language in ordering experience is expressed by Erasmus's credo in *De ratione studii:* "Veborum prior, rerum potior." Without language, there is no social discourse to be sure, but more fundamentally, there is no contact with reality: "For things are only intelligible to us through vocal signs; he who is unversed in the signification of speech is blind also in the discernment of things; necessarily he hallucinates, he is delirious."[4]

By placing maximum stress on the relation between *verbum* and *sensum* in *Utopia,* More underscores the trade-off between the critical and performative aspects of translation. The transformations of translation are revealed as both goal and potential danger. More outlines Utopia not as a *merely* metaphoric place, but as a place that can only be apprehended in translation or described or enacted through translation.

More was well aware that translations—no matter how faithful or how literal—must necessarily result in some distortion, so that the act and product of translation will at once take a reader further away from the original, even as it asks her to recover imaginatively the perfect, uncorrupted source. *Utopia,* obsessed as it is with its origins and with measuring the distance from the source, will offer both a narrative and a graphic commentary on the linguistic, literary, and sociohistorical processes of translation as humanist method and subject.[5]

Inscribing Utopia

The Utopian alphabet is spare, orderly, and geometric.[6] The sequence of letters in this imaginary alphabet follows a metamorphosis from circle

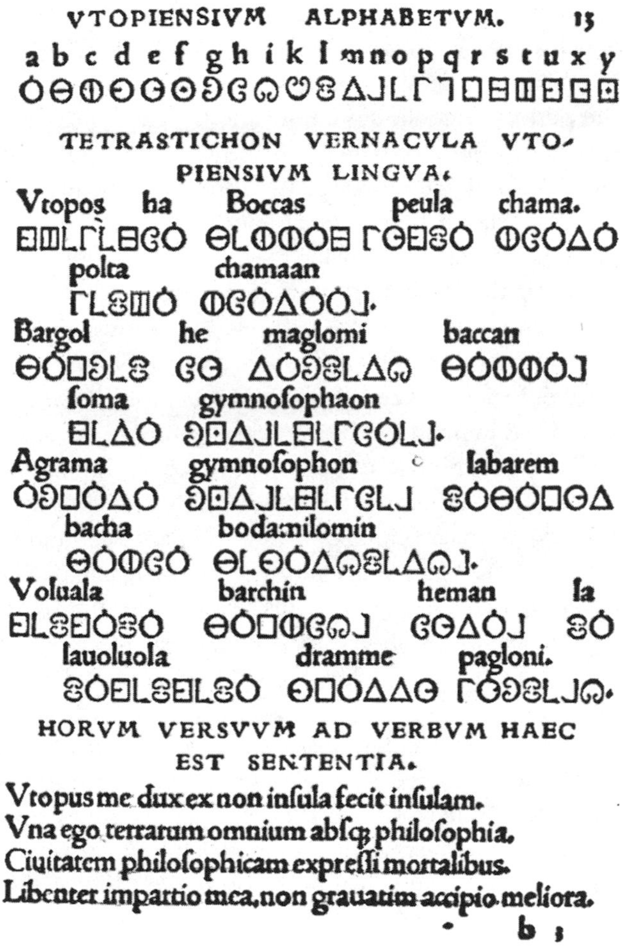

VTOPIENSIVM   ALPHABETVM.   13

a b c d e f g h i k l m n o p q r s t u x y

TETRASTICHON VERNACVLA VTO-
PIENSIVM LINGVA.

Vtopos   ha   Boccas   peula   chama.

polta   chamaan

Bargol   he   maglomi   baccan

foma   gymnofophaon

Agrama   gymnofophon   labarem

bacha   bodamilomin

Voluala   barchin   heman   la

lauoluola   dramme   pagloni.

HORVM VERSVVM AD VERBVM HAEC
EST SENTENTIA.

Vtopus me dux ex non infula fecit infulam.
Vna ego terrarum omnium abfq; philofophia.
Ciuitatem philofophicam exprefli mortalibus.
Libenter impartio mea, non grauatim accipio meliora.

b ;

Figure 5. The Utopian Alphabet. From Thomas More, *Utopia* (Basel, 1518). By permission of the Beinecke Rare Book and Manuscript Library, Yale University.

to square, announcing emblematically both its impossibility and its perfection as the ostensible solution to the classical conundrum of the quadrature: the squaring of the circle.[7] Although this may seem a fanciful speculation, More's interest in just such geometric games is amply illustrated by the text's repeated insistence on taking impossible measures, a methodological impulse that very much links the Utopian alphabet and the Utopian map. The circular dimensions of the island must be measured against the quadrilateral plan of Utopia's fifty-four identical cities, but as Louis Marin has shown, these figures do not add up to produce either a geographically or politically coherent system.[8] Geometry's ability to embrace both rational and irrational ratios also provides the perfect symbolic system for the Utopian language, in which the rational progression represented by the Utopian letters must be balanced against an irrational language that produces meaning principally through paradox.[9] Ralph Keen has pointed out that More would have found precedent in Plato for using "geometrical truths" as "graphic means of ensuring the conviction of the interlocutor."[10]

Roger Bacon and Alexander Hales, similarly interested in securing belief, articulated the connection of geometry to theology for the Middle Ages. These theologians argued that the higher spiritual sense could be grasped only by examining the literal sense with the aid of geometry.[11] Roger Grosseteste would follow the same line of reasoning to argue that geometry holds the key to natural philosophy.[12] In *Utopia,* geometry seems to provide a similar bridge between the particular and the universal, the literal and the figurative aspects of Utopian language. But such connections are not characterized in this text by their transparency, and, indeed, geometrical propositions are more often than not played off against geometrical puzzles to heighten the paradoxical dimension of the text.

Utopia's fanciful geometry—found both in its urban plan and its alphabet—may have its source in *The Birds,* in which Aristophanes uses the squaring of the circle to lay the groundwork for a city in the clouds. Meton, the great astronomer and mathematician, appears to land-survey the air of Cloudcuckootown in a foundation that both declares and confounds measure:

> With the straight rod I measure out, that so.
> The circle may be squared; and in the centre
> A market-place; and streets be leading to it
> Straight to the very centre; just as from
> A star, though circular, straight rays flash out
> In all directions.[13]

The impossible measure taken at the foundation of Cloudcuckootown finds its parallel both in the geographical mapping of Utopia and in the translation of the Utopian language, where two systems of meaning and measure attempt and fail to find equivalence. The presence of the alphabet, the Utopian verse, and the Latin version sets up translation as both method and metaphor for negotiating the path to (and through) Utopia.[14] The direction, procedures, and success of translation are, however, in a continual state of redefinition and revision.

These processes of translation are exemplified by the Utopian tetrastichon, which appears under the alphabet in the *parerga*. The utopian verse is first transliterated from Utopian characters into Roman letters and then translated (*ad verbum*) into Latin.[15] This double or progressive translation of the quatrain prepares the reader for the way in which the Latin text will also require sequential translations, both because much of the Latin text's naming and punning go on in Greek, and also because it is a text whose speakers translate the practices, actions, and ideas of others. Hythlodaeus translates what he understands of Utopian practice; More translates what Hythlodaeus (whose Greek was better than his Latin) said to him. The manifest impossibility of the perfect or complete translation, and the ultimately unbridgeable gap between original and version, anticipate the many ways in which this text constrains attempts to decipher the Utopian original with(in) the European terms that make it legible. James Holstun sees *Utopia* as a fantasy of objective anthropology and perfect translation, but I would argue that, if this is so, More takes pains to expose the degree to which this is indeed a fantasy.[16]

To de-cipher the language of no-place is to learn to read the cipher both in its role as a component of the Utopian alphabet and as the sign of Utopia itself. In both cases the utopian cipher has meaning only when transferred and applied to another context.[17] In his discussion of the problem of an object-based utopian theory of figures, Ernst Bloch writes that "real ciphers are not static, they are figures of tension, they are tendentious process forms and, above all in fact, on this path, symbolic ones."[18]

Tracing this circular text back to its point of origin proves, at last, impossible.[19] Things change along the way, and despite Hythlodaeus's successful circumnavigation, he finds he can't go home again. Hythlodaeus's suspension between two worlds, between two systems of measure and value, and his inability to persuade More either of Utopia's superiority or the possibility of its various reforms being realized "in nostris ciuitatibus" registers the pathos of this failure of translation, even as it relies on our ability to comprehend (and read through) the absurdity of an exchange in which the fiction fails to persuade its own author.

Jonathan Swift was later to draw his own connections between utopia, geometry, and language in "The Voyage to Laputa," one of the several utopian travesties of *Gulliver's Travels*. In Laputa, not only the language is geometrically derived, but also the measure of Gulliver's new suit (taken by quadrant, rule, and compass), the abstractly conceived and impractically constructed Laputian architecture, and dinner.[20] The extravagant frivolity of the excessively rational Laputian language and culture was to find its real-world source and referent in the Royal Society's *Philosophical Transactions,* which provided a wealth of raw material for Swift's satiric grand Academy of Lagado.[21] More, on the other hand, insists on a plausible presentation of a place he calls "nowhere," and by insisting on both its authenticity and its impossibility by definition, he destabilizes the direction and the force of its satiric reference.

Whereas Swift distills pure, unadulterated nonsense out of this hyper-rational and scientific language, More will suggest a more dialectical relation between sense and nonsense. *Utopia* achieves this in part by creating its own intertextuality. In her analysis of the interdependence of the domain of nonsense and the domain of common sense, Susan Stewart argues, "The concept of intertextuality relies upon two basic assumptions: first, that various domains of meaning are contingent upon one another, and second, that the common-sense world may be considered as a base from which other provinces of meaning are formed. . . . It is not only that the common-sense world is characterized by certain relations we hold to time, space and causality, but that time, space, and causality are themselves constituted in the common-sense domain."[22] By shaping a fictional domain that embraces both common sense and non-sensical worlds—both the everyday world of More and Giles and the strange worlds reported by Hythlodaeus—*Utopia* compromises the autonomy of the commonsense world, even as it lends an aspect of respectability to the nonsensical. Indeed, throughout the tale Hythlodaeus presses his ordinary-world audience to accept that they live in the domain of nonsense and that it is the Utopians who embody and enact virtuous commonsensicalness. The rhetorical basis for Hythlodaeus's appeal is neither satiric nor inverted, but it sets the stage for a conversion of terms. The representation of the alphabet and verse and their Latin translations heightens this "conversion" process, because it is here that the act of making sense (both common sense and nonsense) is enacted.

Hythlodaeus's proper name enacts a double confusion of these domains. As Richard Halpern has pointed out, Hythlodaeus's name, formed by combining the Greek *hythlos* and *daios,* is not well-served by the English translation, "expert in trifles" or "well-learned in nonsense," offered by the Yale edition. Halpern argues that *bythlos* suggests not vain chatter but "nonphilosophical speech. . . . [S]peech that aims at pleasure rather than knowledge." Conversely, *daios* does not mean scholarly knowledge but " 'experienced,' 'cunning,' 'skilled' as an artisan might be skilled at his craft" (142). Halpern offers instead the translation: "skilled in pleasant speech" (142). Thus Hythlodaeus's name, instead of dissolving into a simple contradiction or oxymoron, announces the very rhetorical skills in which his character declares himself entirely deficient—a contradiction not in terms but in performance.

The tetrastichon in the utopian vernacular is in several respects worth noting, although it has often escaped the notice of *Utopia*'s readers.[23] Utopia's boast to have alone represented the philosophical city "without the aid of abstract philosophy" (Una ego terrarum omnium absque philosophia/ Ciuitatem philosophicam expressi mortalibus [18/19]) provides a direct challenge to Plato's speculative construction of the ideal city-state in his *Republic*. Moreover, More's rebuttal to Plato's banishment of poetry is cunningly accomplished in the personification of Utopia as/in a poem. In Utopia, poetry is not only tolerated; it is the essential embodiment, the very voice, of the philosophical city.

The tetrastichon offers itself as no mere dialectical speculation, but as the enactment of Utopia, an enactment in itself deeply dialectical. Utopia describes itself as a threshold state, freely giving of its benefits and yet adopting without reluctance better ways. This theme is taken up again in the text when Hythlodaeus remarks with some bitterness at the lack of symmetry between this Utopian policy and the European: "And just as they immediately at one meeting appropriated to themselves every good discovery of ours, so I suppose it will be long before we adopt anything that is better arranged with them than with us. This trait, I judge, is the chief reason why, though we are inferior to them neither in brains nor in resources, their commonwealth is more wisely governed and more happily flourishing than ours" (108/109).

Such giving and taking, then, form the basis of evaluation for that which is or should be Utopian, and this commerce makes Utopia a sort of membrane or filter through which ideas are passed. Utopia's openness to persuasion is thus represented in the prefatory alphabet and verse as an invitation to translation, both into and out of the Utopian. The translation of Utopian verse into Latin is the first act of Utopian commerce, and it is at once an act of giving and an act of taking. Thus any critique of the static or sinister nature of the Utopian enterprise must also register that any failure of the Utopian imagination is implicitly, or rather *explicitly,* represented as a rhetorical failure—a failure of performance that links the deficiencies of Utopia directly to the inability of any other polity (or its representing agents) to make its own superiority evident.

The Utopian word for philosophy, "gymnosophaon," is the most transparently Greek in derivation of any in the quatrain.[24] The term is glossed by the Yale editors as an allusion to the sect of Hindu philosophers known as the "gymnosophists," whose ascetic nakedness and practice of solitary mystical contemplation were reported by Plutarch, Lucian, and Cicero, among others, and mentioned by St. Jerome in his letter to Paulinus.[25] But the referent of "gymnosophaon" in the Utopian language is at once more figurative and more literal than its indological source. Utopian philosophy declares itself as naked and unadorned wisdom, and in this sense it is neither mystical nor given in solitude. The secret alphabet has at its heart, then, a naked wisdom through which we decipher a hermeneutic mythos like Andersen's story of the emperor's new clothes, but with the reverse moral. We are invited to look beneath the ornate coverings of wisdom (to peep, as it were, under the robes of scholastic dialectic), and to admire wisdom's naked form—however amusing such a form might be. Rather than pointing to a cryptic message,[26] the Utopian language announces the absurdity of such an esoteric project of translation, even as it teases the reader to make the attempt. And, indeed, it is essential that we make the attempt, for Utopian words like Erasmian sileni are important not for what they disguise but for what they disclose.[27]

Émile Pons has pointed out how ingeniously and inevitably the Utopian language serves as a vehicle for Utopian ideas: "The word [parole] is reason in action, in motion; it is its most characteristic realization and its most comprehensible. That is why grammar, in utopian literature, is inseparable from philosophy, as it was from dialectic in the trivium of the middle ages, and why philosophy dissolves into metaphysics, ordinarily denounced by the author, and into logic, which is most often confused with grammar. Thus, nine times out of ten, grammar in and of itself constitutes a method for conducting thought."[28] Utopian words, insofar as they express the complete culture, cannot disclose their wisdom to the unlearned. Latin is, of course, assumed—the letters and syntax will correspond on a one-to-one basis to the universal language of learning.[29] Additionally, a knowledge of Greek is required, as is enough exposure to the oriental languages to appreciate the Utopian affectation of a Persian morphology.[30] Moreover, because we can only read the Utopian verses backward against the literal translation that accompanies them, making sense of this New World language must entirely depend on a thorough mastery of the languages and cultures of the Old.[31] Reading Utopian will depend on a systematic analysis of the interplay between original and version, between the thing named and the function of its name(s). Wittgenstein, in his analysis of word games, puts it as a question: "naming is something like attaching a label to a thing. One can say that this is preparatory to the use of a word. But what is it a preparation *for?*"[32]

The fanciful invention of a Utopian language would seem to demand equally fanciful interpretations in which "the spirit" rather than "the letter" takes precedence. Despite the Utopia's reputation as a "jeu d'esprit," however, the philological and etymological direction of the exercise of reading and translating the Utopian verse does not rely principally on figurative or anagogic readings but on literal ones.[33] This imperative to read literally grows out of the basic premise of *Utopia,* which is simply to take straight the notion of the commonwealth or *res publica* and therefore to ask what it would mean to take such terms at face value.[34] The revelation that emerges from the exercise of translating the Utopian verse is not the distinctiveness of Utopia's cultural inheritance per se but rather its *expression* of that inheritance. Thus it is that Utopia offers its own literalness as precisely the grounds for its superiority over Plato's republic in the hexastichon: "The reason is that what he has delineated in words I alone have exhibited in men and resources and laws of surpassing excellence" (18/19). This claim to go beyond the figurative will become a standard topos of Utopian fiction, and Bacon makes precisely the same gesture toward More when he wishes to establish the superiority of his genuinely utopian *New Atlantis* over More's "Feigned Commonwealth."[35]

When Utopia is literally cut from the mainland, it is clear that all kinds of connections remain, figurative and otherwise. Raphael Hythlodaeus, we may note, similarly refuses any kind of connection to his family by passing on his patrimony. Nonetheless, the difficulty of denying one's relations can be deduced by considering the authorship of the hexastichon, attributed to "Anemolius, poet laureate, nephew of Hythlodaeus by his sister" (20/21).[36] This poet would seem to link all the worlds of *Utopia.* His name identifies him with the Anemolian ambassadors, whose dismal failure to impress the Utopians with their magnificence is one of the more vivid tales in Book 2. His title of poet laureate suggests that he is a native son of Utopia, and yet his relation to "Uncle" Hythlodaeus raises thorny or even potentially embarrassing questions about this unknown and unnamed sister. Is she blood relation or in-law? European or Utopian? There seems to be, pointedly, no way to determine from what quarter this windy poet originates. Utopia does not speak for itself again, and the beguiling simplicity of its poetic discourse is quickly complicated by the multiplicity of voices that contend for dominance and priority in the rest of the text.[37]

And yet, significantly, the voice of Utopia is discovered to be the product of the union of the Utopian and the non-Utopian. The polyphonic and monologic modes of discourse that divide the total *Utopia* into two books as we move from the dialogue in Antwerp to Hythlodaeus's Utopian monologue are both epitomized here, as Utopia's historical singularity is shown to be deeply connected to its rhetorical malleability, its desire and talent for self-transformation. The authorship of the hexastichon is ultimately left in doubt, as Giles does not disclose its origins, claiming neither himself nor Hythlodaeus as its source. But the multiple possibilities and their radical indeterminacy makes even Utopia's soliloquy a kind of conversation. If the quest for Utopian origins represented by/in the Utopian verse seems to lead us to the very questions of reform that Book 1 leaves unresolved, this circularity seems part of their design. We are led away from history as nostalgia to history as reform, from reading backward to reading forward.

This dialectical aspect of translation links Utopia to the rest of the world, and more particularly to the central concerns of the humanist translators. Translation in the sixteenth century was—in all senses of the word—a radical act.[38] The philological efforts of humanistic scholarship produced and defended scores of new translations of both profane and sacred texts. Erasmus would repeatedly formulate the project as a quest for origins, a return *ad fontes*. But although the translator's goal was generally understood and expressed in nostalgic or spiritual terms, the humanists rendered translation an increasingly visible (and controversial) art and an ever less invisible medium. As the authority of pagan and sacred texts began to be understood in great part as a textual question, the skill and moral authority of the translator/grammarian grew in importance. This shift follows logically; nonetheless, it proved a sort of moral paradox for those defenders of ancient learning, for although the humanist philologist, returning as he was *ad fontes,* would presumably arrive at the true, authoritative text by effacing himself as a reader and releasing the meaning in the text,[39] the newly understood historical contingency of those texts made the breadth of knowledge and virtuosity of the reader the greatest claim for the authority of the reading.

Humanist scholars and translators claimed their authority and, when necessary, their innocence from either or both sides of this contradiction. More's spirited defense of Erasmus in his letter to Martin Dorp claimed for the "poor grammarian" (albeit, after bridling a bit at the term) the greatest and most inclusive form of wisdom and knowledge:[40]

> In the letter to Erasmus more than once you ride roughshod over our theologians, over Erasmus, and over our grammarians, as if, while occupying a throne high up among the ranks of theologians, you were shoving him down among the poor grammarians. You take your place among the theologians, and rightly so, and not just a place, but the first place. Still he should not be shoved from the throne of the theologians down to the benches of the grammarians. Though I do not think Erasmus will scorn the title of grammarian, which you laugh at with more frequency than wit. As a matter of fact, he deserves the title most of all perhaps. But he is so modest, he does not admit it, since he realizes that the name "grammarian" is synonymous with learned; the function of the grammarian penetrates all types of letters—that is, all the arts. Consequently, a person who has made a thorough study of dialectics can be called a dialectician, of arithmetic, an arithmetician; likewise in the other arts. But it is my definite opinion that only the man who has investigated all the branches of knowledge has the right to be called learned.[41]

Rather than insist on Erasmus's qualifications as theologian, More undermines Dorp's hierarchy from below by revaluing the role of the grammarian, whose solid grounding in "all types of letters" is discovered to be the most extensive and inclusive basis of learning.[42] As Eugenio Garin has pointed out, "the expositions of the grammarians about the language of ancient texts began to involve all other texts and all other languages, i.e. institutions, habits, norms, procedures in logic and visions of the world."[43]

The grammarian's penetration into all the arts is based not only on his ability to speak the native idioms of the various arts but also on his capacity to explicate and facilitate those connections between languages and cultures.[44] In *De ratione studii,* Erasmus describes this breadth of learning with a metaphor of circumnavigation: "In order that the teacher might be thoroughly up to his work, he should not merely be master of one particular branch of study. He should himself have travelled through the whole circle of knowledge."[45]

Ultimately, *Utopia* posits the experience of history as a double translation—first linguistic and second cultural or conceptual—as the reader becomes aware that understanding Utopia in its own terms is to revalue one's own. George Steiner describes this aspect of translation in a passage that applies as much to Utopia's map as to its language: "One's own space is mapped by what lies outside, it derives coherence, tactile configuration, from the pressure of the external. 'Otherness' particularly when it has the wealth and penetration of language compels 'presentness' to stand clear."[46]

Of course, linguistic and cultural translations were never entirely separate or consecutive textual procedures even though the Renaissance debate over whether works were to be translated *ad verbum* or *ad sensum* suggested that these two "methods" were held up as mutually exclusive choices. The basic question raised in such debate was not simply the choice between imitation or invention, anachronism or modernism in diction or syntax; at issue was whether the locus of meaning in the original lie in its historical particularity or in its atemporal universality. Brian Copenhaver describes the famous fifteenth-century philosophical debate on translation between Leonardo Bruni and his critic, the Spanish bishop Alonso de Cartegena (Alfonso de Cartagena), as follows: "Where Bruni insisted on fidelity to the historically contingent language of the original, Alonso (de Cartegena) required fidelity to a privileged metachronic structure (ratio) discoverable in the text but unconstrained by history and expressible in any language. 'Reason (ratio) is common to every people' he argued, 'though it is expressed in various idioms. So let us discuss whether the Latin Language supports [a translation] . . . whether it agrees with reality (res ipsae) not whether it accords with the Greek.'"[47] As the preceding discussion makes clear, the issue could never be decided as a choice between two opposed techniques for while the theoretical goals of humanist translation were being debated, individual efforts could take their place only along a continuum whose defining poles were, in practice, equally impossible to achieve. Perfect representation of either the original or *res ipsae* necessarily remained an elusive goal, a utopian destination.

Humanist translators and pedagogues defined and classified the variety of relations that their texts might have to the classical models they reproduced or imitated. Humanist handbooks provided exercises and examples to rehearse the differences between *translatio, paraphrasis, imitatio,* and *allusio*—techniques ranging from the most literal reproduction to the most free adaptation. Nonetheless, as Thomas Greene has pointed out, "Most Renaissance translations are already interpretations. . . . The wider the cultural gulf, the more inevitable this interpretive element."[48]

After its prefatory verses, *Utopia* is not offered in any strict or literal sense as a translation. It is, nonetheless, an important meditation on the problems of cultural translation and transmission. The text confronts its reader with an enormous cultural gap, and yet More seems reluctant to interpret the materials before him. Just when editorial interpretation (that is, cultural intervention) would seem most necessary, More plays the naif.[49] The reader is left to translate for herself, and the act of translating will depend in large part on the measure taken between Utopia and Europe, between the cranky yet (if the *parerga* is to be believed) persuasive Hythlodaeus and the skeptical and unpersuaded More. Indeed, to be comprehensible, *Utopia* must be read against the comprehensive strategies of Renaissance translation.

Problems of translation are legion in *Utopia.* For example, the act of naming distinguishes not between Utopian and Latin versions but between new and old Utopian versions. The doubling of Utopian names is further complicated in that each Utopian name, old or new, tends to have etymologically encoded double meanings. Thus Utopian meanings multiply by two principles: "polyonomasia" and "polyetymologia," which push the act of definition in two directions at once.[50] For example, the official elected by every thirty families is called in the newer language "phylarch" ("head of a tribe" or "lover of power"),[51] and yet Hythlodaeus persists in referring to the office by what he declares to be its old name, "syphogrant" ("sty-ward," "steward," or "silly old man"). Over every ten syphogrants and their families presides a "protophylarch," or, in the old language, as Hythlodaeus continues to refer to the post, a "tranibor" ("bench-eater" or "master-trencherman").[52] Hythlodaeus's insistence on using the older language allegedly not in use is, doubtless, a reflection of the humanists' defense of the study of Greek and Hebrew and the value of original texts. Yet paradoxically, for the Utopians, Greek is a new language, against which they measure their independent and yet parallel philosophical and scientific traditions, thus allowing for a contest between ancients and moderns that is completely removed from European chronology.

The old and new Utopian languages, taken with the Greek letters newly introduced by Hythlodaeus (and yet already archaeologically embedded in Utopian names), form a trilingual system. More and Giles may have had in mind a language system comparable to that proposed by Roger Bacon in the thirteenth century or established in the trilingual college (Hebrew, Greek, and Latin) at Louvain in 1518.[53] But where Roger Bacon or the Collegium Trilingue enlisted a diversity of languages in the pursuit of singular scriptural truths, the antipodal languages are often (though not consistently) self-divided and contradictory.[54] The Utopian language is not a "natural" language in the sixteenth-century sense of an original, unfallen tongue, nor does Utopian naming replicate the Adamic task. Nonetheless, it may come very close to describing the true nature of things in the postlapsarian world.[55]

The compromising and self-condemning Utopian names have most often been taken to indicate an implicit critique of Utopia's ostensibly improved political order. If the postlapsarian status of the Utopian languages is revealed by their failure to idealize, however, it is in just this regard that they are least distorting. In the *Cratylus,* law is associated with name-giving, and the legislator is the namer and maker of names. More reconsiders Plato in *Utopia* as the namer of legislators. The names for Utopian offices offer an inversion of the vanity of European metaphors for rule, where, as Hythlodaeus points out, the rulers and guardians of people neither rule themselves nor guard their flock. The cautionary names for Utopian stewardship—the ambiguity, for example, of whether the tranibor is a steward or glutton, or whether the phylarch is tribal chief or lover of power—ask that we read both possibilities literally against the performance of the office. On the other hand, the debased literalization of European metaphors for rule suggests an unambiguous critique. Thus we see the secular or ecclesiastic shepherds of the people enact the letter rather than the spirit of such epithets, when, as under the enclosure laws, they take care of sheep rather than men.[56]

More sets up the irony by first referring to the "pastoris officium" in Book 1 as part of the extended hypothetical speech of Hythlodaeus to the king who retained his service: "For this very reason it belongs to the king to take more care for the welfare of his people than for his own, just as it is the duty of a shepherd, insofar as he is a shepherd, to feed his sheep rather than himself" (94/95). But this is part of a speech that cannot be spoken, whose unfolding shows why it must fall on deaf ears. For Hythlodaeus, who is more nominalist than idealist, it represents the counterfactual analogy that cannot be spoken until the conditions that enable it are in effect. Conversely, the seemingly counterfactual or self-canceling Utopian terms—whereby Utopia is nowhere, its river without water, and its prince without subjects—are best understood as literally true. Whatever critique these terms imply shifts in its reference to the conditions that make Utopia impossible.

More's neologisms that deal with the non-Utopian are not systematic in their inversions. Some names, such as those of the Achorians (without place, region, or district), appear self-denying; others, such as those of the Macarians (Blessed Ones), seem anabashedly self-lauding. But the process of ascertaining the relation of the place name to the place named almost always brings us to some utterly literal rendition, in part because the act of reading demands that we square the name with the thing. We learn that the Achorians are without land by choice, having forced their king to choose among his kingdoms, and that it is precisely this voluntary landlessness that affords them the stability and the prosperity they enjoy. In the case of the Macarians, that which makes them happy among men is the compulsory impoverishment of their king. Here again, More transforms a self-declared virtue into a self-evident one, through a dramatic inversion of contemporary monarchical values. Curiously enough, the Achorian's place-name seems to mirror Utopia in meaning. Both are national oxymorons—places defined by negation or lack of place. But the Achorian's defining civic virtue is quite different from Utopia's aggressive colonial practice. Understanding the aptitude of these New World names tends to redirect the paradox from name to practice, and consequently from the expression to the conception of the values they reflect.

The original act of Utopian translation might properly be assigned to Utopus when he "translates" the old Abraxa into the new Utopia in a staggering feat of civil engineering, making an island out of what was "formerly not an island" (Utopus me dux ex non insula fecit insulam [18/19]). This act of translation is in itself an act of authorship and transformation, whereby Utopus is *arche,* beginning and foundation principle. But Utopus must also translate his wisdom into a code that does not depend on his personal interpretation or administration when he sets up

Utopia as a self-perpetuating system. The first act will separate Utopians from others in a quite literal fashion; the second will bind them to one another. Utopian letters, like the Utopian map, perform both as metonymy and as metaphor. To be a fully effective text, *Utopia* can be read neither as wholly one or the other, just as the Utopian game of Vices and Virtues is deployed on a game board and yet relies implicitly on the ability of the player to translate the lessons of the game from the field of play to the real world.[57]

Such translations, however, necessarily require a complete reconception of terms, suggesting the difficulty facing the "ideal" textual transmission. Budé's letter to Lupset concludes by praising More for providing "a nursery of correct and useful institutions from which every man may introduce and adapt transplanted customs (*translatitios mores*) to his own city" (13/14). Budé thus indicates a double transformation, both of the "translatitios mores" (suggesting a pun on More's name) and their new context. Budé's metaphor suggests that translating and transplanting are, in fact, the same thing. But if imitation is, in effect, the process of dissemination, the ultimate impossibility of perfect reproduction requires deconstruction, for, at least according to the Derridean understanding of this term, "[dissemination] is what foils the attempt to progress in an orderly way toward meaning or knowledge, what breaks the circuit of intentions or expectations through some ungovernable excess or loss."[58]

Eutopia/Heterotopia

It is precisely this issue of whether Utopia describes a place of excess or of loss that has governed contemporary readings of *Utopia* specifically and utopian fiction generally; yet it seems worth considering how such irreconcilable characterizations can offer what have come to be interchangeable alternatives. If the garden world suggested by Budé's preceding organic analogy has not satisfied all of Utopia's readers, one form of resistance (as we have seen illustrated in Berger and Freeman) argues that the garden or pastoral world of utopia is ultimately an artificial world, sterile rather than productive. Michel Foucault's complaint about utopias, however, takes the opposite tack. In *The Order of Things,* he makes the following distinction between "utopias" and "heterotopias" to account for the effects he discovers in Jorge Luis Borges:

> *Utopias* afford consolation: although they have no real locality there is nevertheless a fantastic, untroubled region in which they are able to

unfold; they open up cities with vast avenues, superbly planted gardens, countries where life is easy, even though the road to them is chimerical. *Heterotopias* are disturbing, probably because they secretly undermine language, because they make it impossible to name this and that, because they shatter or tangle common names, because they destroy "syntax" in advance, and not only the syntax with which we construct sentences but also that less apparent syntax which causes words and things (next to and also opposite one another) to "hold together." This is why utopias permit fables and discourse: they run with the very grain of language and are part of the fundamental dimension of the *fabula;* heterotopias (such as those to be found so often in Borges) desiccate speech, stop words in their tracks, contest the very possibility of grammar at its source; they dissolve our myths and sterilize the lyricism of our sentences.[59]

What to my mind is most remarkable about Foucault's linguistic portrait of heterotopia is how clearly it describes the operations of the eponymic *Utopia,* suggesting that the first utopia was, at least according to Foucault's definition of the term, a heterotopia. Foucault offers the qualities of desiccation and sterility as a *tribute* to Borges's achievement, yet it is these very features that, when discovered in More, tend to aggrieve his critics. That Foucault does not identify such qualities with *dystopia,* but rather with *heterotopia,* can perhaps provide an expanded model for *Utopia* as neither untroubled *fabula* nor dystopian disavowal. But it may seem less important to coin a new term for utopian fiction that resists idealization if we can properly historicize utopia's origins as just such a critical discourse.[60] It is, rather, the historical situation of utopia since the nineteenth century as the antithesis of history, its erasure or denial, that drives the insistence on such alternatives, not *Utopia* itself. More knew as well as Wittgenstein that "to imagine a language is to imagine a form of life."[61] But by inventing a deeply paradoxical, self-denying, and reduplicating language and alphabet, More and his collaborator, Giles, imagine not an ideal world—for Utopia is not that—but a set of wor(l)ds whose connections are very much in doubt.

The problem of Utopian language and representation will resurface repeatedly in later utopian (or dystopian) writers.[62] The unity or perfection of utopian language is often characterized by the absence of—or an inability to represent—that which is not utopian. Swift's peaceful Houyhnhnms ("who have not the least idea of books or literature") cannot lie; indeed, the closest they can come to the word or even the concept for falsehood is to say elliptically, the thing which is not."[63] The hero of

Bellamy's *Looking Backward,* Mr. Julian West, can describe an impressive novel of the future only by saying that "what impressed me was not so much what was in the book as what was left out of it."[64]

Yet the Utopians, unlike the Houhnhynms, are worldly polyglots. In contrast to the politics of omission in the future novel of *Looking Backward,* or the pastoral world of Morris's *News from Nowhere,* in which the word for politics is itself omitted, what gets included in Utopian discourse is in many ways as disturbing as what gets left out.[65] Utopian language practice is both imperialistic and quite literal in its comprehensiveness. The Utopians are acquainted enough with the letters and customs of other cultures that when it becomes "necessary" to wage war, they rely on the power of language to undermine a culture from within. Printing up huge placards that offer substantial rewards for the capture of their enemies, they manage to conquer without bloodshed, by appealing to motivations that should ostensibly be incomprehensible to members of their own society. Indeed, the entire power base of Utopia is generated by advantageous translations. The Utopians' only real power over their neighbors is based on their ability to transmute gold, which is to them intrinsically worthless, into tokens of far greater value: soldiers who hold their lives dear, citizens who hold their loyalties cheap, kings who put their national security up for hire. The Utopians thrive explicitly on their ability to speak to the worst instincts of their neighbors. This is not the linguistic distortion that Bacon was to call the "Idols of the Marketplace." This, rather, is deliberate translation of and traffic in ideals, a question not of meaning but of use. And it is this operational property of language that connects Utopian language most problematically to the transformations required by rhetoric.

European Authority and Utopian Counterfeits

The relation of translation to original in *Utopia,* as I have suggested, is not always to the advantage of the original. More "reminds" Giles how he was relieved of the labor of gathering materials, their arrangement or style (inventio, dispositio, or elocutio), because "I had only to repeat what in your company I heard Raphael relate" (38/39). More goes on to characterize Hythlodaeus's speech—first as hurried and impromptu and then as "the product of a person, who, as you know, was not so well acquainted with Latin as with Greek." Giles's prefatory letter to Busleyden attributes such eloquence to More that he suggests that this text is more vivid to him than when he heard "Hythlodaeus's own words sounding in [his] ears" (20/21). Challenging Plato's notion of written language as a corrupted form of oral discourse, Giles insists not on the priority of textual representation to oral transmission but on its evident superiority, asserting that "we tell more effectively what we have seen than what we have heard" (22/23). Strikingly, Giles associates sight here not with Hythlodaeus's first-person experience or reportage but with the experience of reading More's represpresentation of that account.

Even though Hythlodaeus lived in Utopia and was apparently an impassioned convert, Giles attributes to More the better description: "Nevertheless, when I contemplate the same picture as painted by More's brush, I am as affected as if I were sometimes actually living in Utopia itself. By heaven, I am even disposed to believe that in all the five years which Raphael spent on the island, he did not see as much as one may perceive in More's description" (22/23). The dialectic of praise here is a playful meditation on the question of textual authority. By claiming a superior status for More's Utopian imitation over Hythlodaeus's Utopian experience, Giles claims for the humanist translator and historian a status of highest authority in the re-creation and elevation of his materials. Such a declaration is much more than a veiled acknowledgment of More's authorship. Humanists such as Poggio Bracciolini attributed to themselves the status of author (scriptor) for their translations. Valla and Dolet, following Cicero, saw their task as translators to improve on the original. In so doing, they were simply following the oratorical ideal of the humanist rhetoricians who privileged eloquence and expression (*oratio*) over philosophical wisdom (*ratio*). But significantly, More will make no such claims for his own eloquence, and Hythlodaeus is a supremely reluctant orator.

Hythlodaeus's refusal of eloquence in Book 1's Dialogue of Counsel is both striking and disturbing, and more than one critic has ascribed Hythlodaeus's disavowal of public service to a covert or even overt misanthropy, which to varying degrees implicates More himself.[66] Whatever Hythlodaeus's misanthropic tendencies, his objections to serving as an adviser to kings seem both reasoned and practical enough.[67] Advising princes, declares Hythlodaeus, is possible only if you tell them what they wish to hear. The *speculum principis* must always be flattering and thus can never be sufficiently corrective. Thus, as Hythlodaeus makes clear in Book 1, *Utopia* is not prescriptive but descriptive; indeed, it is most descriptive in its outline of the ways in which it could only fail as a prescriptive text for any English or continental king. Although More is obviously making a point for Henry VIII's benefit, Hythlodaeus's refusal of service does more than allow More to state obliquely the terms under which he can accept such service.[68] Hythlodaeus declares quite clearly in Book 1 that he has no desire and less hope of persuading before launching into his long monologue of Book 2. If More's skeptical remarks at the end of the book are any indication, Hythlodaeus's doubts were well-founded.

Arthur Kinney and others have suggested that the weakness of Hythlodaeus's character is that he is a bad rhetorician.[69] But it is not at all the case that Hythlodaeus is an inarticulate speaker; he is, rather, a self-declared anti-Sophist. And there are reasons to fear rhetoric for hire that need not be connected to the ineffectiveness of counsel in *Utopia*. On the contrary, in his prefatory letter, William Budé declares that he was so affected by the book that "I almost neglected and even forsook the management of household affairs. I perceived the trumpery in all the theory and practice (artem omnem industriamque) of domestic economy and in absolutely all anxiety for increasing one's revenue" (4/5). The more persuasive Hythlodaeus's zealous defense of the other world, the greater the potential disengagement it provokes with this one. Indeed, Hythlodaeus—in himself a cautionary tale—has become one of the disengaged. His cynical conviction that there is no proper European audience for his discourse—and More's demonstration that he remains unpersuaded—makes explicit the failure of a rhetorical defense of *Utopia*. Because the ideal reader is not provided *in* the idealizing text, the project becomes one of conversion—the creation of an ideal audience. Here More's authorial pragmatism seems to anticipate both critical and idealist responses, and to tie them in close and problematic relation to each other. The problem of audience is closely related to the problem of authorship and authority, and this is most clearly emblematized by More's own position as author/audience for his text.

Budé's letter to Lupset underscores the reversibility of Utopian authority in another striking passage in which More, Hythlodaeus, and the Utopians each vie for the position of author, exemplar, and model:

We owe knowledge of this island to Thomas More, who has made public for our age this model of the happy life and this rule of living. The discoverer, as More himself reveals, is Hythlodaeus, to whom he ascribes the whole account. On the one hand, Hythlodaeus is the one who has built their city for the Utopians and established customs and laws for them; that is to say, he has borrowed from them and brought home to us the pattern of the good life. On the other hand, beyond question it is More who has adorned the island and its holy institutions by his style and eloquence. (12/13)

In this passage each act of imitation, every reproduction of the paradigm, becomes in turn an act of authorship, and More's true authority is doubled rather than concealed in the text's fictional origins. The double status of the "model" and its ambiguous claim to superiority—both as that which is original and that which is to be made over—is featured as a central component of the problematics of praise in *Utopia*. In his prefatory praise of More, Busleyden terms *Utopia* the "absolutissimum simulacrum" (31/32); indeed, the status of the copy, counterfeit, or simulacrum is one of the very serious questions raised by the stylistic and institutional formulation of Utopia. The problem is particularly vexed because the text's putative "original" is the extravagantly fictional island nation of Utopia. If the original is "noplace," then arguably there can exist nothing but counterfeits. More manages to evade one of the most thorny questions of Renaissance imitation—that is, whether art or nature was the principal object of mimetic practice—by hopelessly confusing the status of the "original."

The counterfeit is discussed explicitly in two interesting passages in *Utopia* to elaborate the difference between true and false pleasures. In the commentary with which he concludes the story of the ostentatious display of the Anemolian ambassadors and their ultimate humiliation, Hythlodaeus remarks, "The Utopians wonder that any mortal takes pleasure in the uncertain sparkle of a tiny jewel or precious stone when he can look at a star or even the sun itself" (156/157). Although the pleasures of looking at the sun may have their limits as well as their hazards, the moral of the tale, following the platonic hierarchy of forms, seems to be "accept no substitutes." The original is shown to be the transcendent form rather than the diminished, material image. The marginal gloss to this passage notes, "The Narrator Terms the Sparkle 'Uncertain' because the Gems are Imitation or at Least Does So Because their Sparkle is Tiny and Faint" (156/157). The gloss fixes not on solar pleasures but on the double doubtfulness of the gems. That all gems are an imitation of light is a given; the only question that remains is the degree of the remove from the ideal form. Thus the "real" counterfeit paradoxically helps us to an understanding of true value by dramatizing the limitations of sense experience and the true nature of (false) imitation. This model suggests how the "false" utopia can perform a similar hermeneutic function, creating an interpretative crisis that requires the reader to measure not just Utopia's distance from the ideal but its distance from the real.

In a later discussion of the counterfeit pleasures (fucatae voluptatis), Hythlodaeus describes how the Utopians class those who imagine themselves noble because of a long line of ancestors rich in landed estates ("now the only nobility") with those fools who dote on jewels and gems:

> With these persons (the Utopians) class those who, as I said, dote on jewels and gems and who think they become a species of god if ever they secure a fine specimen, especially of the sort which at the period is regarded as of the highest value in their country. It is not everywhere or always that one kind of stone is prized. They will not purchase it unless taken out of its gold setting and exposed to view, and not even then unless the seller take an oath and gives security that it is a true gem and a true stone, so anxious are they lest a spurious stone in place of a genuine one deceive their eyes. But why should a counterfeited one give less pleasure to your sight when your eye cannot distinguish it from the true article? Both should be of equal value to you, even as they would be, by heaven, to a blind man! (168/169)

This passage goes through several curious turns. First, gems are bad because they are falsely believed to confer value on the owner, but the argument quickly takes a paranoid turn when the attention focuses on the uncertain value of the gems themselves. On the one hand, the owner is faced with the problem of shifting fashions and the absence of any guarantee of stable value. But clearly worse is the nagging uncertainty of whether the value of the goods is ever knowable, and the disconcerting fact that the more clever the counterfeit, the more insecure the position of the buyer or owner. The reader is both implicated and made all the more anxious by the sudden shift from the moralizing third person to an accusing second-person assault. The personal tone may owe something to the fact that Erasmus tells a very similar story in his *Praise of Folly,* in which More seems to be named a principal: "I know a certain man named after me [Folly/Morus] who gave his bride some imitation gems, assuring her (and he is a clever jokester) that they were not only real and genuine but also that they were of unparalleled and inestimable value. I ask you, what difference did it make to the girl since she feasted her eyes and mind no less pleasantly on glass and kept them hidden among her things as if they were an extraordinary treasure?"[70] Folly's perverse argument is, of course, that the happy fool who gazes at images is at least as well off as the sober wise man who leaves Plato's cave "and sees things as they really are." And, indeed, where we might expect an inversion of Folly's view, the argument that More (Morus) makes in *Utopia* is strangely parallel. If, in the larger context of the Utopian "model," value is not absolute but only an act of the imagination ("Opinio hominum precium addit, aut adimit gemmis" [168]), then the counterfeit's status is elevated at least as much as that of the genuine article is debased. But More's counterfeit is still an object of suspicion, as the difference between good imitation and bad imitation is that good imitation is infinitely the more problematic, both epistemologically and ethically.

The suspicious—even destructive—role of the imitator is exemplified in the figure of the monkey who destroys part of Hythlodaeus's Theophrastus during the voyage. Marin has pointed out the long tradition of *simia-similis* this incident amusingly caricatures, for the overliteral consumption of the book clearly ends its usefulness.[71] Thoughtless incorporation equals mutilation.

From a rhetorical point of view, More's inability to let himself be persuaded at the end of Book 2 suggests either that Hythlodaeus's performance was lacking and that he only imperfectly represented the perfection of the Utopians, or that the imperfection was in the Utopians themselves. It is worth pointing out that *neither* More nor Hythlodaeus shows any hope of Utopian customs taking root at home. The *transformatio orationis* is suspended, remaining to be accomplished. Nancy Struever has suggested that "the rhetor's realm of effectiveness is in the realm of the probable (eikos) perceived by the senses, structured by phantasia and mimesis,"[72] a description that suggests why Hythlodaeus must fail. If Utopian practice is improbable, the chance of like reforms occurring in England is held out as impossible. The mimetic text and the idealizing text are shown to be at cross-purposes. Patriotism, heroism, honor, glory—all tools of the rhetor's and the early modern historian's trade—are rendered suspect. All the anxieties of the text come to reside in the figure of the counterfeit, wherein both performance (the act of imitation) and source (the object of imitation) are completely compromised.

In the end *Utopia* leaves its readers no place, but this is not the same place where we began, it having taken the entire course of the text to get there. And it is only here, in the uncertain location between the cynical pragmatism represented by More and the unyielding idealism represented by Hythlodaeus, that reform can theoretically be conceived.

Engaging both philological and rhetorical methods, More pushes the text toward a heuristic crisis as it lurches backward and forward at the same time. He invites us to read literally and then shows the futility of the attempt, providing along the way a number of disturbing details, which, paradoxically, grow increasingly alienating the more familiar they become. By representing and foregrounding an imperfect transmission between the mimetic and the ideal text, *Utopia* can begin to suggest why More greatly feared the translation of his text. *Utopia* was clearly a text meant only for the learned, who might read it closely enough to know that Utopia is not easily approached and less easily reproduced; common sense was not to be confused with vulgar knowledge. Despite its political teaching of communal property and shared labor, *Utopia* was never intended as a text for the masses. And More later classed the work with Erasmus's *Praise of Folly* as texts he would sooner destroy than have misconstrued: "Yf any man wolde now translate [Eramsus's] Moria in to Englyshe, or some workes eyther that I haue my selfe wryten ere this, all be yt there be none harme therein/folke yet beynge (as they be) geuen to take harme of that that is good/I wolde not onely my derlynges bokes but myne owne also, helpe to burne them both wyth myne own hands, rather then folke sholde (though thorow theyr own faute) take any harme of them, seynge that I se them lykely in these dayes so to do."[73] Because the import of method and its reform in *Utopia* is not always fully considered, such sentiments have been too often regarded as a change of heart brought on by the upheavals of the Protestant Reformation. But it seems unwarranted to regard as a retraction, or change of view, More's appreciation that the profound change in *Utopia*'s political position during the Reformation, and the change of its potential readership in vernacular translation, had the potential utterly to transform the conception and reception of his text. Indeed, *Utopia* offers the object lesson in how such transformations occur. Finally, the work cannot properly be considered either an ideological idyll or a revolutionary credo. Interpretations that oppose these as exclusive alternatives in measuring the text's success or failure cannot help taking *Utopia* as the failure of history or history as the failure of Utopia.

Chapter Four

The *New Atlantis:* Bacon's History of the New Science

Those however who aspire not to guess and divine, but to discover and know; who propose not to devise mimic and fabulous worlds of their own, but to examine and dissect the nature of this very world itself; must go to facts themselves for everything.

—FRANCIS BACON, *The Great Instauration*

And all depends in keeping the eye steadily fixed upon the facts of nature and so receiving their images simply as they are. For God forgive that we should give out a dream of our own imagination for a pattern of the world; rather may he graciously grant to us to write an apocalypse or true vision of the footsteps of the Creator imprinted on his creatures.

—FRANCIS BACON, *The Great Instauration*

These passages from Bacon's *Instauratio Magna* (1620),[1] demanding the philosopher-scientist's unwavering commitment to the mundane facts of nature, may (and indeed should) seem ostensibly problematic assertions from the author of the *New Atlantis,* a manifestly imaginative, fabulous, and inevitably fictional utopia. Unless we are to construct a theory of a late-career recantation around the *New Atlantis,* the most plausible explanation is that the preceding exhortations are not leveled against fictional productions per se but against the fantastic syllogistic productions of scholasticism that stand in the place of (and in the way of) a true natural history. Nonetheless, it is at least perplexing when attempting to situate the *New Atlantis* among Bacon's works to note that such passages are exemplary of a refrain that would make him seem positively hostile to the imaginative enterprise we might naturally assume a utopian fiction to represent.

Indeed, we can find in the *Novum Organum* a far more direct and emphatic refutation of fiction as well as the authority and dignity of Atlantean recovery:

> But for my part, relying on the evidence and truth of things, I reject all forms of fiction and imposture; nor do I think that it matters any more to the business in hand, whether the discoveries that shall now be made were long ago known to the ancients, and have their settings and their risings according to the vicissitude of things and course of ages, than it matters to mankind whether the new world be that island of Atlantis with which the ancients were acquainted, or now discovered for the first time. For new discoveries must be sought from the light of nature, not fetched back out of the darkness of antiquity. (4.108–109)

To construct a coherent reading of the *New Atlantis,* it is necessary at the very least to frame explicitly the larger questions raised by these passages that many readers manage to elide entirely; that is, if Bacon identifies his project in opposition to the construction of fabulous worlds, and manifests complete indifference to the identity or recovery of the Old Atlantis, what is the *New Atlantis* doing among his philosophical works? Indeed, isn't a utopia just such a "dream" taken for a "pattern of the world," not as it is, but as it should be? Doesn't the utopian writer eschew the recording of nature as it is in order to display its perfection in humankind's culture and institutional elaborations? Is the *New Atlantis,* then, an exemplum or an anomaly—an allegory of or a crime against the method proposed?

To note, as commentators on the *New Atlantis* must, and do, that Bacon's utopia has exactly those features we would expect of its author (the domination of nature achieved by a rationally ordered society guided by its revered scientist-priests) should not too quickly distract us from the problems that inhere in the nature—and in the very fact—of this Baconian utopia. Remarkably, this technological utopia is described in a text that does not deal with facts, proposes no particular scientific works, shrouds its imaginary House of Salomon in secrecy, offers itself as fulfillment of prophecy, and seems to base its scientific authority in miracles.

Although the religious tenor of Bacon's philosophy has been discussed both sympathetically and critically, the religious idiom of the *New Atlantis*'s fictional frame has too often been ignored or treated as a textual act of bad faith, because of its failure to correspond to what we have learned to read as a future-based technological fantasy. By investigating the parabolic construction of the *New Atlantis,* however, we can begin to answer some of the most basic questions about the historical form and function of Bacon's fiction. If we do not locate the utopian "method" of this text exclusively in the scientific practice of the House of Salomon but instead understand the tensions in those operative metaphors of secrecy and apocalypse, veiling and revelation, mystery and illumination to be essential features of Bacon's utopian project, then the intimate connections between the *New Atlantis*'s fictional and institutional frames can be brought to light. It is only by taking fully into account the nature of Bacon's antipathy to Atlantean projects of recovery "out of the darkness of antiquity" that we can begin to understand the historical situation of the *New Atlantis.* For Bacon, putting the practices of his work into history depends to no small degree on putting a new sort of history into practice, one that both assimilates and revises the models offered by universal and civil history to make way for and record the production of the new natural history. Rather than reiterate claims for the *New Atlantis* as proleptic science fiction, this chapter redirects attention to the historical framing of the *New Atlantis* to outline Bacon's utopian fiction as a myth of origins—a myth that is anything but nostalgic.[2]

We do not have to assume that Bacon was cynically applying religious window dressing to an utterly mechanical secular model, if we understand why and how Bacon would use a religious idiom to tell a parable of reformed history. Bacon's utopia needs to be viewed, then, not simply as an expression of the ambivalence of his philosophical inheritance (the medieval Christian vs. the scientific modern) but as the *locus* where he most explicitly works out a synthesis of genres to negotiate a new narrative for the *production* of history. As such, the *New Atlantis* is not best understood as a fabulous history of the future, a fanciful interlude from the present, or even a design for an ideal research institute, but as the outline—from its origins—of a fictional (that is, imagined) History of Learning that would reveal Bacon's project to be more than a fiction.

Bacon and the Fables of History

While it has always been widely read, the *New Atlantis* has only recently begun to receive the attention and critical scrutiny it deserves.[3] Historically, scholars interested in Bacon's scientific and philosophical oeuvre have too often treated the *New Atlantis* as merely illustrative material, which has had the effect of reducing the text to a sort of *Amazing Stories* cartoon version of Bacon's program for the reform of learning. Those who have placed the *New Atlantis* in the context of utopian fiction have tended to fall in one of two categories. Some readings have tended to ignore the work's strangeness to treat it as a straightforward blueprint or a self-evident polemic on the role Bacon believed technology should play in shaping the perfect society.[4] Others have relished its strangeness at the level of detail while ignoring the strangeness of the project as such, proceeding instead to decode (or encode) the perceived allegory of science without providing either a context in Bacon's work for such an unabashed exercise of fancy or a persuasive argument of why Bacon's science would require a veiling, allegorical representation.[5]

In general, neither approach comes around to explaining *why* Bacon would construct a utopian fiction at all when he had already written scores of New Science manifestoes outlining every institutional reform his utopia "enacts," as well as a number decrying the invention of such idle fancies as the mythopoetic *New Atlantis* would seem to embody. Too often both types of reading evaluate this and other utopian texts in terms of their "success" or "failure"—terms that sometimes confuse historical and ethical registers. Moreover, arguments for the "failure" of the *New Atlantis* very often reproduce the same arguments used to make the case for its "success"—that is, the degree to which this utopian fiction actually anticipated or produced institutional, cultural, or epistemological change. Denise Albanese, for example, argues that Bacon's *New Atlantis* is not a true utopia at all but "a simulacrum of the utopian form," precisely because it "works to produce in actual practice what it summons in the representational."[6] Thus, for Albanese, Bacon's text represents a failure of the utopian form in direct and inverse proportion to its success in achieving its ideological program—a critique that could be said to unite her with such diverse and famous readers of Bacon as the Frankfurt School's Horkheimer and Adorno and the conservative Catholic Count Joseph de Maistre.[7]

Offering her own answer to the question "Why fiction?," Albanese detects in the *New Atlantis* a "colonized utopianism," whereby "the discursive terrain of humanism, dominated as it is by *literae,* by literature, is appropriated by the emergent ideology of science."[8] Attributing to the ideology of science an efficacy (however negative) denied to the "true" literary utopia raises theoretical as well as rhetorical difficulties, however. How does history confirm that Bacon's utopianism is "appropriated by" or transformed into ideology or that More's is not, when the history of criticism, as well as the history of colonialism (viz. de Quiroga), offers rather mixed evidence?

The word "appropriation," like "co-optation," is generally used by new historicist readers to suggest that a work, act, or gesture is—by design or default—subsumed by a dominant political power or enlisted to justify and legitimate it. Bacon is naturally eager to persuade others to his view, and his text is clearly far more polemical in its design than is More's paradoxical *Utopia.* Nonetheless, despite Bacon's inevitable association with power as the author of modernism's credo "knowledge is power," his access to and expression of power is, at the time he wrote the *New Atlantis,* far more rhetorical than real. Composed during Bacon's disgrace after his fall from office, the *New Atlantis* failed to persuade its most important and powerful reader, James I, to support either its author or his ideas.[9] A close reading of the *New Atlantis* and its evasion of sovereign political power may suggest why this was so. This does not, of course, prevent the work from participating in its ideological context; indeed, it can scarcely fail to do so. But to measure the "appropriation" of a text's utopian content by its potential or perceived "application" means, paradoxically, that no utopian text offering itself as genuinely reforming can be genuinely utopian.

Indeed, if history is, as we have seen, almost inevitably identified as the inversion or annulment of utopia, the *New Atlantis,* insofar as it is understood to enter or produce history, can *only* be read as not-utopia. But this reflects more the determined anti-utopian bias of contemporary new historicist poetics than a full historical delineation of Bacon's utopian vision. Gerald Graff is instructive on the strategic as well as logical impasse facing the new historicism's alertness to any and all species of ideological "co-optation": "What makes 'co-optation' a paradoxical concept is the negative value it assigns to something that we usually think of as desirable—being accepted or successful, persuading others to one's point of view. The word 'co-optation' makes every form of appropriation sound sinister, even the kinds of appropriation normally

presupposed as ends of social action." [10] Bacon's influence on his Enlightenment heirs is enormous and indisputable. Nonetheless, the vicissitudes of his reputation, both during his lifetime and in the 372 years
since his death, suggest that the ideological work done by and in his
writings has been open to a wide variety of interpretations, applications,
and potential appropriations. [11]

My concern here is not to forget the historical magnitude of Bacon's
impact on Enlightenment and post-Enlightenment thought, but, rather,
to remember that Bacon wrote the *New Atlantis* at a moment when
power had slipped entirely from his grasp and when his legacy may
well have seemed to him very much in doubt. I would like, therefore, to
pursue the connection between literature and history by reconsidering
the manner in which the *New Atlantis* designs its own history, situates itself with respect to its European cultural and philosophical inheritance,
and attempts to control and put into effect its utopian legacy in a parable of history.

Bacon's animation of his most ambitious and global vision of reform
in an exercise of poesy demonstrates the need for a greater consideration of the role imagination played in the relationship between representation and reformation. The confusion about the "method" of the
New Atlantis is perhaps most clearly revealed by the myriad of generic
categories used—often interchangeably, or in hybrid form—to describe
it: prophecy, allegory, myth, technological utopia, allegory of science,
"utopia of science," [12] "mythic parable," [13] "philosophical fable," [14] "speculative myth," [15] or even "a theater for the presentation of an allegory of
science." [16]

William Rawly, Bacon's secretary and biographer, in his preface to the
New Atlantis, describes the work as a "fable" that contains a "model":

> This fable my Lord devised, to the end that he might exhibit therein a
> model or description of a college instituted for the interpreting of na-
> ture and the producing of great and marvellous works for the benefit of
> men, under the name of Salomon's House, or the College of the Six
> Days' Works. And even so far his Lordship hath proceeded, as to finish
> that part. Certainly the model is more vast and high than can possibly
> be imitated in all things; notwithstanding most things therein are within
> men's power to effect. (3.127)

Rawly here both provokes and finesses the taxonomical confusion
that has surrounded interpretations of the text since its posthumous

publication in 1627. "Fable," of course, could suggest a range of meanings: a fiction, a myth, a moral tale. But whatever resonances Rawly is deploying, if the *New Atlantis* is a fable, it requires deciphering, unfolding, interpretation—if only to discover what kind of fable it is. If, however, it is a model, it suggests that we look to it for a pattern, a structured facsimile, an image rather than an allegory of perfection, where problems of interpretation are supplanted by problems of implementation. If it is, as Rawly suggests, a model "more vast and high than can possibly be imitated in all things," contained by and reflected through an allegory, then a coherent interpretation of the text must co-ordinate or subordinate these paradoxically described, and inevitably competing, representational schemata.

Readers most sensitive to the inclusiveness of Bacon's work have demonstrated the methodological connections between Bacon's "literary" output and his scientific writings. Stanley Fish's analysis of Bacon's *Essays* and Michael Hattaway's work on Bacon's aphorisms persuasively challenge the traditional divisions between the writer's literary and scientific projects by pointing out methodological analogies (and their limits) previously unnoticed and unremarked.[17] Ironically, however, the connection between the *New Atlantis* and the New Science has been perceived historically as so transparent, so obvious, and so exemplary that commentators have generally overlooked the strange and ambiguous nature of that connection, with regard both to method and matter. Even Charles Whitney, a sophisticated reader of Bacon's methodological contradictions and complexities, has suggested the self-evidence of the *New Atlantis*'s "fictionality and representational simplicity," remarking that "since Bacon's special problem is the relation of text-bound to text-free truth, an explicitly fictional story offers a relief."[18] Of course, relief and succor are precisely what the *New Atlantis* offers both its shipwrecked sailors and the weary reader, but that this should be the "experience" (as Fish defines this term) of the text is, in fact, part of its complex representational scheme.

Although Shelley declared "Lord Bacon was a poet" and William Hazlitt enthused that Bacon was "one of the strongest instances" of men who are "at once poets and philosophers, and see equally into both worlds," this has not been the niche that modern literary history has carved out for him.[19] L. C. Knights blames Bacon for delivering the fatal blow that irrevocably severed man's reason from his imagination and, following T. S. Eliot, declares this "dissociation of sensibility" to be a condition "from which we have never recovered."[20] In fact, I would argue that it is modernism's persistent association of Bacon with "dissociation" from which we have not yet adequately recovered.[21]

Lamenting Bacon's "mechanistic" style, Knights complains that the function of images in Bacon's work "is not to intensify meaning, to make it deeper or richer, but simply to make more effective a meaning that was already formed before the application of the illustrative device" (115). This critical view of Bacon's style that distinguishes absolutely between a language proper to things in themselves and a language used for ornamentation, "intensification," or illustration makes the mistake of accepting as accomplished the most extreme and naive claims of Bacon's Royal Society followers for the reform of language.[22] Although Bacon viewed himself as a reformer of language, he neither proposed nor attempted the mechanistic style that Knights attributes to him. Certainly, Bacon's description of the "idols of the marketplace" reveals his deep and abiding suspicion of the mediation of language and its power to "overrule the understanding, and throw all into confusion"; yet it is also true that he never strays far from a complex metaphoric mode of discourse.

Reading Bacon retrospectively against Eliot's historical account of the etiology of "dissociation," Knights concludes that "the process leading to the division within the mind and feelings—within the human psyche as a whole—began in the seventeenth century; and the work of Francis Bacon points forward to the conscious and unconscious utilitarianism of the nineteenth century of which we ourselves are the embarrassed heirs" (125). While Knights's yearning for organic wholeness through the reparations of poetry is located historically in the essentially conservative formalism of the New Criticism and his own critical descent from Eliot, his assumptions about Bacon's use of language ally him in some perhaps unexpected ways with the views of Horkheimer and Adorno, who believe that Bacon's legacy is nothing less than "the disenchantment of the world; the dissolution of myths and the substitution of knowledge for fancy" (3). But if Eliot's New Critical disciples, no less than the Frankfurt School philosophers, treated Baconian ideology with equal parts contempt and nostalgic regret, it is not because the former regarded Bacon as a destructive instrument of capitalist imperialism. Indeed, Eliot himself was arguably far more worried about Bacon as a proselytizer of revolution, and his anxieties about "dissociation" may well be drawn from Bacon's later importance to the English Revolution as a theorist of radical social transformation.[23]

I point out this interesting feature of the history of Bacon's reception not to collapse the distance between such writers but to show how some of the most influential modern critiques of modernity from left and right treated Bacon as not just exemplary of a historical moment but in no small part responsible for bringing it about, specifically by severing our connection to our mythopoetic origins. The convergence of these two familiar and perpetually rearticulated attacks on Bacon has made his continued villification in some recent new historicist criticism both doubly satisfying and politically suspsect, for it is not so clearly a move away from formalism to a fuller reckoning of history to return Bacon to the long textual history that recounts as established fact his deleterious impact on posterity. Bacon continues to be identified so fully with his Enlightenment heirs and the epistemological production of modernity that it has been difficult to read Bacon's historical situation in any mood other than the future indicative. This has only meant, however, that Bacon's own mythographic treatment of history and language continues to be slighted.

It seems particularly ironic that Bacon should continue to be associated with theories of "dissociation," as his "division" of human learning in *De Augmentis* (1623) into poetry, history, and philosophy, corresponding to the human faculties of imagination, memory, and reason, suggests, rather, an anatomy of correspondences to a whole and irreducible body of human knowledge. And it is in the highly synthetic *New Atlantis,* in which the self-perfecting body of knowledge is animated, that such generic divisions are most elided in Bacon's poetic parable of philosophical history.

In his anatomy of poetry in *De Augmentis,* Bacon elaborates the direct correspondences between poetry and history. Each of the three classes of poetry—the Narrative, the Dramatic and the Parabolical—is shown to correspond to a type of history, each form being, as Bacon puts it, "nothing but an imitation of history at pleasure." Narrative poesy is a "mere imitation of history." Dramatic poesy is "history made visible." Parabolic poesy is the "typical History by which ideas that are the objects of the intellect are represented in forms that are the objects of sense" (4.440). Thus only Parabolic poetry, which Bacon classifies as the highest of the three forms, offers sufficient escape from the material circumstances of history to provide a reforming lesson in the history it would describe.

The *New Atlantis* recovers the Old Testament temple of Solomon and situates it on a Christian island whose civil origins figure importantly in classical history. This piece of patchwork proves a resilient structure, and yet one whose constituent elements resist the concrete situatedness of a "plan." The very title of the *New Atlantis* suggests the nature of the paradox and the project at hand. It is the new Old World and the old New World, a revision and a recovery that represents as it calls for a "great instauration," a word that, for Bacon, represented both restoration and beginning again.

Bacon's vision of a technologically ordered society, where the scientific dominion over nature provides "the relief of man's estate," establishes him as one of the first of the truly modern utopian authors.[24] Such modernity notwithstanding, his vision is nonetheless framed as part of a Providential order and is indebted to ancient and newly revived traditions of mytho-historical, prophetic, and apocalyptic literature. Robert K. Merton, Ernest Tuveson, Charles Webster, and others have discussed the connections of seventeenth-century science and utopian thought to Puritan eschatology,[25] and Bacon scholars, such as John Briggs and Charles Whitney, have recently brought attention to the providential basis of Bacon's new science.[26] Still, little particular attention has been given to the ways in which Bacon's *New Atlantis* both engages and challenges eschatological models of history to wrest from the providential scheme a forum for human accomplishment.[27]

The intersection of sacred and secular historical paradigms in fact allows Bacon to translate the literal expectations of millennialism into a metaphor for a universal scientific transformation of the world. As an allegory or parable, the *New Atlantis* creates an interpretive imperative whereby the local fiction must be dismantled in order to enable its more universal function. Maureen Quilligan has discussed the essentially inverted relation of literal to figurative in allegory, and Bacon's *New Atlantis* foregrounds the conditions of this transference.[28] Metaphors of discovery, revelation, and illumination are literalized and held forth for examination and discrimination to determine exactly those conditions that enable and reveal utopia.

The *New Atlantis*'s conversions of and translations between literal and spiritual domains bring to mind More's utopian reflections on the language arts of humanist translation and the interplay of literal and figurative meanings. While the two utopian writers can be connected by their mutual privileging of scriptural hermeneutics and their interest in tracing things back to their origins in "natural" language (interests that are intimately connected to the history of history as a discipline), the differences between the humanist theory and practice of translation and the new science are profound. Bacon seizes the humanist method of "translation" as a metaphor for an entirely new project that represents (or re-presents) the language of Nature "herself," an idiom that Bacon believes requires not just "reading" but rewriting. Indeed, it is the religious allegory that allows the differences to stand clear, as Bacon calls not for a simple translation but a complete transfiguration.

Bacon's apocalyptic "transfiguration" has a double effect. First, it offers a circular authority for its apocalyptic vision as it confirms and is confirmed by millennial expectation. Second, by bringing the miraculous into sharp focus at Renfusa while figuring Salomon's House as the epicenter of a far-reaching discourse of illumination, Bacon offers a perfect inversion not simply of literal and figurative, but of spiritual and material worlds. While some readers have cautioned that Bacon's use of prophetic language cannot be "reduced to a symptom of millenarianism,"[29] it is important to point out that, for Bacon's purposes, the invocation of millennial expectation is quite the opposite of a reduction: it is instead a profound expansion of the domain of revealed knowledge and, consequently, of a power that moves between and connects the spiritual and the material realms.

The only character to offer an explicitly millennial vision in the *New Atlantis* is Joabin, the Jewish merchant who is a native of Bensalem and the narrator's guide. Joabin believes that "Moses by a secret cabala ordained the laws of Bensalem which they now use; and that when the Messiah should come and sit in his throne at Hierusalem, the king of Bensalem should sit at his feet, whereas other kings should keep a great distance" (3.151). Those few readers who have commented on Joabin's presence have taken him to represent the Christianized jewry that Protestant theologians such as Theodore Beza and William Perkins believed would betoken the beginning of the millennium.[30] Certainly, Joabin's presence was intended to encourage such millennial speculations; however, the problem with this interpretation is that Joabin is quite explicitly an unconverted Jew: "He was a Jew, and circumcised: for they have some few stirps of Jews yet remaining among them, whom they leave to their own religion" (3.151). Joabin is a prominent and respected citizen of Bensalem, but his millennial views are dismissed as "jewish dreams." On the other hand, if Joabin's presence is supposed to offer an argument or exemplum for religious tolerance, it does not seem to call for universal application, especially as the suggestion that Joabin's distance (and difference) from the European Jew defines and measures the virtue of his character retains an unmistakable anti-Semitic bias. The primary significance of Joabin's inclusion and depiction in the *New Atlantis* seems to be very much connected to the process of invoking and yet discounting immaterial millennial expectation. The Christian reader who overlooks or rejects the possibility of Bensalem's worldly achievements by fixing on the promise of millennial transformation is analogized to the Jew who waits dreamily for another messiah, while rejecting the incarnation of God on earth.

Joabin offers, moreover, a resolution of Old and New Testament typology that does not require the erasure of history as a precondition of its final fulfillment. Joabin's proper name provides a vital clue to understanding his double role. The apparent link to Joab, who served David as captain of the hosts seems, at first glance quite odd, given that Joab falls when he supports Adonijah *against* the anointed Solomon. But Joabin's name suggests that he is twice a Joab, serving not only the father of wars but the "son of peace," a literal translation of Bensalem.[31]

The promise of Bacon's *New Atlantis,* then, does not depend on a return to Edenic origin but on a retrospective recasting of history that allows a perfected Christian nation to exist in the present and does not require the end of history in chiliastic rule as a precondition of its accomplishment. In the end, the *New Atlantis* interposes itself in the place of eschatological vision and millennial promise, for it was vital to Bacon's project that his utopia be understood as contemporary and historically rooted—more remarkable for its present human accomplishments than for a passive fulfillment of an indefinitely deferred divine destiny. Rather than quoting Revelation or the fiery vision of Daniel's apocalypse on the famous frontispiece of the *Instauratio Magna,* Bacon takes from Daniel the forecast of a period of intensified intellectual commerce in the time before the end: "Multi pertransibunt et augebitu scientia" ("Many shall runne to and fro and knowledge shall be increased" [Dan. 12:4]).[32]

From the beginning of the *New Atlantis,* the discovery of Bensalem entails a discrimination between the literal and spiritual role of salvation. When the narrator and his crew arrived at Bensalem it is to them life after certain death: "It seemed to us that we had before us a picture of our salvation in heaven; for we that were awhile since in the jaws of death, were now brought into a place where we found nothing but consolations" (3.136). The conspicuous metaphor of Bensalem as a "picture" of heavenly salvation opens a window through which the reader is asked to perceive and distinguish between the divine and human planes. Even as the image attributes to Bensalem a transcendent dimension, it raises the question of the spiritual or temporal situation of what is being viewed. Reading this picture and situating Bensalem in its proper relation to the salvation of heaven becomes here the explicit problem for interpretation. If the crew's salvation is no picture, but real, though transcending the limits once thought to bound mortal powers, what role has divinity in it? The question of the "supernatural" is both raised and suspended to allow for a redefinition of the "natural." The care, treatment, and healing of the voyagers is not supernatural at all but entirely natural—that is, artificial and human. The reader is challenged to view Bensalem not as a locus of transcendence or longing but as an image of a state (neither entirely spiritual nor entirely institutional) worthy of emulation: a "picture of salvation," requiring both belief and works.

Bacon's most explicit elaboration of his religious allegory in the *New Atlantis* is in story of Bensalem's Christian origin, recounted by the governor of the Stranger's House in response to the voyagers' first question: " '[A]bove all,' (we said) 'since that we were met from the several ends of the world, and hoped assuredly that we should meet one day in the kingdom of heaven (for that were both parts Christians,) we desired to know (in respect that land was so remote, and so divided by vast and unknown seas from the land where our Savior walked on earth) who was the apostle of that nation, and how it was converted to the faith'" (3.137). Asking after the apostle who brought Bensalem to Christianity, the international crew seems to assume the mediation of some itinerant Christian missionary bearing the Word (like, for example, the would-be bishop of Utopia). They discover, however, that the revelations brought to light by the great miracle at Renfusa are twofold. The voyagers (or ten of the better born of their company) learn that the high level of Bensalemite culture actually predates the influence of Christian doctrine, and that the Bensalemite knowledge of God is not an indirect influence from abroad but accomplished directly by a miracle sent by St. Bartholomew of the original twelve disciples "about twenty years after the ascension of our Savior" (3.137). Bensalem is thus shown to have a completely independent Christian apostolic tradition, one that never knew an Augustine or an Aquinas.

The spiritual birth of the nation, notable for its precocity, dramatizes a national conversion at a point in history when the crew's European forebears would have been pagan barbarians. But as early as the institution of Christianity on the island was—occurring before all of the New Testament had even been written—the House of Salomon was older still. Indeed, it is the wisdom of one of their men that allows the Bensalemites to recognize and praise God's work. A pillar of light with a large cross at its top is seen a mile out to sea. Those who approach it find their boats fixed and immovable. As the governor relates the tale, the wise man from Salomon's House ("which house or college, my good brethren, is the very eye of this kingdom" 3.137) throws himself down in prayer:

> "Lord God of heaven and earth, thou hast vouchsafed of thy grace to those of our order, to know thy works of creation, and the secrets of them; and to discern (as far as appertaineth to the generations of men) between divine miracles, works of nature, works of art, and impostures and illusions of all sorts. I do here acknowledge and testify before this people, that the thing which we now see before our eyes is thy Finger and a true Miracle; and forasmuch as we learn in our books that thou never workest miracles but to a divine and excellent end, (for the laws of nature are thine own laws, and thou exceedest them not but upon great cause,) we most humbly beseech thee to prosper this great sign, and to give us the interpretation and use of it in mercy; which thou dost in some part secretly promise by sending it unto us." (3.137–38)

Reason and not rapture ascertains the authenticity of this miracle, and it is demonstrated that the wise man's training has been good and that his sources are reliable when his boat is unbound and he alone is allowed to approach. When he does, the light breaks up "and casts itself abroad, as it were, into a firmament of many stars." What is left is a small ark holding the book containing the Old and New Testament, moreover, "the Apocalypse itself, and some other books of the New Testament which were not at that time written, were nevertheless in the Book" (3.138).

Accompanying these texts is a letter from St. Bartholomew giving the full interpretation of the miracle requested by the fellow of Salomon's House: "I Bartholomew, a servant of the Highest, and Apostle of Jesus Christ, was warned by an angel that appeared to me in a vision of glory, that I should commit this ark to the floods of the sea. Therefore I do testify and declare unto the people where God shall ordain this ark to come to land, that in the same day is come unto them salvation and peace and goodwill, from the Father, and from the Lord Jesus" (3.138). This miracle is certainly notable for its documentation, and such sacred truths are scarcely text-free. The wise man shows himself to be a good reader of nature, knowing its limits well enough to know God's hand, and into his hands are delivered God's texts. Yet despite the distinction given to the fellow of Salomon's House, he remains anonymous, and the benefit of the miracle is not restricted to a single interpreter. An ancillary miracle accompanies these texts:

> There were also in both these writings, as well the Book as the Letter, wrought a great miracle, conform to that of the Apostles in the original Gift of Tongues. For there being at that time in this land Hebrews, Persians, and Indians, besides the natives, every one read upon the Book and Letter, as if they had been written in his own language. And thus was this land saved from infidelity (as the remain of the old world was from water) by an ark, through the apostolical and miraculous evangelism of St. Bartholomew. (3.138–39)

Howard White has emphasized the universal culture created by this miracle that reverses the curse of Babel in the fulfillment of the promise of Bacon's New Science.[33] But it is equally important to note the remarkable cultural diversity that this miracle in fact allows. Bacon's confidence in the universality of science as a shared language permits his utopia to be less culturally uniform or coercive than the idealizing "pagan" republics created by either Plato or More or the roughly contemporary ideal Christian republics designed by Campanella or Andreae. Despite its undisguised fantasy of power, Bacon's utopian narrative is driven by change and social transformation rather than an imposed or prescribed constitutional order—features not lost on his growing audience in the period leading up to the Civil War.[34]

The miracle at Renfusa has a strange double status. It endorses the House of Salomon as it is endorsed by it, a symmetrical if principally secular reciprocity. Within the fiction, it is a miracle proved beyond doubt, requiring less faith than most, as it is so well and unambiguously documented. Yet paradoxically, by virtue of its very textual depiction, this miracle advertises itself as a poetic invention, a sign that no reader—however devout—would take for an authentic wonder. Bacon's invention thus delimits even as it invokes sacred authority. The Christian origin story's most important lesson is that a properly instructed and instructive science will teach man to recognize and to praise both divine and human works, and, most important, to distinguish between them. The import of the fable may be different for the true believer than the cynic, but the demonstrations are designed to benefit either with a grace that surpasses belief. Here begins a history of learning that illuminates and yet goes beyond sacred history.

The usefulness of universal history to his utopian vision nothwithstanding, Bacon describes "Sacred or Ecclesiastical History" in *De Augmentis* as a subcategory of Civil History. This was not entirely to subordinate "matter of divinity" to the realm of the secular, but rather to acknowledge that material of history was in either case expressed through and made visible by the "deeds and works" of nature (4.293). Nonetheless, Bacon asserts in *De Augmentis* that "among the writings of men there is nothing rarer than a true and perfect Civil History" (4.302). Bacon complains that "Civil History is beset on all sides with faults," "because in ancient transactions the truth is difficult to ascertain, and in modern it is dangerous to tell" (4.302).

In his "history" of Bensalem, Bacon assiduously avoids the essentially political "great chain of causation" offered by classical and Renaissance civil historians. The political tales they told about tyrants, kings, or model states were—insofar as they were exemplary—too often nostalgic in mood or tragic in form, their moral lessons more cautionary and retrospective than forward-looking and visionary. Even Walter Ralegh's reworking and integration of historical models in his providential *History of the World* focuses on ancient stories of politics and intrigue that reveal God as "the author of our tragedies."[35] In "Of Fortune," however, Bacon maintains that "chiefly the mould of Mans fortune is in himselfe" (6.574). Yet in *The History of Henry VII*, Bacon's emphasis is not on the king's *virtu*. As he declares in his dedicatory letter to Prince Charles of his subject, "I have not flattered him, but took him to life as well as I could" (6.25). His interest, rather, is to detail Henry's skillful manipulations of his political fortunes through those "accidents" and "mutations" (6.25) brought about by the "vicissitude of things."

Because Bacon seeks to situate his *New Atlantis* somewhere between divine providence and political determinism, neither sacred history nor civil history (in its restrictive sense) provides the ideal model for the origins or operations of Bensalem. Finally, it is the third type of Civil History described in *De Augmentis*, the "species" of history that Bacon

declares does not yet exist, that most captures the "historical" project of
the *New Atlantis*—that is, "The History of Learning and the Arts." Although Bacon is forced to concede that "a complete and universal History of Learning is yet wanting," his description of what this history
should document reads like a precis or gloss of Bensalem's history in
the *New Atlantis:*

> The argument is no other than to inquire and to collect out of the
> records of all time what particular kinds of learning and arts have flour-
> ished in what ages and regions of the world, their antiquities, their pro-
> gresses, their migrations (for sciences migrate like nations) over the
> different parts of the globe, and again their decays, disappearances,
> and revivals. The occasion and origin of the invention of each art
> should likewise be observed, the manner and system of transmission,
> and the plan and order of study and practice. (4.438)

The value of such a history, Bacon goes on to suggest, is that "it
would assist very greatly the wisdom and skill of learned men in the use
and administration of learning; that it would exhibit the movements and
perturbations, the virtues and vices, which take place no less in intellectual than in civil matters; and that from an observation of these the best
system of government might be derived and established" (4.439). Here
Bacon clearly asserts that it is the model of history that does not yet exist
that has the best chance of providing a model for the best system of
government. The *New Atlantis* does not substitute for this undocu-
mented history of learning (for to stand *for* would be to stand *in the way
of* the real production of that history), nor does it codify a perfected government. As an allegory or parable of history, however, Bacon's utopia
shows the nature of the connection. The fiction of the *New Atlantis* suggests that the perfect government would be a natural byproduct of the
self-perfecting arts of Natural History. Bacon's division of all history into
Natural History and Civil History in *De Augmentis* is based implicitly on
an anatomy of correspondences, and his description of a "History of the
Arts" figures as importantly "as a species of Natural History" (4.294) as it
does in his Civil History. The neglect of this as a branch of Natural History, Bacon maintains, is the result of "a subtle error which has crept into
the human mind; namely, that of considering art as merely an assistant to
nature" that "has bred a premature despair in human enterprises"
(4.294). Bacon's proposal for a vastly expanded program of history pro-

vides not just a storehouse of precepts or examples but the only coherent basis for a reformed natural and civil philosophy.

Although Bacon's secretary and biographer William Rawley suggests in his preface to the *New Atlantis* that Bacon meant to compose a "frame of laws" or "the best state or mould of a commonwealth," Rawly also asserts that "[Bacon's] desire of collecting the Natural History diverted him, which he preferred many degrees before it." *De Augmentis* can suggest the theory, and the *New Atlantis* the practice, of the intimate connection between these two projects.

Visions of Empire and the Politics of Praise

If the *New Atlantis* is a call to action and Bacon is the *bucinator novi temporis* ("trumpeter of our times" [1.579]), who are to be the actors and precisely what are they to do? Those who have not based their answer on the tale's hermetic obscurity have treated the answer as much more obvious than it is. Numerous readers have seen the *New Atlantis* as a tract or a proposal to attract King James's support (as well as a number of well-situated financial backers) for the foundation of an academy based on the House of the Six Days Work. F. H. Anderson, in his discussion of Bacon's "suit for science," points to a diary entry of July 26, 1608, in which Bacon sketches plans for the "Foundation of a College for Inventors," a project that bears a number of formal resemblances to the House of Salomon.[36] But whereas Bacon was certainly interested in academic reform, the *New Atlantis* is not in any simple sense an institutional proposal. And while the king would certainly have been an important and an assumed audience for his works, Bacon's relationship to James I in 1624, when he was writing the *New Atlantis,* was, to say the least, strained. Bacon did not publish the work in his lifetime.

Although Bacon would continue to seek support for the new philosophy from James after the House of Lords charged him with accepting bribes and brought about his political fall, this utopia, not surprisingly, is designed in such fashion that it might flatter the English Solomon (as James was described by Bacon and others), while at the same time achieving perfect autonomy from political authority and contingency.[37] Only two kings are worthy of mention in the annals of Bensalemite history: Altabin, for defeating the old Atlanteans in a bloodless battle, and Solamona, who put scientific utopian practice in place by setting up the

College of the Six Days Work. The wisdom of subsequent kings is un-worthy of mention and based presumably on their ability to let well enough alone. No mention of the currently reigning monarch is made in the narrator's account. On Bensalem it is the Fathers of the House of Sal-omon, and not an enlightened monarch, who will constitute the new and divinely sanctioned ruling order in which human knowledge and human power are united.

The effaced position of the monarch in Bensalem can perhaps be bet-ter understood by returning to the dialectic of secrecy and revelation in the *New Atlantis.* John Archer, also interested in the work's preoccupa-tion with secrecy, describes Salomon's House as "a state apparatus of scientific investigation that depends partly on techniques of political in-telligence gathering that were familiar to Bacon from his early career as a servant of Elizabethan sovereignty."[38] Archer situates Bacon's utopia historically as the place of convergence between the consolidation of sovereign power and the emergence of the modern political state, whose mechanisms of social control through surveillance the *New At-lantis* was seen, in part, to inaugurate. For Archer, the *New Atlantis* is the place where the separate domains of knowledge and power meet "through the mutually productive relationship between sovereignty and intelligence" (2). This analysis is extremely suggestive for much of Bacon's work, but by casting the *New Atlantis* as an essentially *political* fantasy of the conjunction of knowledge and power, Archer may, I be-lieve, underestimate the significance (as well as the political motives and potential applications) of Bacon's apocalyptic articulation of knowledge as power.

As Archer notes, Bacon elaborates the connection between power and knowledge most fully in "Of Heresies," an essay published among the *Meditationes Sacrae* (1597). In this essay Bacon argues that the cause of all heresies is twofold: "The ignorance of the will of God, and ignorance or superficial consideration of the power of God." Bacon identifies the third degree of heresy with those who discover in human actions, "which partake of sin," a force capable of opposing God, "which actions they suppose to depend substantially and without any chain of causes upon the inward will and choice of man; and who give a wider range to knowledge of God than to his power; or rather to that part of God's power (for knowledge itself is power) whereby he knows, than to that whereby he works and acts" (7.253). To discover in human will to sin a power that challenges God's is for Bacon a species of Theomachy, for, as he argues, "whatever does not depend upon God as author and principle, by links and subordinate degrees, the same will be instead of God, and a new principle and kind of usurping God."

Archer describes the equation of knowledge and power in this essay as "Bacon's attempt to idealize knowledge by completely identifying it with a power that does not have to be produced, a divine power" (2). But Bacon's identification of divine knowledge and power is not designed to disguise or shield the mechanisms of either, so much as to bring them to light. Bacon emphasizes the reach of divine knowledge as power in order to liberate human action and inquiry from the taint of sin. If it is heresy to believe that man's actions can escape God's knowledge, then no pursuit of knowledge can escape God's will. Indeed, what makes the *New Atlantis* invisible is not the state apparatus of secrecy but the conspicuous failure of belief on the part of Europeans to think Bensalem possible:

> That king [Solamona] also, still desiring to join humanity and policy together; and thinking it against humanity to detain strangers here against their wills, and against policy that they should return and discovery their knowledge of this estate, he took this course: he did ordain that of the strangers that should be permitted to land, as many (at all times) might depart as would; but as many as would stay should have very good conditions and means to live from the state. Wherein he saw so far, that now in so many ages since the prohibition, we have memory not of one ship that ever returned; and but of thirteen persons only, at several times, that chose to return in our bottoms. What those few that returned may have reported abroad I know not. But you must think, *whatsoever they have said could be taken where they came but for a dream.* (3.145; my emphasis)

The providence of this plan is that it captures information by capturing the loyalties of those who visit, not by force or secrecy but by "conversion." The inability of returning Europeans to persuade their compatriots of the truth of Bensalem shows a double failure of faith, for to regard the reports of Bensalem's accomplishments as "a dream" is to doubt God's will to bestow knowledge of his work, and consequently to doubt God's power to unveil his work to men.

To begin an analysis of Bacon's specular politics, it is useful to turn to a work of his that dates to an earlier period of political expectation. In *The Advancement of Learning* (1609), the first of Bacon's books addressed to James I, the king's perfection is attributed to the "triplicity" of his greatness, having "the power and fortune of a King, the knowledge and illumination of a Priest, and the learning and universality of a philosopher" (3.263). This confluence of roles will perfectly describe the father of Salomon's House, though the cautious corrective address given to a thrice great ruler will have to take a different course than one given by the father to his humble and attentive servant. In defending the New Science and defining the role and function of mind in *The Advancement,* Bacon finds himself playing figuratively with light and mirrors.

Bacon declares that "God hath framed the mind of man as a mirror or glass capable of the image of the universal world, and joyful to receive the impression thereof, as the eye joyeth to receive light" (3.265). These absorbing metaphors of "imaging" delay the reflections they suggest, for if mirrors not only receive images but also display them, then the faithful mirror, like the unflattering advisor, may suggest room for improvement. In the lines that follow, Bacon quotes Solomon twice. Both allusions offer more active images of the mind's light, but the reversal in the direction of that action recapitulates the suspended activity-passivity of the first image. Bacon first quotes Proverbs 20:27: "The spirit of man is as the lamp of God, wherewith he searcheth the inwardness of all secrets" (3.265). Next he quotes Ecclesiastes 2:13,14: "I saw well that knowledge recedeth as far from ignorance as light doth from darkness and that the wise man's eyes keep watch in his head, whereas the fool roundeth about in darkness: but withal I learned that the same mortality involveth them both" (3.266). The inquiring mind of the first passage is shown in the second on the run, receding before an encroaching ignorance, and the wise man's vision has retracted to an exclusively interior view. Bacon's problem in establishing the direction of the mind's light does not ultimately reside in his epistemology but derives, rather, from the difficulty of constructing a narrative that must describe and yet veil Bacon's own position as a lesser but instructing light to a not entirely "receptive" patron.[39] The problem illuminated is the *condition* of knowledge, which begs for correction, and not its natural mechanisms, which need only to be brought to light.

These images finally resolve themselves in a paradox that Bacon takes from Philo Judeaus: "And therefore it was most aptly said by one of Plato's school, that the sense of man carrieth a resemblance with the sun, which (as we see) openeth and revealeth all the terrestrial globe; but then again it obscureth and concealeth the stars and celestial globe;

so doth the sense discover natural things, but it darkeneth and shutteth up divine" (3.267). In fact, Philo's emphasis is quite the opposite of Bacon's. Whereas Bacon stresses the importance of the sun in both revealing the temporal world and at the same time maintaining the safety and remoteness of divine secrets, Philo is describing "the course of sacred revelation," which comes in divine dreams only when sense perception is eclipsed: "When the light of our senses has risen like a sun, the various forms of knowledge, so truly heavenly and celestial, disappear from sight: when it reaches its setting, radiances most divine and most star-like sent forth from virtues come into view: and it is then that the mind also becomes pure because it is darkened by no object of sense" ("On Dreams" 1.84).[40]

Bacon's reorientation of his source is only one of several deflections represented in this passage. His metaphor seems to invite an exegetical discrimination between "spiritual" and "literal" applications, as divine secrets are not the only secrets that might require protecting. Indeed, Bacon seems to be offering a veiled political lesson, giving the solar image a pointed sublunary application. Whereas Philo's metaphor is cautionary, Bacon's represents good policy. It offers James the reassurance that he might sponsor a popular reform of learning without licensing heretical or treacherous inquiries.[41] Furthermore, Bacon's allegory suggests that the brighter James shines on the labors of the New Science, the less its inquiring view will probe the constellations of court; that, indeed, the more one knows, the less one need be known. This is the promise of power offered as the threat of its loss.

Jonathan Goldberg connects mirrors and lights to state secrets in his reading of Ben Jonson's masque, *News from the New World*. In Goldberg's analysis of the masque, King James is discovered as the figure for both poet and text "in the essential configuration of poetic transformation, as a 'mirror' (line 308) offering 'the sun's reflected light' (line 309)."[42] Unlike Jonson, however, Bacon seems to be offering James a palatable invisibility in place of a dazzling centrality, which may explain, in part, his difficulty in persuading the king to support his efforts. The secrets Bacon asks James to license were not those produced by—or centered on—the sovereign. Not surprisingly, therefore, James's response to Bacon's proposals demonstrates that he found them more opaque than illuminating, and quoting Scripture in turn, he paid Bacon the ambiguous and often-quoted compliment that his writings were "like the peace of God which passeth understanding."

The rhetorical problems posed by a defense of learning can thus provide some clue as to why Bacon would turn at the end of his career to a poetic utopian discourse to promote the New Science. Bacon, no longer tied to the seductive metaphors of politician or courtier, is free to literalize and fictionally enact his proposed reforms. The images of light in the *New Atlantis,* rather than being concentrated in the great center of mind or monarch, tend to be diffused among the enlightened Bensalemites. The great pillar of light that brings about the conversion of Bensalem is scattered when properly interpreted, and the sacred texts left behind in a cedar ark are miraculously intelligible to the citizens of all the nations occupying the island.

Among the brethren of Salomon's House are the Merchants of Light, who conceal themselves in their travels to other nations and bring back "the books, and abstracts, and patterns of experiments of all other parts" (3.164). The light they represent greatly extends over the world and yet provides illumination only as it is directed back to its source, "the very eye of this kingdom" (3.137)—the House of Salomon—where the three fellows they call "Lamps" look at the materials gathered "to direct new experiments of a higher light, more penetrating into nature than the former" (3.165). The governor of the Stranger's House compares Bensalemite commerce to European practice: "But thus you see we maintain a trade, not for gold, silver, or jewels; nor for silk; nor for spices; nor any other commodity of matter; but only for God's first creature, which was Light: to have light (I say) of the growth of all parts of the world" (3.146–47).

Bacon will materialize the properties of light in two quite distinct ways. His use, for example, of Cherubim will embody light in a highly symbolic fashion. But whereas Bacon will use light as a figure for knowledge, he also insists on the *defiguralization* of light, which allows it to be a material presence with its own nature and qualities to be explored and documented. This literal treatment of light, far from diminishing the fiction, actually intensifies the allegory by focusing on the quest for knowledge rather than the materiality of its promised rewards.

The quality of light is investigated not by analogies but by "perspective-houses," wherein, according to the father of Salomon's House, the fellows

> make demonstrations of all lights and radiations; and of all colours; and out of things uncoloured and transparent, we can represent unto you

all several colours; not in rain-bows, as it is in gems and prisms, but of themselves single. We represent also all multiplications of light, which we carry to great distance, and make so sharp as to discern small points and lines; also all colorations of light: all delusions and deceits of the sight, in figures, magnitudes, motions, colours: all demonstrations of shadows. We find also divers means, yet unknown to you, of producing light originally from divers bodies. We procure means of seeing objects afar off; as in the heaven and remote places; and represent things near as afar off, and things afar off as near; making feigned distances. We have also helps for the sight, far above spectacles and glasses in use. We have also glasses and means to see small minute bodies perfectly and distinctly. . . . We make artificial rain-bows, halos and circles about light. We represent also all manner of reflexions, refractions, and multiplications of visual beams of objects." (3.161–62)

With such abilities to manipulate the properties of light (including the manufacture of halos!), one might begin to wonder whether the miracle at Renfusa was nothing but a simple light show put up to impress the natives, especially because we know the House of Salomon was in place before the national conversion. And, indeed, the fellows are expert in all kinds of deceits:

We also have houses of deceits of the senses; where we represent all manner of feats of juggling, false apparitions, impostures, and illusions; and their fallacies. And surely you will easily believe that we that have so many things truly natural which induce admiration, could in a world of particulars deceive the senses, if we would disguise those things and labour to make them seem more miraculous. But we do hate all impostures and lies; insomuch as we have severely forbidden it to all our fellows, under pain of ignominy and fines, that they do not shew any natural work or thing, adorned or swelling; but only pure as it is, and without all affectation of strangeness.

These are (my son) the riches of Salomon's House. (3.164)

Although the fathers have the skill of deceit, they are forbidden to practice this knowledge for show. Yet to the degree that Bacon insists that the fellows of Salomon's House do not practice deceitful games with perception for public display, he also insists on their ability to do so. Credibility paradoxically depends on the fellows' ability to tell the true miracle from the false illusion, and their authority is based in their great skills with the latter. Among the Bensalemites, the lie of sense perception is an acknowledged fact of nature, which is "represented," anatomized, and cataloged in the encyclopedia of natural phenomena. Bacon carefully itemizes the powers of true miracles and the powers of lies to enable his utopia to stand somewhere in between in the natural domain subject to human control with powers that are not fictions, though they depend in large part on their control and understanding of fiction. Bacon answers Plato's objection to poetry in the *Republic* with a *poesis* that masters rather than shadows its materials, in which the distance between the original and its image is essentially erased, and each counterfeit is new made in its own image.

Thus Bacon's *New Atlantis* offers the idealized locus where the practice of natural simulation makes political dissimulation unnecessary.[43] If the English Solomon did not choose to perform the role of King Solamona, Bacon's utopian fantasy suggests that the *arcana imperii* could themselves be anatomized and reproduced at will.

The "Virgin of the World": The Poetics of History and the Art of Nature

The Bensalemite civilization forces a redefinition of the shape and nature of human empire, preserved, but not defined, by political tools. The world to be explored and "conquered" is not principally the terra nuova but rather the terra incognita, which for the fellows of Salomon's House turns out in many cases to be in fact the Old World revisited. Bensalem's perfection, based on a "grounding" in science, is depicted as a geography of knowledge. "I have taken all knowledge to be my province," says Bacon in an often-quoted letter to his uncle, the Lord Treasurer Burley, in 1592. "I hope I should bring in industrious observations, grounded conclusions, and profitable inventions and discoveries; the best state of that province." But if the geography of knowledge is one of the important, operative metaphors for the *New Atlantis* and the boundaries of human knowledge will establish the coextensive boundaries of human empire, it is curious to note that Bensalemite politics are strongly insular whereas their culture is quite the opposite. Their knowledge of the outside world is universal and comprehensive, yet they do not seek to extend their borders with overtly coercive martial prowess—as do, for example, the Utopians. Thus, John Archer has argued, the *New Atlantis* "presents us with colonialism's mirror image."[44] As a locus of perfection Bensalem designs itself to be overlooked. Its discovery involves a larger recovery of the overlooked properties and practices that make it possible.

In Bacon's utopian vision, it is not first necessary to show people new things but to get them to see anew, and thus the control of the reader's gaze will be of central importance. The images of secrecy and veiling, continually counterpoised against the central themes of discovery and revelation, will be paradigmatic for the controlled and properly instructed gaze. When Joabin praises Bensalem as the most "chaste" of nations and the "virgin of the world" (3.152), the implications of his description go beyond the social practices he relates to the narrator, for it is curious that Bensalem is described not simply as chaste but as in fact "virgin," when the highest social honor of the land is conferred on its most progenerative (male) citizens. In describing this "virgin" utopia, Bacon constructs his ideal state as active but unacted upon. Bensalem is pure, unconsummated possibility, but the fruitfulness of this virgin state is a mystery that seems to shield itself from penetration. Although Bacon often uses an eroticized language to describe (or incite) man's pursuit of Nature to her secret hiding places, Bensalem's discovery deflects this kind of eroticized desire of knowledge.[45] The spirit of the chastity of Bensalem, says Joabin, would "appear in the likeness of a beautiful fair Cherubin" (3.151), a class of angels whom Bacon calls the "angels of knowledge and illumination" in *The Advancement* and to whom he gives—in accordance with the heavenly hierarchy of pseudo-Dionysius the Areopagite—pride of place before the angels of "office and domination."[46]

The allegorical discontinuities between the featured virginity (or even angelic asexuality) of Bensalem and the fecundity of its citizens creates a figurative paradox analogous to the text's vacillation between secrecy and revelation. Both tensions point to the problems of an idealized poetics in which representation may bring about the possibility of the violation of the ideal even as it allows for textual "productivity." This paradox of chaste production, however, is probably best approached through Bacon's proposed solution, celebrated in the Bensalemite ceremony known as the "Feast of the Family," for it is in this passage that the symbolic marriage of mind and universe, art and nature, history and destiny is consecrated.

The Feast of the Family connects the origins of the family and the state in a myth of natural and self-reproducing and genealogically derived order. This celebration, honoring at state expense those males "that shall live to see thirty persons descended of his body alive together" (3.147), is described in more particular detail than any other aspect of Bensalemite society. The elaborate and ornamental description of this section has been taken by some readers as a reflection of Bacon's obsession with ceremonial display, and a distraction from the real business of Bensalemite (utopian) science or politics. The prominence and function of the Feast of the Family and its genealogical alliance of art and nature can perhaps be more fully understood in comparison with Spenser's description of the Bower of Bliss in Book 2 of *The Faerie Queene,* which offers some provocative and unexpected parallels in what can only be understood as a highly conventional debate.

Whereas the Feast of the Family, like Acrasia's bower, features a commingling of artful and natural elements, Bacon's feast corrects the corrupting sensuality of Acrasia's bower, both its excesses and its sterility, with a chastity more accommodating and productive than Guyon's. Spenser will, of course, offer his own corrections of the Bower of Bliss, most notably in the platonic order of the Garden of Adonis presided over by a very different Genius. But Bacon is profoundly uninterested in mystical forms, and his correction will be much more immediately concerned with the radical consequences of this "garden-variety" contest between art and nature than with Spenser's neoplatonic resolutions.

At the center of the ceremony of the Feast of the Family is the Tirsan (the patriarch of thirty living offspring) and his chair of state:

> Over the chair is a state, made round or oval, and it is of ivy; an ivy somewhat whiter than ours, like the leaf of a silver asp, but more shining; for it is green all winter. And the state is curiously wrought with silver and silk of divers colours, broiding or binding in the ivy; and is ever the work of some of the daughters of the family; and veiled over at the top with a fine net of silk and silver. But the substance of it is pure ivy; whereof, after it is taken down, the friends of the family are desirous to have some leaf or sprig to keep. (3.148)

Compare the preceding description with the ivy draping the fountain at the center of the Bower of Bliss:

> And in the midst of all, a fountaine stood,
>> Of richest substaunce, that on earth might bee,
>> So pure and shiny, that the siluer flood

> Through euery channel running one might see;
>   Most goodly it with curious imageree
>   Was ouer-wrought, and shapes of naked boyes,
>   Of which some seemd with liuely iollitee,
>   To fly about, playing their wanton toyes,
> Whilst others did them selues embay in liquid ioyes.
>
> And ouer all, of purest gold was spred,
>   A trayle of yvie in his natiue hew;
>   For the rich mettall was so coloured,
>   That wight, who did not well auis'd it vew,
>   Would surely deeme it to be yuie trew;
>   Low his lasciuious armes adown did creepe,
>   That themselues dipping in the siluer dew,
>   Their fleecy flowres they tenderly did steepe,
>   hich drops of Christall seemd for wontones to weepe.
>   (2.12.60–61)[47]

The "ouer-wrought" layers of art that bury and overwhelm nature in the Bower are contrasted by the mutually enhancing cooperation of art and nature in the Bensalemite ceremony. The Bower's ivy is bad because it is a cunning and insinuating replica of nature, and its corrupt art feigns a nature it is not. Bensalem's ivy is, on the other hand, both natural and an improvement on nature, more shining and evergreen. J. P. Zetterberg has rightly pointed out that Bacon did not reject "the doctrine of art as *imitatio naturae* itself. For it was not the doctrine *per se* to which he objected."[48] It was, rather, the servile place appointed to the mimetic arts in ancient and medieval natural philosophy that he attempted to reform. Even ornamented as it is by a silk and silver net, the natural ivy is not disguised, although it is transformed. This metamorphosis, is not, however, a feigning art but an art of cultivation.

A second comparison can be made between Bacon's and Spenser's description of the fruit of the vine. Guyon, the knight of Temperance, and the Palmer first penetrate a gate artfully carved of ivory and come at last to a second gate formed by the "clasping arms" of branches:

> So fashioned a Porch with rare deuice,
>   Archt ouer head with an embracing vine,
>   Whose bounches hanging downe, seemed to entice
>   All passers by; to taste their lushious wine
>   And did themselues into their hands incline,
>   As freely offering to be gathered:

> Some deepe empurpled as the Hyacint,
> Some as the Rubine, laughing sweetly red,
> Some like faire Emeraudes, not yet well ripened.
>
> And there amongst, some were of burnisht gold,
>   So made by art, to beautifie the rest,
>   Which did themselues emongst the leaues enfold,
>   As lurking from the vew of couetous guest,
>   That the weake bowes, with so rich load oppreast,
>   Did bow adowne, as ouer-burdened. . . .
>   (2.12.54–55)

Under this porch sits the fair but "disordered" Excess, a bad hostess who tries to force Guyon to drink from her golden cup. On Bensalem, where hospitality has been both naturalized and regulated, and excess is unknown, a "cluster of grapes of gold" will symbolize and celebrate the fruitfulness of the family. In the ceremony a young boy carries the "long foot or stalk" of these grapes in the company of another who carries a scroll of the King's Charter:

> Then the herald taketh into his hand from the other child the cluster of grapes. But the grapes are daintily enamelled; and if the males of the family be the greater number, the grapes are enamelled purple, with a little sun set on the top; if the females, then they are enamelled into a greenish yellow, with a crescent on the top. The grapes are in number as many as there are descendants of the family. This golden cluster the herald delivereth also to the Tirsan; who presently delivereth it over to the son that he had formerly chosen to be in house with him: who beareth it before his father as an ensign of honour when he goeth in public, ever after; and is thereupon called the Son of the Vine. (3.149–50)

In contrast to Bacon's description of the ceremonial ivy, his grapes symbolize rather than demonstrate an artfully improved nature. The gem-like Spenserian grapes are, on the other hand, neither wholly natural nor entirely artificial. Their seductive properties are based in their ability to make natural bounty a sort of booty, thus stimulating baser appetites with the natural. Bacon's grapes, however, are entirely artificial, but their only raison d'être here is as symbol of the "natural" order of the Bensalemite social structure. In both cases, the grapes suggest a harvest of men, but whereas the Bower of Bliss displays the seductive powers of art to take men in, the Feast of the Family celebrates through art the process of natural generation, and the power of art both to celebrate and regulate that process. Where Spenser animates a nature corrupt with human sins (the wanton and weeping ivy, the grasping vines), Bacon's Bensalemites control the symbolic order—as they do nature—and dominate it.

In his reading of the Bower of Bliss, Stephen Greenblatt notes the tremendous violence with which the chaste Guyon responds to the intemperate and idolatrous arts embodied by Acrasia.[49] According to Greenblatt, the threat that Acrasia's excess represents not only sanctions institutional power but effectively creates it: " 'Excess' is defined not by some inherent imbalance or impropriety, but by the mechanism of control, the exercise of restraining power. And if excess is virtually invented by this power, so too, paradoxically, power is invented by excess" (177). Bacon's revision of Spenser seems designed, by contrast, to highlight both the generative and the temperate properties of his patriarchal art of nature.

Bacon's lavish ritual depends for its chastity on the display of a very different emblem of female sexuality in the veiled wife of the Tirsan. Unlike the women with exposed breasts who populate the Bower of Bliss, the Tirsan's wife is staged as chastely hidden, viewing the ceremony—which she makes possible through the fruit of her body—from the carved window of a screened compartment placed above the proceedings. Her symbolic centrality to the ceremony as preserved-from-spectacle suggests how Bacon's patriarchal festival enacts Protestant iconoclasm without its violence, by abjuring its customary obsession with (and hence dependence on) what are inevitably represented as feminine or feminizing idols. As John Archer astutely notes, "The mother, though excluded from the open display of power, is in the same position in relation to her family that Bensalem is to the rest of the world" (148).[50] This allegorical positioning of the Tirsan's wife as a figure for Bensalem offers a complexly gendered poetics of power if a reductive and oppressive gender politics. The mother's chastity offers the emblem of national chastity, a function not of Bensalem's isolation per se, nor, certainly, of its reverence of the feminine, but of its control and management of the sources of production, both symbolic and literal, sacred and secular. And it is this control of production that suggests a more complete freedom from Rome than severing religious and political ties could have, or had, brought about. That this Bensalemite practice should be admired by the crew of a Spanish ship returning from Peru offers the *New Atlantis*'s English audience a complex model of identification—one poised, it would seem, between envy and emulation, between the exotic booty of Incan gold and the domestic "bliss" celebrated by the feast of the Tirsan, which Spanish pistolets cannot buy.

At the end of Bensalem's temperate feast ("which in the greatest feasts with them lasteth never above an hour and an half"), a poet of the state comes forth and sings a hymn, "varied according to the invention of him that composeth it, (for they have excellent posy,) but the subject of it is (always) the praises of Adam and Noah and Abraham; whereof the former two peopled the world, and the last was the Father of the Faithful: concluding ever with a thanksgiving for the nativity of our Saviour, in whose birth the births of all are only blessed" (3.150).

Bacon does not banish poets from his ideal state, but neither will he recuperate them for the reasons Sidney employs in his "Defence of Poetry"—reasons that rest on assumptions of poetry's ability to compensate for the richness that nature and man's life cannot supply. Both Sidney's defense and Spenser's attack on art cited earlier assume a certain antagonism between art and nature. According to Sidney, the poet's art is unparalleled in nature: "Nature never set forth the earth in so rich tapestry as divers poets have done; neither with so pleasant rivers, fruitful trees, sweet-smelling flowers, nor whatsoever else may make the too much loved earth more lovely. Her world is brazen, the poets only deliver a golden."[51]

Spenser describes the competition on more even (though nonetheless aggressive) terms:

> One would haue thought, (so cunningly, the rude,
>   And scorned parts were mingled with the fine,)
> That nature had for wantonesse ensude
> Art, that Art at nature did repine;
> So striuing each th'other to vndermine,
> Each did the others worke more beautifie;
> So diff'ring both in willes, agreed in fine:
> So all agreed through sweete diuersitie,
> This Gardin to adorne with all varietie.
>
>   (2.12.59)

In Bacon's utopian scheme, however, the perfected scientific and social arts of men necessarily reform the poetic arts. While Bacon allows some room for individual invention, the Bensalemite poet's subject is always the same. Whereas one of Socrates's principal reasons for disallowing the poets in Plato's *Republic* was that the poets, notably Homer, slandered the gods by casting them in ridiculous and compromising fictions, Bacon seems quite simply to assume that his poets will have no reason to do anything but praise their maker, their savior, and the great patriarchs of the human race. On Bensalem the poets will not (or cannot) practice the corrupting arts of the rhapsode because world-distorting fiction becomes obsolete in a world where more potent arts are themselves actively *world-transforming,* and artifice becomes the new nature. The poet is not censored, but his realm of effectiveness—for good or ill—is radically reduced. The new poet of nature, ensconced in the House of Salomon, does not cater (to) events but is now himself the utopian patron and pattern maker.

While Bacon's stolid prose description of his utopia has none of the punning polysemy of Spenser's poetic garden, this cannot, or should not, be entirely attributed to an absolute comparison of their powers as poets (a contest that Bacon, I fear, could never win). Indeed, their stylistic differences have important thematic consequences for their respective allegories. Spenser's etymologically driven moral schema rely on our understanding of the deep signifying structure of names. The priority and authority of verbal relations generate the narrative so that the ends are always a recovery and renewal of the original meaning and nature. The animation of persons, places, and actions forms an organic syntax of verbally constructed and derived meanings in which both the critique and the correction is *implicit*—that is, folded into the very fabric of the narrative's discourse. Bacon, having no such confidence in philologically derived truths, constructs his allegory as a narrative of *explicit* correspondences—that is, the *New Atlantis* proceeds and unveils itself through a series of explications that are at once the subject and the method of its allegory. Finally, if the *New Atlantis* offers an allegory of a place where allegory is at last unnecessary, the nature of the paradox is for Bacon more tragic than ironic.

As other readers have pointed out, the *New Atlantis* strives to represent what, in Bacon's view, the human project is or should be. But this is not, as many readers seem to assume, a fiction of final causes (which Bacon consistently repudiated). The fictional "ends" of the *New Atlantis* are, as we have seen, directed principally toward an understanding of its origins. As the governor of the House of Salomon explains to the narrator, "The End of our Foundation is the knowledge of Causes, and secret motions of things; and the enlarging of the bounds of Human Empire, to the effecting of all things possible" (3.156). Where Aristotle maintained that "the end aimed at is not knowledge [*gnosis*] but action [*praxis*]," Bacon asserts that the two are the same.[52] If this is true, then the project of designing utopia would be tantamount to founding it. But the burden is on the designer to make the design complete, and according to Bacon, this is beyond the capacities of any one man.

Although this seems to ally Bacon's *New Atlantis* with the collaborative design of More's *Utopia,* Bacon's preoccupation with originality and the recognition of his genius—not to mention his stunning lack of appreciation for important contemporaries such as Galileo,[53] Gilbert,[54] Kepler,[55] and Harvey[56]—suggests that his call to collaboration may be fraught with ambivalence. Bacon's utopia is, after all, the work of a man in solitude at the end of his career, whereas More's is the product of a man early in his career, in dialogue with the greatest minds of his age. Bacon's noncontribution to the increasingly important art of experimentation is legendary and makes him an odd figure in the history of the science of his times. His *Sylva Sylvarum* (which Sidney Warhaft calls "a vast, dreary and remarkably unoriginal collection of 'scientific' facts, scraps and observations")[57] provides Bacon's experimental base, but he did not feel compelled to expend his labors processing these "scraps." His project was to be a designer or inventor; the experimenters were simply the laborers in a universal project whose dimensions he was busy outlining:

> Accordingly, if there be any one more apt and better prepared for mechanical pursuits, and sagacious in hunting out works by the mere dealing with experiment, let him by all means use his industry to gather from my history and tables many things by the way, and apply them to the production of works, which may serve as interest until the principal be forthcoming. But for myself, aiming as I do at greater things, I condemn all unseasonable and premature tarrying over such things as these, being (as I often say) like Atalanta's balls. For I do not run off like a child after golden apples, but stake all on the victory of art over nature in the race. (4.105)

This tension between Bacon's desire to convert all men to a tremendous cooperative venture and his desire to run before all—to be the precursor—characterizes much of his work. To reframe the problem with another Baconian metaphor: the designer must not tarry over details but must be concerned, above all, with the master plan; and yet the design must surpass the designer and be capable of perfecting itself, both inside and outside the text. If the cursory gestures of the designer and the fulfillment or control of the design are at cross-purposes, it is the *New Atlantis* that offers the fantasy of resolution—the place where designer and design might enter history. Just before the work breaks off, and just after the governor describes how the fellows of Salomon decide "which of the inventions and experiences which we have discovered shall be published, and which not," there is a description of two "very long and fair galleries." In one of these the Bensalemites "place patterns and samples of all manner of the more rare and excellent inventions: in the other we place the statua's of all principal inventors" (3.165). Bacon would certainly have known Polydore Vergil's popular encyclopedia, which was organized along historical or genetic principles according to the "inventors of things." But Bacon does not trace inventors only, creating instead two distinct commemorative traditions.

His reasons for doing so are probably best understood if we ask how Bacon himself would be honored were the two galleries merged and the presence of the inventor depended on the material form of the "pattern" he produced. Indeed, such a separation is necessary if Bacon himself were to be understood as a principal player in the history of science. Although several European inventors are honored here, the governor forbears describing the Bensalemite inventors and their inventions to his European guest, "which since you have not seen, it were too long to make descriptions of them; and besides, in the right understanding of those descriptions you might easily err" (3.166). The list of Old World inventors honored by the Bensalemites begins with the accomplishments of the age and reaches back into the mythic past: "There we have the statua of your Columbus, that discovered the West Indies: also the inventor of ships: your monk that was the inventor of ordance and of gunpowder: the inventor of music: the inventor of letters: the inventor of printing: the inventor of observations of astronomy: the inventor of works in metal: the inventor of glass: the inventor of silk of the worm: the inventor of wine: the inventor of corn and bread: the inventor of sugars: and all these by more certain traditions than you have" (3.166). Here is a history of learning that bridges the gap between science and fable, the science of letters and the art of science, and thus seems very far from the division of the "two cultures" so often traced to Bacon. No art or material is spared in the commemoration of mankind's benefactors: "These statua's are some of brass; some of marble and touch-stone;

some of cedar and other special woods gilt and adorned: some of iron; some of silver; some of gold" (3.166).

In this gallery, progress is "measured by men" whose metal (mettle) transfigures Hesiod's ages of man. The inventors stand among their true historical peers, rather than their contemporaries, and are protected from errors of judgment by those deemed best qualified to evaluate their contribution and to manage the course of history. It is worth noting that for all his antipathy to Bacon, T. S. Eliot's notion of tradition, outlined in "Tradition and the Individual Talent," bears a strong ressemblance to Bacon's. For both men, "the existing monuments form an ideal order among themselves, which is modified by the introduction of the new (the really new) work of art among them." Bacon's scientist, like Eliot's artist, "cannot be valued alone; you must set him, for contrast and comparison among the dead."

Rereading *the* New Atlantis

The prominence of the House of Salomon has led many readers—most significantly its Restoration readers—to treat the *New Atlantis* as an institutional prophecy whose fulfillment, if denied Bacon himself, was shortly thereafter achieved in the founding of various scientific societies of the mid to late seventeenth century, and most particularly in the founding of the Royal Society. Many of the early readers of the *New Atlantis* were eager to see the text as a kind of charter for institutions devoted to scientific research. Perhaps not surprisingly, however, even the most direct invocations of Bacon's utopia did not consult the text as a blueprint or as a methodological handbook for experimental research; the *New Atlantis* is not legible in such terms. It was used rather than read as an authorizing fiction and myth of origin. The figured divine endorsement of Bensalem's Christian science was taken as a literal prefiguration of the new Royal Society. The House of Salomon was not invoked as a model for Baconian science but as a vision fulfilled.

John Glanvill, the author of a sequel to Bacon's utopia,[58] declared that Lord Bacon's "Salomon's House in the *New Atlantis* was a Prophetick Scheam of the Royal Society," and Cope and Jones, editors of *Sprat's History of the Royal Society,* who begin their introduction with this quotation, add affirmingly that "our age has amply documented the assertion."[59] The prescience with which the *New Atlantis* anticipated actual

institutional changes in scientific research is persistently described by
even its modern readers as "prophetic," even where the prophecy has
been understood to be a dark and foreboding one.

It is more than a historical irony (though decidedly less than a
prophecy) that Bacon, in delineating the three classes of false prophecy,
refers to the tradition of Plato's *Timaeus* and "Atlanticus" (*Critias*),
which, he notes, some might turn into a prediction of the discovery of
the New World, as "probable conjectures and obscure traditions many
times turn themselves into prophecies, while the nature of man coveteth
divination, thinks it no peril to foretell that which indeed they do but
collect" ("Of Prophecies," 6.465). It might be said that the Royal Society
sought exactly such divination when it collected its New Science from
the *New Atlantis*. In his "Ode to the Royal Society," Abraham Cowley
pushes to its limit the notion of Bacon as prophet, imagining him as the
Moses of the New Science:

> From these and all long Errors of the way,
> In which our wandering Predecessors went,
> And like th'old Hebrews many years did stray
>   In Dessarts but of small extent,
> Bacon, like Moses, led us forth at last,
>   The barren Wilderness he past,
> Did on the very Border stand
>   Of the blest promis'd Land,
> And from the Mountains Top of his Exalted Wit,
> Saw it himself, and shew'd us it.[60]

Rather than feature the Royal Society's iconoclastic, anti-scholastic innovations, Cowley gives a typological reading of the Royal Society as a
vision fulfilled in the Judeo-Christian prophetic tradition. Although there
is no reason to assume that Bacon would have objected to his invocation as patron saint, it is noteworthy that the way in which Bacon anticipated and outlined the shape of modern empirical scientific enquiry was
not treated by his followers and enthusiasts as a contribution of intellec-
tion or academic influence, but, rather, as vatic inspiration.

Although Cowley discovers his prophetic vocabulary *in* Bacon's
utopia, taking sacred authority to reside in rather than be revised in the
New Atlantis is radically to alter its use as a text. Bacon's construction of
a rival prophetic "tradition" in the creation of an ur-myth for the fictional
world of Bensalem is replicated by the Royal Society in taking Bensalem

as the ur-myth for a modern scientific society. In this gesture, however, what was conceived as a world-transforming utopia becomes a nostalgic Christian epic. Retrospective typological readings supersede utopian strategies of reform (whether activist or analytical) at the very moment the vision offered is taken as the vision fulfilled. By establishing Bacon as the anti-type of Moses (or King Solamona), Cowley completes—and in so doing exhausts—the meaning of the model text. Such a reading puts contemporary events in relation to a particular and fulfilled past rather than revising the reader's understanding of origins with respect to a reimagined future.

The problems inherent in the literary reproduction of utopia become clear when we examine Cowley's use of the *New Atlantis* in his Christian epic, *Davideis.*[61] Cowley figures his relation to the House of Salomon as one of "anticipation" by casting Samuel as the patron-founder of a Prophets College at Ramah. In the gilded synagogue, the prophets' prayers delineate and praise "the Work of the Six Days." In this context, however, the prophets cannot offer much in the way of improvement, which is the very charter of Bacon's "College of the Six Days Work." Further, as a monastic order, the Prophets College is established not as a new world but as a world apart, whose epic construction declares it to be immutable and complete. Bakhtin describes "the world of epic" as "the national heroic past: it is a world of fathers and of founders of families, a world of 'firsts' and 'bests.'"[62] At first glance, this might well seem an apt account of the originary emphasis of Bacon's utopia, but in Bensalem the fathers are in fact the sons of generations of improvements. Though the first fathers are praised, the "best" are in effect our contemporaries, the sons of "Bensalem" (son of peace), and they are exemplary precisely—if paradoxically—for being *typical* (as Bacon declares the function of the parable) of their generation. Nameless men are not the regular sort of heroes, and yet neither the explorers, the fellows, nor the governors of the Stranger's House or Salomon's House are given proper names. Rather than establish an absolute, immutable origin, the *New Atlantis* establishes a *tradition* of origins and new beginnings.

Cowley's translation of the plain prose style and dialogic structure of Bacon's *New Atlantis* into the heroic couplets of his *Davideis* produces a violent paradigm shift: what was once offered as "true vision" becomes memory; what was once universalizing as a utopian "nowhere" becomes concretized and locally defined and defining. The *New Atlantis,* thus considered, ceases to be a parable of reform and becomes a far more conservative, self-inscribing mythology in which the beginning is taken for the end and the ends for the beginning. Which is to say that although the use of utopia may indeed be the ends of utopia, in such a case it is just as certainly the end of utopia.

If one side of utopia borders on epic with its monolithic tales of national heroes, the other clearly borders on dystopia with its satiric tales of degeneration. To construct Bacon's utopia as an institutional fantasy and the Royal Society as its fulfillment gives Cowley his inspiration, but it also provides Jonathan Swift with all the material he needs to produce his satirical dystopia in Book 3 of *Gulliver's Travels,* in which resident "Projectors" of the Grand Academy of Lagado attempt to extract sunbeams from cucumbers, reduce human excrement to its original food, or devise methods for building houses from the roof down.[63]

It is precisely this "degeneration" of utopia to dystopia that anticipates and replicates the history of the genre. From its inception in the Renaissance, the utopian form was Janus-like, for the utopian impulse has always been shadowed by its twin, the anti-utopia or dystopia, which tells stories about the misuse and abuse of utopia. For every ardent, reforming Bacon or Campanella, there has been an irreverent and subversive Rabelais or Cervantes. More continues to defy definition, so double is his original conception of Utopia. All utopias, however, even the most earnest ones, are stories of opposition and revision. More's original utopia declares its superiority to Plato, and it would seem that most utopian visions thereafter have similarly placed themselves in opposition to other utopias. They are necessarily corrective, insofar as they set their ideal state in contradistinction to what are perceived or represented as lesser, failed, or corrupted ideals (always more fearful than simple human failures).

That Bacon calls his utopia the "New Atlantis" when "Bensalem" or "The House of Salomon" would seem more obvious titles suggests that much of the idealizing force of his fiction will be generated by his opposition to and correction of Plato. Bacon casts himself not as prophet—particularly unnecessary, as everything in the *New Atlantis* is depicted as historically accomplished fact—but as the rival historiographer and cosmologist to Plato. The story does not require a charismatic prophet-narrator, only a rather featureless and nondescript narrator-discoverer who will record how a tiny island-nation, unknown and unseen, could accomplish what all of Europe could not.

Chapter Five

Revisiting Utopia in Margaret Cavendish's *Blazing World*

A learned woman is thought to be a comet, that bodes mischief, whenever it appears. To offer to the world the liberal education of women is to deface the image of god in man, it will make women so high, and men so low, like fire in the housetop, it will set the whole world in a flame.

—BATHSUA MAKIN, "An Essay to Revive the Antient Education of Gentlewomen"

When Bathsua Makin wrote these words in 1673, decrying contemporary views about the education of women, she had before her the example of Margaret Cavendish, a woman whose writings and personal comportment elicited both wonder and alarmed suspicion.[1] Not only did Cavendish promise a world on fire in the very title of her utopian fiction, *The Description of a New World Called the Blazing World* (*The Blazing World*), but she delivered her new world into the safekeeping of a brilliant heroine whose meteoric rise to absolute power is treated as a matter of course.[2] Redirecting rather than neutralizing masculine fears, Cavendish presents the powerful woman as a natural wonder of the world. Makin, by contrast, issues a sober warning: "Let not your Ladiships be offended, that I do not (as some have wittily done) plead for Female Preeminence. To ask too much is to be denied all" (4).

Makin's cautionary remarks for learned women may well draw their

moral from the case of Margaret Cavendish. Although Cavendish tire-
lessly sought recognition from poets, critics, scientists, university men,
and other women, in works of every genre, her contemporaries dubbed
her "Mad Madge," regarding much of her work as unreadable. Samuel
Pepys described her as a "mad, conceited, ridiculous woman," and
Dorothy Osborne declared that "there are many soberer people in
Bedlam."[3]

Not only her contemporaries found her writing difficult to manage.
Virginia Woolf, combing the British Museum for historical models of female writers in *A Room of One's Own,* describes the example of Margaret Cavendish with some exasperation: "What could bind, tame or
civilize for human use that wild, generous, untutored intelligence? It
poured itself out, higgledy-piggledy in torrents of rhyme and prose, poetry and philosophy which stand congealed in quartos and folios that
nobody ever reads."[4] In this image, the congealed torrent of Cavendish's
writing seems not so much to span genres as to overpour them, forming
in their place an undifferentiated mass. Cavendish is thus deemed to be
undisciplined and incoherent, her body of work illegible, relegated to a
place outside of genre and therefore lost to history.

Although Woolf disparaged Cavendish's writing as an undisciplined
hodgepodge of genres, some of her recent apologists have regarded the
ways in which she exceeds or dissolves generic boundaries as an asset
rather than a liability. Rachel Trubowitz, for example, reads *The Blazing
World*'s "generic transgressiveness" as the method by which Cavendish
"dissociates the utopia from the repressive force of discipline and newly
associates it with a suspension of rationally conceived laws and institu-
tionally imposed order."[5] But even if this analysis is offered as praise,
Trubowitz may well overestimate the degree to which Cavendish rejects
rational or institutional order. Nor is it clear that Cavendish is able to
construct sui generis an "unrestrained site" (230) for feminizing utopia.

In this chapter I argue that Cavendish's manipulations of genre in *The
Blazing World* speak directly to the vicissitudes in the history of her reception and the assumptions of her legibility or illegibility. I also want to
establish, however, this synthetic and revisionary utopia as the locus at
which Cavendish works through her own exercise in historical revisionism, constructing neither a nostalgic nor a "progressive" version of history but an alternative account of her own times. In this regard *The
Blazing World* offers an interesting counterpart to her biography of her
husband, *The life of the Thrice Noble, High and Puissant Prince William
Cavendishe, Duke, Marquess, and Earl of Newcastle. . . . written by the*

Thrice Noble, Illustrious, and Excellent Princess, Margaret, Duchess of Newcastle, his wife (*The Life of William Cavendish*), which she published one year later, in 1667. In her preface to that work, Cavendish outlines the three "chiefest" sorts of histories: "General," "National," and "Particular," corresponding to the three sorts of governments: democracy, aristocracy, and monarchy. Given this taxonomy and the project at hand, it is not surprising that she favors the third sort of history, the Particular, which treats "the life and actions of some particular person." This is the form of history, she argues, that is "the most secure because it goes not out of its own Circle, but turns on its own Axis, and for the most part, keeps within the Circumference of Truth" (n.p.). To write the narrative of a particular life is to offer a complete yet self-contained world. This description of her project suggests both a metaphoric and a methodological connection between her account of her husband's life and the imaginary life of the empress of the Blazing World. Interestingly enough, in both cases she is willing to play a supporting, scribal role, although she will be intent on calling attention to—and redefining the importance of—her role as author.

The Particular History she offers in *The Life of William Cavendish* is happily both the only kind she is qualified to write (allowing her to gather her materials directly from her subject and firsthand experience) and the only species of history that qualifies as "heroical."[6] Cavendish concludes her prefatory letter addressed to her husband by declaring for herself a heroic role as author, comparable to her husband's in the field:

> Indeed, My Lord, I matter not the Censures of this Age, but am rather proud of them; for it shews that my Actions are more than ordinary, and according to the old Proverb, It is better to be Envied, than Pitied: for I know well, that it is merely out of spight and malice, whereof this present Age is so full, that none can escape them, and they'l make no doubt to stain even your Lordships Loyal, Noble and Heroick Actions, as well as they do mine, though yours have been of War and Fighting, mine of Contemplating and Writing: Yours were performed publickly in the Field, mine privately in my Closet: Yours had many thousand Eyewitnesses, mine none but my Waiting-maids. But the Great God that hath hitherto bless'd both your Grace and me, will, I question not, preserve both our Fames to after Ages, for which we shall be bound most humbly to acknowledge his great Mercy. (n.p.)

The Blazing World offers not so much a fantasy of role reversal—a place where Cavendish herself is able to practice "noble and heroic ac-

tions" in the field—but the place where contemplation and writing are fully revealed to be active, heroical, and world-transforming. It is perhaps ironic that Cavendish's "historical" project in *The Blazing World* has been too often occluded by autobiographical readings of the work that do not fully account for the historical framing of biography as a genre or the conditions for fame outlined in Cavendish's oeuvre. In the following reading, I want to begin to tease apart, in order to reconsider the relation between, Cavendish as a romantic figure constructed by history and Cavendish's utopian romance of history in which women might appear as world-historical individuals.

Cavendish's eccentricities, as well as her endlessly reiterated desire to be taken as an extraordinary rather than a representative woman and writer, have contributed to her representations as an isolated figure, alternately seen as mad or heroic. Here I argue that *The Blazing World* is not most fruitfully read as either a "private" fantasy of wish-fulfillment or as an isolated feminist province to which women must flee or retreat in order to be free and self-determined agents. Instead, I survey how Cavendish reworks the ground, connecting literary and historical genres at (and as) the intersection of representation and experience. This negotiation between the fictional and factual realms of *The Blazing World* is a tricky one and quite clearly fraught with peril for both Cavendish's characters and the author herself. Although Cavendish challenges and revises generic boundaries, she also seeks inclusion in male literary and philosophical canons, and in order to gain recognition, she must also to some degree be recognizable within such canons. For this reason, Cavendish's complex engagement with both the shifting discursive practices of the seventeenth century and the established generic conventions that shaped and bestowed the textual authority she so ardently desired deserves fuller attention—even if the history of Cavendish's reception tells us she was not always able to make her texts legible in such terms.

Sandra Sherman has usefully argued for Cavendish's construction of an "authorial" model of empowerment in *The Blazing World* and other works.[7] Nonetheless, her representation of Cavendish's solipsistic retreat into a textually constructed self does not entirely capture, I believe, the nature of Cavendish's project. In Sherman's view, Cavendish's strategy is to show that "her own acts of creation are always already original, exempt from the intertextuality and hence from the authority of shaping discourses" (193). Consequently, Sherman finds it inconsistent or contradictory that Cavendish, despite her authorial strategies for "eluding a

dominating power by excluding external discourse" (191), also seeks to "lodge herself in cultural memory" (203) through a fame that can only be achieved or affirmed through intertextuality. This is no contradiction at all, however, if one does not identify Cavendish's "withdrawal into fancy" as a rejection of "external discourse." In the preface to *The Blazing World,* Cavendish outlines fancy or the "fantastical" as the third generic component of the narrative's structure, "the first part whereof is romancical, the second philosophical" (124). Furthermore, in arguing that "the end of fancy is fiction" (123), Cavendish demonstrates that fancy not only is textually productive but also brings with it a long history of textual defenses.[8]

The mixed genre of Cavendish's utopia—its blending of imaginative romance fiction, natural history, and philosophy—links it clearly to Bacon's own utopia. And her decision to attach *The Blazing World* to her *Observations upon Experimental Philosophy* was almost certainly influenced by the publication of Bacon's *New Atlantis,* with his natural history, *Sylva Sylvarum.* Nonetheless, despite such formal parallels, the historical reception of Cavendish's writings offers a mirror image of Bacon's. As I have argued, Bacon's *New Atlantis* has been (mis)understood as transparently productive of history, whereas Cavendish's utopia has, until quite recently, been regarded as so obscure, so fantastic, so *personal,* that it could make no claim to historical relevance, let alone historical or scientific veracity.

Yet it is, precisely, if somewhat ironically, the recent historicizing turn in feminism and in literary studies that has brought Cavendish's writings, including her utopia, back into view. Woolf's assessment that Cavendish's work is something "nobody ever reads" is certainly no longer true. Nonetheless, how we read Cavendish's work continues to be marked in interesting ways by the history of her reception—in which her literal and her literary self-presentations are often conflated or confused. Cavendish's inclusion of herself as a character in *The Blazing World* has certainly contributed to this confusion, but it is important not to overlook the literary model she would have found for this in More's *Utopia.* Moreover, even the understandable confusions of "the Duchess" as persona and author in Cavendish's utopia do not entirely explain why critics so insistently identify *The Blazing World*'s heroine, the empress, with Cavendish herself.

Cavendish's obsessive reiteration of her originality need not be taken at face value and, indeed, must be weighed against her persistent fear that her works would be credited to other (male) hands. In her dedicatory epistle to her husband in *The Life of William Cavendish,* she remarks on the malice of "spightful tongues" who denied her authorship: "for your Grace remembers well, that those Books I put out first, to the judgment of this censorious Ages, were accounted not to be written by a Woman, but that somebody else had writ and publish'd them in my Name."[9] The depiction of Cavendish's exile by gender—even after the Restoration and her return from political exile on the Continent—from the authority of masculine institutional learning has taken both pitying and admiring turns, in Cavendish's time and our own. It is unhelpful at best and dangerous at worst, however, to let either her declarations of her singularity or her complaints about her lack of formal training blind us to her profound engagement with, and revision of, her intellectual and cultural milieu. Cavendish herself had no affirmative desire to place herself outside of genre, tradition, or history.

In recent criticism, *The Blazing World* has probably most often been classified as a utopian text, although many of Cavendish's readers have focused on the particular ways in which the text revises a "masculine" utopian tradition. Before particular claims can be made for Cavendish's utopian revisions, however, it is important to remember that utopia has always been a hybrid, synthetic, and revisionary genre, drawing on a variety of literary, historical, theological, and philosophical forms. To the standard variations of saturnalia, travelogue, Platonic dialogue, natural philosophy, and "historical" accounts of a secular golden age or a sacred paradise, Cavendish will add romance, beast fable, and cabbala. But as this study should amply demonstrate, utopian fiction has remained remarkably unconstrained by a fixed set of formal features. Moreover, insofar as it is the custom of utopian narratives to reject or transform their literary precursors, Cavendish is nowhere more orthodox a utopian than in her revisions of others' utopian models.

For this reason it may be more helpful to consider the ways in which Cavendish, as an early-modern feminist, seizes upon the potential of this nascent genre, rather than to assume that she strains against its peculiar limitations. I believe that Cavendish exploits both the novelty and tremendous range of utopian narratives to authorize a revisionary project that subsumes and transforms a number of more intractable generic models for representing female nature, authority, and experience. In this chapter I am particularly interested in focusing on the interrelation and realignment in *The Blazing World* of three dominant discourses for representing women: the misogynist strain of narratives depicting the "woman-on-top,"[10] the literary conventions of romance, and the emerging textual practices of natural philosophy. While each of these aspects of Cavendish's utopian project has been discussed before, I want to avoid discussing *The Blazing World*'s generic elements in isolation to suggest how Cavendish conjoins these discursive practices—like so many worlds—to establish an axis of female agency that resists the simple inversions of a world turned upside down. By connecting the Blazing World, as well as the empress's home world, to her own world, Cavendish explicitly reorients generic expectations to allow for a new reading of the Old World. The historical dimension of this reconfiguration is immediately suggested by her heroine's arrival in Paradise, the capital city of the Blazing World, a place of considerable material as well as spiritual rewards. The world of the fall, she is told—the place to which "Adam fled" (170)—is the world from which she comes. The setting of *The Blazing World* is thus given both contemporary and prelapsarian coordinates, a place of restoration and reparation. But if Cavendish wants to insist on the proximity of these worlds, she also knows that the spiritual distance between a Paradise in which woman rules and a Paradise ripe for a fall was very much in question for many of her readers. Blazing new trails will not be as important in the journey to *The Blazing World* as passing safely through all too familiar terrain.

Women on Top of the Blazing World

The title *The Description of a New World Called the Blazing World* invokes the utopian commonplace of New World discovery figured as the superimposition of epistemological and geographical frontiers. Although Cavendish has been claimed as the first female author of a utopian text,[11] it was not possible for Cavendish to describe an entirely new world; indeed, the topos of the female utopia had long been discursively colonized. The "utopian" narrative of the woman-on-top has, indeed, a double ancestry, both along paternal lines, in which Plato, whose female guardians share rule with men in the *Republic*, and Aristophanes, whose female tyrants lord it over men in the *Lysistrata* and *Ecclesiazusae*, each play a seminal role. As noted earlier, Robert C. Elliott has argued that utopia and satire are both rooted in the prehistory of saturnalian rituals.[12] But the differences between satire's inversions and utopia's corrections of social norms are notoriously unstable where the advancement of women's station is concerned. Sexual inversions of power drive much of Aristophanes' bawdy comedy. Yet even Plato seems to indulge a stifled giggle in the *Republic* when Socrates, Glaucon, and company are forced to imagine women (naked women, perhaps naked old women) in the gymnasium with the men.[13]

In early modern literature, Book 2 of Joseph Hall's *Mundus Alter et Idem,* "Viraginia, or New Gynia," offers just one of the many examples of satirically constructed "female utopias" in which the ladies have their day.[14] Hall's text, published in 1605 under the pseudonym Mercurius Britannicus, was popular enough to go through two Latin editions, one German edition, and two editions of the English translation, which appeared under the title *The Discovery of a New World.*[15] But if Hall's narrative constructs a world predicated on female gratification, readers were, of course, expected to perceive beneath the sardonic humor the horror of the very possibility of such a distempered world, a land "perfectly fertile but badly husbanded" (57).

It might reasonably be protested here that *The Blazing World* is no sneering satiric tract but instead posits an affirmative feminist utopia. While such a characterization seems obvious enough, I want to underscore the difficulty of Cavendish's task in maintaining this very distinction, given the generic overdetermination of the narrative of the woman-on-top.[16] Historically, the antipodal logic of satiric inversion cut a very direct and generally one-way path between female utopia and male dystopia. In the world where female desires prevail, men are feminized and controlled by debasing passions. If, however, Cavendish's full title, *The Description of a New World Called the Blazing World,* indicates that her utopia may itself represent an inversion or revision of Hall's satirically inverted *Discovery of a New World,* or texts like it, then Cavendish cannot be said simply to reject a genre that she exploits by layering fictional travelogue with social commentary. A more complex rhetorical analysis of what she attempts or accomplishes in *The Blazing World* is clearly necessary.

Lee Cullen Khanna has suggested that Cavendish "relocates 'utopia' at the borders of feminine desire and masculine models of meaning."[17] Thus, one might argue, utopia emerges not so much as a location but as a situation, where female desire must confront its mirror image, already constructed and constrained by masculine discursive models. In other words, putting a positive spin on the topos of the woman-on-top was not entirely subject to Cavendish's textual control. Cavendish avoids the specter of what John Knox called the "monstrous regiment" only by defining her heroine's power in largely spiritual terms.

Cavendish's dematerialization of female power, however, has led feminist readers such as Janet Todd to complain that "her fantastic utopias are firmly placed in her own head."[18] Todd, Sara Heller Mendelson and others have consequently questioned Cavendish's feminism and criticized her for limiting the benefits of her fictional worlds to thinly disguised versions of herself.[19] Responding to such charges, Catherine Gallagher, Kate Lilley, and others have outlined the important historical and theoretical relationship between Cavendish's conservative, absolutist politics and her feminism, tracing, in Gallagher's felicitous phrase, "the paradoxical connection between the *roi absolu* and the *moi absolu*."[20] In light of such studies, it no longer seems necessary (or possible) to establish a perfect correspondence between *The Blazing World*'s utopian content and its articulation of an "ideal" feminist vision relevant for contemporary practice. "Locating" Cavendish's fabulous world requires, instead, a fuller consideration of the discursive tactics and constraints of her utopian methodology, especially because she attempts to revise the world already re-constructed in a variety of narratives, either utopian or misogynist or both. In this context, the cerebral perambulations of Cavendish's utopian heroines, the empress and the duchess, are probably best measured as the critical distance between her utopia and Aristophanes' or Hall's dystopian satires, which fix wholly on the grotesque physicality of women's desires.[21] But this distance also threatens to destabilize the generic principles that make this text recognizable as either utopia or dystopia, and it helps to explain why generations of readers, who could not but believe Cavendish to be earnest, were forced to believe her mad.

Diagnosing Utopia

The long-standing judgment that Cavendish produces in *The Blazing World* a limited personal fantasy rather than a recognizably utopian text reappears in Frank and Fritzie Manuel's utopian encyclopedia, *Utopian Thought in the Western World*.[22] Their reading of Cavendish offers a fascinating instance of contemporary resistance to distinguishing between female utopias and topsy-turvy representations of feminine disorder. I want to consider the example of the Manuels here in some detail because I think their account of the intimate and paradoxical connection between being "truly" utopian and being historically significant offers an important "symptomatic" reading of Cavendish. And I believe that some of the assumptions underlying their assessment of Cavendish can be found even in more sympathetic accounts of the utopian aspect (and impact) of her writing—accounts that insist on reading *The Blazing World* as an essentially personal—and therefore an ahistorical—fantasy.

Although the Manuels describe their definition of utopia as "latitudinarian and ecumenical," they do not judge Cavendish to be the author of a true utopia. Reviewing their honor roll of utopian thinkers in their introduction, one can't help but notice that there is not a single woman in the list: "More and Patrizi, Bacon and Campanella, Andreae and Morelly, Fénelon and Condorcet, Restif de la Bretonne and Edward Bellamy, H. G. Wells and Theodor Hertzka, Wilhelm Reich and Norman Brown, Erich Fromm and Herbert Marcuse, Julian Huxley and Pierre Teilhard de Chardin all have a place on the roster of utopians—some, to be sure, against their will" (7). While they may desire to extend the boundaries of utopia to include the unwilling, the Manuels do not propose to include just anyone, and in the next paragraph they explain their principle of exclusion, which features Margaret Cavendish as the prime negative example:

> But if the land of utopia were thrown open to every fantasy of an individual ideal situation the realm would be boundless. The personal daydream with its idiosyncratic fixations has to be excluded. The ideal condition should have some measure of generality, if not universality, or it becomes merely a narcissistic yearning. There are utopias so private that they border on schizophrenia. *The Description of a New World, called the Blazing World* (1666) by Margaret Cavendish, Duchess of Newcastle, has much in common with the delusions of Dr. Schreber analyzed by Sigmund Freud in a famous paper. Uncounted utopian worlds of this stripe, many of them highly systematized, are being conjured up every day, in and out of hospitals, though few of them are ever set in print. (7)

The Blazing World, according to this view, provides something closer to a pathological profile than a universal utopia. The Manuels' objection to the text is clearly not based on a narrow formal definition of utopia, for among the approved forms the Manuels count "extraordinary voy-

ages, moon-travelers' reports, fanciful descriptions of lost worlds in a
state of nature, optimum constitutions, advice to princes on the most
perfect government, novels built around life in a 'proper' utopian society, millenarian prophecies, architectural plans for ideal cities" (7). In
the Manuels' account, Cavendish's text again escapes a generic structure
of any sort because they view *The Blazing World* not as a constructed
alternative world but as a frightening glimpse into Cavendish's dissoci-
ated interior world. *The Blazing World* is thus dismissed as a degenerate
form, a private and narcissistic fantasy, with paranoid tendencies.

What is perhaps *most* remarkable about their assessment, however, is
the comparison they make between Cavendish and the case of Dr.
Schreber. Daniel Paul Schreber, a former Senatspräsident in Dresden
who had captured Freud's attention, suffered from the delusion that he
had a mission to redeem the world and to restore it to its lost state of
bliss—but only after he was transformed from a man into a woman.
Freud, who never met Schreber, undertook an analysis based entirely on
a reading of Schreber's 1903 *Memoirs,* an account of his illness in which
he described hearing voices and dressing himself in "feminine finery." [23]
In the Manuels' juxtaposition of texts, the transgendered delusions of
Schreber become themselves transgendered as allusions to Cavendish.
Where Schreber's transsexual fantasy functions to enact a "heterosexual"
union with a disciplining father figure, the homoerotic union of the
characters of the empress and the duchess in *The Blazing World* is designed to evade masculine sexuality and authority altogether. The comparison of Cavendish and Schreber reverses, or collapses, the gendered
ambiguities in each figure. A fiction in which a woman is represented in
a position of absolute power is quite tellingly analogized to the feminized male's delusion that he could redeem the world in the form of a
woman.

Cavendish's actual practice of cross-dressing, and her reputation as
"Mad Madge of Newcastle," are doubtless part of the well-known biographical "evidence" the Manuels have in mind for their psychoanalytic
reading. But such details are drawn from the portrait of the author constructed out of diaries and letters by Pepys, Osborne, Evelyn, and others, rather than a close reading of her utopian text. [24] The "perversions"
or transgressions of *The Blazing World* are doubtless perceived as the
more disturbing and profound, because the representation of female
rule, and the female homoerotic subtext, subordinate the masculine to
the feminine in both public and private spheres, destabilizing gendered

norms and utopian ideals in ways not "corrected" either by therapeutic solutions or by costume changes in the closing scene.

What the Manuels' comparison features goes beyond the assumption that Schreber and Cavendish share delusions of grandeur and unstable gender identities. The analogy depends specifically on the conflation of their "symptoms" in a gendered, that is, *female* megalomania. And this way madness lies. Yet it should go without saying that, even if she were power mad, Cavendish is scarcely mad for imagining herself a woman, nor can she (or any of her fictional heroines) be considered clinically perverse for seeking control as a woman.[25]

In the final analysis, it seems clear that the most striking comparisons that can be drawn between Cavendish and Schreber point not to the visions they share but to the fears they provoke. Indeed, their comparison is comprehensible *only* when considered in terms of the anxiety caused by the blurred gendered categories and the emasculation attributed both to the effeminate male and to the dominant woman. The Manuels' reading powerfully suggests the duration, as well as the tenacity, of the topos of the woman-on-top as a cultural narrative that continues to discover a symmetrical identity in female power and male paranoia, female utopia and male dystopia.

Cavendish's exclusion from the utopian canon is justified by the tacit assumption that she, like Schreber, violates the boundaries not only of sanity but also of social decorum, sexual preference, gender identity, and ultimately therefore, legibility. Following a kind of inverted mimetic fallacy, this view would seem to suggest that Cavendish cannot be understood to author a "real" utopia precisely to the degree to which her compensatory world is (mis)taken for reality, although it is arguably the Manuels who, in mistaking character for author, confuse fiction and reality. The possibility that Cavendish might be a bad writer (a not entirely insupportable conclusion) rather than a mad one is never entertained. Indeed, these represent functionally opposed rather than interchangeable readings, as the former suggests the failure of Cavendish's prose to communicate her vision, whereas the latter depends on the transparency of her text to portray her distempered mind.

The Manuels' exclusion of Cavendish is ultimately predicated on their separation of mere wish-fulfillment fantasies from productive utopian speculations. The authors acknowledge that they have, by necessity, left many utopias out of their survey, but they go on to assert that "when a writer has imprinted his personality upon a movement of ideas he is singled out" (7). But if each utopian author must make an imprint upon the age in which "he" lives to merit inclusion, then the use of the masculine pronoun is necessarily more descriptive than generic.[26] The Manuels' stated purpose is not to provide an exhaustive utopian bibliography or catalog but to write "a true history" (6). Ironically, however, the "true history" of utopia must in such a case be forced to reproduce the very suppression of female agency that Cavendish's utopian fiction was created to revise and transform. The Manuels *disallow* Cavendish utopian status precisely because she does not transform the conditions she critiques; however, as we have seen, actual historic impact has not been a standard measure for the utopian genre. In Chapter 4 I discussed how More has been attributed utopian status on the grounds that he does not attempt to produce a social blueprint for world transformation, whereas Bacon has been found a false utopian by critics of Enlightenment science or colonialism by virtue of the assumed or demonstrated historical impact of his vision. History has been invoked as a flexible measure of utopian design and content, or, put another way, utopia offers the ultimate vindication of one or another romance of history. For the Manuels, Cavendish's utopian romance is verified by history to be all in her head.

"The Whole Story of This Lady Is a Romance"

By declaring that the first part of *The Blazing World* is "romancical,"[27] Cavendish offers romance generic pride of place notwithstanding her frequent criticisms of the genre.[28] Khanna argues that *The Blazing World* "begins with a deconstruction of the romance plot and the image of woman as simple object of male desire" (18). Yet Cavendish's deliberate reliance on the generic force of the romance plot may offer something closer to a reconstruction than a deconstruction of the form, for her revision still very much depends on viewing woman as "object of desire," even as she romances the reader to a new consideration of woman as desiring subject. To illuminate the particular nature of Cavendish's revision of the romance plot of disaster, exile, and restoration, I want to read *The Blazing World* against Shakespeare's utopian romance, *The Tempest,* a text that serves as one of this utopia's important subtexts. I do not mean to suggest here that Cavendish's only source or point of reference for *The Blazing World* is *The Tempest*. There are certainly any number of romance heroines who are more obvious counterparts for the powerful and worldly empress than the mild and naive Miranda. But if readers have found more obvious romance analogs for the empress in martial maids such as Bradamante or Britomart, Cavendish's heroine bears perhaps an even more significant resemblance to the romance hero, Prospero. While it becomes less easy to dismiss *The Blazing World* as undisciplined scribblings or grandiose delusions when one fully credits the text's romance structure, it is also the force of generic expectation that can suggest why Cavendish's utopian romance would confuse its readers when it is the lady (instead of, say, Prospero) who plays all the parts: victim, hero, and magus. Significantly, Cavendish's utopia, like Shakespeare's play, begins with a thwarted rape and a tempest. Although perhaps the most obvious difference between the romance plot of *The Blazing World* and *The Tempest* is found in the ladies' parts, in both texts the female role is central to political consolidation in the New World and the possibility of restoration in the Old World. Cavendish's boldest revision is simply to make the woman the agent as well as the instrument of these processes.

As *The Blazing World* opens, the unnamed lady is carried by force to the extreme verge of the world by a merchant who "fell extremely in love" with her but who had no hopes of obtaining her hand as he was her inferior in both station and wealth. Before he can ravish her, the gods take pity on our heroine and provide a tempest, which drives the small packet boat to the north pole and through a mysterious passage to a new world connected to the old one at the pole. Obligingly, the merchant and his men soon freeze to death, and it is explained that the lady is preserved "by the light of her beauty and the warmth of her youth" (126). Cavendish manages to make conventional praise the salvation (rather than the undoing) of the lady, by taking it all quite literally. This description can be seen to correct both biological and poetical conventions, for the heat of the lady not only resists the determinism of humoral psychology, which would ally the female with the cold and moist, but it also suggests a reworking of the Petrarchan poetics of an icy feminine virtue, which Cavendish displaces here onto the romance landscape.[29] We know we have arrived at an entirely new world when the lady's virtues are safe even in the company of beastly men who treat her more courteously than the men of her own world, greeting her with wonder and admiration. It is not long before the lady's virtues captivate the emperor who makes her empress of the Blazing World. The romance plot thus turns from a quite conventional narrative of feminine vulnerability to a far less conventional narrative of female power, moving in the process from violent sexual *raptus* to female neoplatonic rapture. Cavendish's use of romance conventions is nowhere more transparent or subversive than when she casts her virtuous female protagonist in the double role of victim and hero. Although it may seem both striking and strange that this utopian fantasy of unbridled female power and autonomy is inaugurated by the abduction and near rape of its heroine, her salvation can be seen to enact simultaneously the fulfillment and the profound revision of generic expectation.

The Tempest also begins with a foiled rape and a tempest; however, it is not until the end of the play that Miranda's imperial role is unveiled (or staged) by Prospero in the "discovery" of the young lovers engaged in a game of chess. Nonetheless, Caliban's unrepentant if frustrated desire to have "peopled else / This isle with Calibans" (1.2.353–54) shows that Miranda's body is, from the beginning, the contested ground for empire construction. Although she herself has no power, she is the center of a power struggle between Caliban, Ferdinand, and her father, Prospero, a contest whose outcome will determine the fate of Milan and Naples as well as the island where the struggle is staged. Caliban's sexually predatory behavior—representing a violation not only of trust but of "natural" hierarchial order—is used to justify enslaving him. But Prospero similarly denies Ferdinand access to his daughter, using his potent powers to press him into service. The structural parallel between Prospero's test for the worldly and aristocratic Ferdinand and his punishment of the "salvage and deformed slave," Caliban—although designed to heighten and contrast their responses—inevitably serves to naturalize Caliban's offense, much as it dramatizes the persistent paternal anxieties motivating Prospero's behind-the-scene manipulations.

In fact, these paternal anxieties relate not only to Miranda's future but also to her origins. After hearing Prospero explain that her father was the Duke of Milan and "a prince of power," Miranda asks, "Sir, are you not my father?" Prospero's reply allows the possibility of doubt even as it assuages it: "Thy mother was a piece of virtue and / She said thou wast my daughter" (1.2.55–57). If Miranda's absolute innocence confirms her own virtue, it also threatens it as a consequence of her inexperience and ignorance in the ways of men. Her potentially dangerous naïveté is belied when she fixes her utopian expectations on the shipwrecked remnants of the Old World. "How beauteous mankind is! O brave new world / That has such people in't," she exclaims, drawing from her father the cynical rejoinder, "Tis new to thee" (5.1.185–87).

Prospero's anxiety about both his daughter's domestic origins and her imperial future explains why Cavendish's heroine remains isolated and why her romance restoration is figured in martial rather than marital or familial terms. Because the emperor is virtually absent, imperial success in Cavendish's romance depends not on controlling the woman's virtue but on the virtue of the woman in control. Feminine virtue becomes a medium for action, rather than the mediation necessary for transmitting political legacies. Although the female body remains potentially vulnerable in Cavendish's romance, the dematerialization of feminine virtue ultimately secures both the female body and the body politic from harm.

The Blazing World contains no conjuring fathers, benevolent or tyrannous; it is the empress who is able both to recognize and to overcome her enemies by virtue of her great learning. Given the emphasis on her mastery of the natural sciences, it is striking that the tempest that initially saves our heroine has divine rather than human origins. This explicit intervention of the gods is unique in this text devoted to the "magic" of natural science, and it contrasts pointedly with Prospero's meteorological manipulations. In *The Blazing World* the divinely sent tempest, far from qualifying the lady's powers, serves to preserve the social order and to ratify the transcendent authority of her imperial rule. But henceforth it is the lady who, like Prospero, is taken for divinity. And just as Prospero did, she will ultimately exploit the confusion with friend and foe alike.

When she is brought before the emperor of the Blazing World, in his capital city, Paradise, he declares that she must be a goddess. (A convention surely, but also, perhaps, an unironic echo of Ferdinand and Miranda's mutual astonishment.) On learning she is mortal, he marries her and makes her empress, this title serving as the only name by which she is known for the remainder of the narrative. The emperor, within the space of two sentences, gives her "absolute power to rule and govern all that world as she pleased" (132) and virtually disappears from the text. Thus, without violating social decorum and with the explicit intervention of the gods, whose instrument is nature, Cavendish gives over to the lady the equivalent of Prospero's authority and his arts. The newly created empress deliberates with the kingdom's beast-men virtuosi, whose natural resourcefulness she corrects and improves on without the ingratitude or curses of Caliban, just as she consults with spirits who do her bidding without the suspicious petulance of Ariel.

During the period 1666–68, when Cavendish produced two editions of *The Blazing World, The Tempest* was very much in the air. Shakespeare's play had an obvious appeal for Restoration audiences, with its story of the exile and return of lawful authority. Not long after Cavendish published the first edition of *The Blazing World* in 1666, Dryden's version of *The Tempest* (subtitled *The Enchanted Island*) was first performed by the Duke's Company at the theater in Lincoln's Inn Fields.[30] Not only would Pepys compare this play favorably with another version of *The Tempest* revived for the Restoration stage, John Fletcher's and Philip Massinger's *Sea Voyage,* but he also compared it favorably with Shakespeare's original, which he declared had "no great wit."[31] Dryden's play, on the other hand, was "the most innocent play" he had ever seen. Shakespeare's play was thus regarded as wonderful source material but capable of improvement. Dryden, nonetheless, declares his debt to Shakespeare in his play's Prologue: "He Monarch like gave those his subjects law, / And is that Nature which they paint and draw."[32] The identification of Shakespeare as nature's poet had become a commonplace that Dryden did much to augment. What is striking in Dryden's tribute here, however, is his identification of Shakespeare not simply as the poet of nature but as nature itself.

Margaret Ferguson has shown how another early modern female author, Aphra Behn, used Shakespeare to justify her own art in an early "Epistle to the Reader":

> Behn becomes the first, to my knowledge, in a line of English women writers who have defended or justified their own writing practices (which, like Shakespeare's and Jonson's, often included substantial imitations and "thefts" from predecessors) by allying themselves with the paradoxical authority of a supposedly unlearned Shakespeare, a figure whose greatness is held to derive more from "nature than from art," and who is therefore an appealing imaginary model for the writer who is, because of her gender, excluded from, or only partly welcomed into, institutions of higher learning."[33]

Cavendish never explicitly compares her art with Shakespeare's, and thus leaves Behn's place in Ferguson's genealogy unchallenged.[34] Nevertheless, Behn and Cavendish can still be compared for borrowing from Shakespeare without attribution, and appropriating his reputation as nature's poet to similar ends.[35] The strong contemporary identification of Shakespeare with nature is doubly suggestive for Cavendish's revision, providing both a source of literary inspiration and the "natural" ground for observation and experimentation. In her *Sociable Letters* (1664), rather than elaborate her indebtedness to Shakespeare, Cavendish praises Shakespeare's ability to represent all types of women as the ability to "metamorphos[e] himself into a woman" (246), feminizing both his skill and his authority for such representations.

That Cavendish was not interested in anatomizing her literary debts does not mean she was suppressing them. As Ferguson reminds us, literary "thefts" were also common masculine practice. Still, the very coherence of this text depends upon our understanding of how Cavendish sorted through and responded not only to romance conventions but also to the entire cultural repertoire for representing the domain of the feminine. Cavendish effects the lady's salvation by "translating" her between worlds. It is the reader's task to assess what is lost or gained in the translation. For wherever the Blazing World is, this is not a place outside of genre. Indeed, the legibility of *The Blazing World* depends on our first taking literary—rather than literal—measure of its distance from the Old World. Toward that end, Cavendish will offer her heroine something resembling a generic grand tour. Her first encounter in the Blazing World takes place in a topos suspended somewhere between Lucian's satiric "A True History" and Aesop's moral fables.[36] Bearlike creatures who walk erect rescue the lady with the aid of "men like foxes" and "geesemen," three species of the Blazing World's vast menagerie of citizens. These anthropomorphized animals are joined by mild-tempered satyrs who gather to admire and assist the lady, in a scene structured like Una's salvation by satyrs in the Book 1 of *The Faerie Queene*. Unlike the satyrs' idolatrous worship of Una, or Caliban's lust for Miranda, however, no correction is needed or offered in *The Blazing World,* in which even such beastly men are "all respect and civility," sharing a common language and subject to universal law (128).

Thus, returning to the topos of the woman-on-top, Cavendish invokes a world replete with satiric conventions to perform her own satyric conversions, establishing from the outset that this is anything but a world turned upside down.[37] Indeed, with its humanized beasts, exemplary purple citizens, and gentle satyrs, this is a world in which disorder can have no purchase. Cavendish carefully shows how the Blazing World's order preexists the empress's arrival, to further guard against the association of female rule with a world of beastly usurpation and upheaval. Cavendish's hybrid generic constructions are not pitched toward carnival release but figure universal restoration to (and as) a state of nature.

Nature and the Anatomy of Utopia

As empress, our heroine is enabled to display her great learning and wisdom. She oversees the intellectual, political, and military affairs of her empire, all to the admiring acclamation of her new citizens. In her full imperial regalia, the empress becomes, as Lilley has noted, a kind of blazon, an allegorical emblem:[38]

> Her accoutrement after she was made Empress, was as followeth: on her head she wore a cap of pearl, and a half-moon of diamonds just before it; on the top of crown came spreading over a broad carbuncle, cut in the form of the sun; her coat was of pearl, mixed with blue diamonds, and fringed with red ones; her buskins and sandals were of green diamonds: in her left hand she held a buckler, to signify the defence of her dominions; which buckler was made of that sort of diamond as has several different colours; and being cut and made in the form of an arch, showed like a rainbow; in her right hand she carried a spear made of a white diamond, cut like the tail of a blazing star, which signified that she was ready to assault those that proved her enemies. (132–33)

This blazon constructs an image at once iconic in its lapidary stillness and dramatic in its staging of the empress as a virago in buskins. But beyond its allegorical and dramatic presentation of the empress, the language of this passage also contains an interesting echo of Bacon's *New Atlantis,* in which the governor of the House of Salomon catalogs the feats of natural science performed by the fellows of that institution. Here, the governor similarly links a description of light shows to precious stones:

> "We make artificial rain-bows, halos, and circles about light. We represent also all manner of reflexions, refractions and multiplications of visual beams of objects.
> "We have also precious stones of all kinds, many of them of great beauty, and to you unknown. . . . Likewise, loadstones of prodigious virtue, and other rare stones, both natural and artificial."[39]

In her utopia, Cavendish will naturalize Bacon's artificial wonders by assimilating both rainbows and precious stones to the charismatic bounty of the empress herself. Nonetheless, although our heroine becomes empress as a consequence of her natural virtues, her imperial tactics are not without artifice. Consequently, if Bacon's fictional virtuosi are in the business of manufacturing halos, we should be not be surprised when the empress, in her attempt to reform the Blazing World's religion, tries one on for size.

Enlisting not only her considerable eloquence in preaching, but also her knowledge of natural science, the empress builds two chapels: one made of a material found in a volcano, which causes the chapel "to appear all in a flame"; and the other, made of a material retrieved from the stars which causes the chapel to be bathed in perpetual light. In the one chapel the empress preaches "sermons of terror to the wicked," and in the other, where she appeared "like an angel," she preaches sermons of salvation and comfort. Thus, as the narration explains, "by art, and her own ingenuity" the empress converted the entire world to her religion "without enforcement or blood" (164).

These so-called miracles are attributed neither to active divine intervention nor to passive virtue, but rather to a manipulated natural science, whose operations the empress is particularly skilled in understanding and controlling. Whereas the conversion of the *New Atlantis*'s Bensalem is brought about by a miraculous pillar of light, the empress converts the citizens of the Blazing World by her own dazzling brilliance. The spectacular light show, in which the empress appears like an angel and performs her own miracles, does not derive from divine origins. Extending well beyond her natural body, the empress's power redefines both the personal and the "natural."

With her knowledge of the natural sciences, the empress not only works spiritual transformations but military ones as well, as when, in the second part of *The Blazing World,* she returns to her native land to rout a menacing navy, using the very firestone she formerly employed in the Blazing World to simulate hellfire. The empress appears before the enemy standing on the waters—a blazing apparition in her garments of light. This is no miracle, but an illusion she achieves by standing on an early prototype of a submarine with the aid of the star-stone. Nonetheless, the victory she achieves is not simulated, for the firestone she brings burns their ships with real fire, and the enemy is utterly vanquished. Thus, she puts to rest—perhaps—the fears of her compatriots, some of whom say she is an angel or a goddess, some who suspect her as a sorceress, and "some of whom said the devil deluded them in the shape of a fine lady" (211). None of these speculations get near the truth of the matter, but neither does the empress's association with the supernatural detract from her accomplishment or diminish the assessment of her powers. Even this most physical demonstration of female power is not so much linked to the female body itself as it is a dramatic escape from its social and material constraints.

For Cavendish, as for Bacon, knowledge is power, and the manipulation of nature as a way of exploring her secrets is a particularly potent tool for a revision of feminine "nature." The fruit of the ideal alliance of the female with nature in *The Blazing World* is neither organic nor egalitarian. For this reason, it has been at times difficult to situate her utopian thought within the context of contemporary feminist critiques of rationalist utopias. Carolyn Merchant's *Death of Nature* explores the "age-old association" of women and nature in a number of utopian texts.[40] She condemns Bacon's "mechanistic" utopia in the strongest terms for its plan for the domination of nature, and she directly traces its legacy to modern efforts to bypass natural reproduction:

> The antithesis of holistic thinking, mechanism neglects the environmental consequences of synthetic products and the human consequences of artificial environments. It would seem that the creation of artificial products was one result of the Baconian drive toward control and power over nature. . . . To this research program, modern genetic engineers have added new goals—the manipulation of genetic material to create human life in artificial wombs, the duplication of living organisms through cloning, and the breeding of new human beings adapted to highly technological environments. (186)

But where Merchant sees a symbolic (but nonetheless real) loss for women in the seventeenth century when mechanistic metaphors for nature began to displace organic metaphors, Cavendish seizes upon the New Science as a powerful means of rereading woman's traditional inscription in the "Book of Nature." *The Blazing World* unapologetically displays artificial manipulations of nature that are not only protective of feminine virtue but also productive of very real female power. Indeed, Cavendish seems to predicate the very possibility of utopian emancipation on liberating the female from her traditional earthbound constraints and reproductive mandates.

Merchant's preference for a nature figured as female nurture seems inevitably nostalgic for a mythic past, in which exaltation of female nature reflects to whatever degree a corresponding valuation of women. But as Judith Butler warns in *Gender Trouble,* "The feminist recourse to an imaginary past needs to be cautious not to promote a politically problematic reification of women's experience in the course of debunking the self-reifying claims of masculinist power."[41] The kind of "trouble" that Cavendish makes may unsettle both traditional and utopian feminist associations of female and nature, but it is in just such a refusal to narrate the female as identical with or constrained by nature that Cavendish most opens the possibilities for illuminating the complex cultural construction(s) of gender.

Cavendish's ambivalence toward the female body as, on the one hand, an object of veneration and, on the other, a trap that must be transcended time and again is a theme running through the work. As Lilley observes in her introduction to *The Blazing World,* "The literal body of female virtue is never available for representation" (27). One of the most striking evasions of the female body is found in a long passage in which it is explained to the empress in rather excruciating detail "how it came, that the imperial race appeared so young, and yet was reported to have lived so long, some of them two, some three, and some four hundred years." The cause of this imperial longevity is a certain gum with quite remarkable side-effects: "It being given every day for some certain time to an old decayed man, in the bigness of a little pea, will first make him spit for a week or more, after this, it will cause vomits of phlegm, and after that it will bring forth by vomits, humours of several colours" (155). After vomiting comes purgation by every orifice, until "lastly. . . . it will make the body break out into a thick scab and cause both hair, teeth and nails to come off; which scab being arrived to its full maturity, opens first along the back and comes off all in a piece like an armour" (155–56). When this gruesome metamorphosis is accomplished, "the patient is wrapped into a cere-cloth." In this state "he continues until the time of nine months be expired from the first beginning of the cure, which is the time of a child's formation in the womb," after which "he will appear of the age of twenty, both in shape and strength" (156).

In making the natal analogy explicit, Cavendish declares both what this process is like and what it is not. By evading childbirth, this imperial family has a security greater than any dependent on dynastic succession—a dicey business at best in the seventeenth century. If Cavendish is interested in celebrating female rule in *The Blazing World,* she clearly has no interest in connecting the political body to maternity and female nurture. Her motives are not hard to discover in this passage, which seems to conjoin the travails of childbirth to the suffering of plague victims, even as it redirects their sufferings toward personal resurrection.[42] Cavendish herself remained childless, and for her this was both a source of disappointment and liberation.[43] For this reason we should not find it surprising that in *The Blazing World,* female fertility is associated with the spiritual and intellectual rather than the material. Again, Cavendish looks to less biologically determined ways to "produce" greatness.

A remarkable exploration and reimagination of the female will to power and spiritual generativity in this narrative comes with the introduction of Margaret Cavendish as a fictional character in her own romance. This is not, of course, without precedent in utopian fiction: in the original *Utopia,* More casts himself as his text's doubting Thomas. But Cavendish will take, not surprisingly, a less self-reflexive and self-effacing stance in her own story. When the empress decides to enlist the aid of a spiritual scribe, her spirit advisors counsel her to choose the soul of the Duchess of Newcastle over the souls of Aristotle, Pythagoras, Plato, Galileo, Descartes, Hobbes, and other great writers and thinkers, because these ancients and moderns alike would be too conceited or wedded to their views to serve as a scribe to a woman. The empress perceives an additional advantage in having Margaret Cavendish's disembodied soul attend her: "This lady then, said the Empress, will I choose for my scribe, neither will the Emperor have reason to be jealous, she being one of my own sex. In truth, said the spirit [advising her], husbands have reasons to be jealous of platonic lovers, for they are very dangerous, as being not only very intimate, and close, but subtle and insinuating" (181). There is no assurance that female spiritual unions are exempt from the status of platonic lovers or this caveat, as Cavendish says explicitly that "truly their meeting did produce such an intimate friendship between them that they become platonic lovers, although they were both females" (183). And there is a patently erotic stamp to this immaterial conjoining of souls. Indeed, I would argue that this homoerotic bond is licensed, rather than constrained, by its "spirituality," as it places the relationship outside the traditional arguments about the biological mandate of male-female relations.

For Cavendish, however, even if souls can't have sex, they can and do have gender, as the empress makes clear when she asks her spirits for "information of the three principles of man, according to the doctrine of the Platonists; as first of the intellect, spirit, or divine light: 2. of the soul of *man herself:* and 3. of the image of the soul, that is, *her* vital operation on the body?" (173; my emphasis). Reversing the Aristotelian principles that identify mind with the male and matter with the female, Cavendish almost dissolves masculine materiality altogether, in order to free the now generically female soul. In doing so, Cavendish draws on traditional Christian representations of the soul as feminine; in this passage, however, she would seem to create a sexual and textual hermaphrodite, combining male and female, classical and Christian.

The relation between material and spiritual worlds is one of the principal preoccupations of *The Blazing World.* John Rogers has brilliantly discussed Cavendish's rejection of contemporary "tenets of mechanism to embrace the animist materialism that had flourished a decade before at the Vitalist Moment."[44] Although her natural philosophy was variously regarded by contemporaries as retrograde, impious, or simply beneath consideration, Rogers argues that "the duchess's revised model of physical agency provided an important model for her interest in female agency" (190). But if Cavendish was vitally interested in what Rogers calls "the volitional power of motion intrinsic to all physical matter" (189), she is equally at pains in *The Blazing World* to dematerialize the textually overdetermined female body.

Following Robert Burton's *Anatomy of Melancholy,* Cavendish links her "personal utopia" to an anatomy of man. She makes explicit, however, that for the former to be possible, the latter must be redefined, and providing a new utopian anatomy is one of Cavendish's principal discursive strategies. Devon Hodges has pointed out that the anatomy comes into currency "when the feudal body was decaying and a whole new body of knowledge was forming."[45] What is interesting to note here is how this new body of knowledge offered even the royalist Cavendish a paradoxically enabling narrative. Despite Cavendish's abhorrence of revolution and the unruly, distempered body politic, it is clear that the Civil War, specifically the military failure of the aristocracy and the unity challenge to priestly authority, provided the context for an allegorized refiguring of gendered hierarchies. The members of the body politic had severed the head, and the destroyed political body had to be reimagined and recast. Despite the bitterness and privations of sixteen years of exile, the unmanning of the aristocracy provided both the opening for, and the necessity of, understanding other avenues to power and authority, even as it provided new self-authorizing allegories for political weakness.

The connection between the Blazing World and the world of the duchess is at the intersection of these volatile and potentially reversible paradigms. Under the benign rule of the empress, the Blazing World is "so well ordered that it could not be mended; for it was governed without secret and deceiving policy; neither was there any ambition, factions, malicious detractions, civil dissensions, or home bred quarrels, divisions in religion, foreign wars, etc. but all the people lived in a peaceful society, united tranquility, and religious conformity" (189). But when the empress asks to see "the world the duchess came from," the latter "used all the means she could to divert her from that journey, telling her, that the world she came from, was very much disturbed with factions, divisions and wars" (189). The world turned upside down is associated here with Cavendish's world—one that the Restoration has not entirely restored. If Cavendish offers the preceding passages to suggest the great divide between the duchess's world and the Blazing World, she does not ever dramatize this as the distance between fact and fiction. Indeed, the guided tour that the duchess provides for the empress of her native world is entirely spiritual, abstract, and textual in nature. As traveling souls, the duchess and the empress "in a moment viewed all the parts of [the duchess's world], and all the actions of all the creatures therein" (190). This is an authorial view, divine in scope, that implies a mastery greater than that of even an "Emperor of a world," who, as the empress reminds the duchess, "enjoys but a part, not the whole" (190).

Significantly, when the duchess and empress arrive in England, their first stop is the theater. The empress wonders that the scenes make a better show than the actors, declaring her preference for a "natural face before a sign-post" (191). The duchess explains that "relation" or narration is something "our poets defy and condemn. . . . into a chimney-corner, fitter for old women's tales, than theatres." To which the empress replies, "Why. . . . do not your poets' actions comply with their judgements? for their plays are composed of old stories, either of Greek or Roman, or of some new found World" (192). The empress's observation and the duchess's description of plays as "new actions" "joined to old stories" allows Cavendish to forge a connection between the materials of history, the art of narration, and theater. When the duchess and empress travel directly from the theater to court, Cavendish further reinforces the association of stagecraft and statecraft, describing how the royal family "attended by the chief of the nobles. . . . made a very magnificent show" (192). The empress is struck with awe at this spectacle of the royal family who "seemed to be indued with divine splendour" (192). But while the scene allows Cavendish to praise the queen's virtue and piety as well as the king's discourse, it seems designed to anticipate the episode in the second book when these virtues will be combined in her own imperial heroine in displays no less—and yet no more—theatrical and yet so powerfully effective against her enemies.

The final section describing the duchess's world recounts the legal wrangle between William Cavendish and Fortune. This allegorical morality play (enlisting characters such as Prudence, Honesty, Folly, Rashness, and Truth) is one of the more "artificial" contrivances of the story, but it is significantly also one of the most "historical," both in its biographical emphasis and in its return to the classical and early-modern historical topic of *virtus* and *fortuna* and the dilemma of how best to determine and represent their relation. In his description of the three rhetorical genres, Aristotle associates each with a historical situation or mode: "Deliberative oratory is concerned with the future (advice about what is to be done), demonstrative with the present (celebration of the values of the community), and the judicial with the past (judgment on what has been done)."[46] Although *The Blazing World* is filled with oratory pitched to each of these temporal registers, the judicial oratory that follows gathers witnesses, interested parties, and their testimony to showcase Personal History at its most personal. As she does in her *Life of William Cavendish,* "the Duchess," Cavendish, speaks in her own voice to play her husband's advocate, although unlike her biography of her husband, the play of forces here is entirely feminized—both the duke's adversaries and his associates. Fortune, "a powerful princess, and as some believe, a deity, overcame him, and cast him into banishment, where she kept him in great misery" for the crime of preferring "his innocence before my power" (197). It is Honesty as Cavendish's surrogate (and the one who taught him everything he knows) who comes forth last to speak for the duke, declaring that "I came not here. . . . to hear Fortune flattered. . . . neither came I hither to speak rhetorically and eloquently, but to propound the case plainly and truly" (199). In similar terms, Cavendish writes in her Preface to *The Life of William Cavendish* that she was forced "to write this History in my own plain Style, without elegant Flourishings, or exquisit Method, relying intirely upon Truth" (n.p.). But if Honesty is willing to let Truth decide the matter in *The*

Blazing World, Fortune is not, and justice is deferred and the trial cut short when Fortune storms off "in a passion" (200).

Representing the utter irresolution of the duke's steadfast virtue and the mutability of Fortune is for Cavendish both a moralizing and a mimetic practice, and she will return to this theme in *The Life of William Cavendish*.[47] On the one hand, Cavendish authorizes a version of history that can account for the reversal of the fortunes of once powerful historical actors. But further, by pointing to possibilities for a powerful female rhetoric in the face of impotent masculine heroism, Cavendish clears the ground for her own historical agency. By making virtue and fame (rather than victory and fortune's favor) the final arbiters of history, Cavendish suggests a utopian model of history in which she can fully participate—as author, as historian, and as historical subject.

Lee Cullen Khanna has suggested that the historical significance of *The Blazing World* for a feminist canon is that it initiates "an alternative utopian tradition in English" (15–16). But, of course, Cavendish's place in a feminist utopian tradition is only clear through the reconstruction of that tradition.[48] Retrospective or anticipatory histories have tended to obscure, or at least underestimate, the historical dimension of what Khanna describes as Cavendish's "struggle for discursive authority" (30). Judith Butler speaks of the temptation of feminist theory to discover in the "prejuridical past"

> traces of a utopian future, a potential resource for subversion or insurrection that promises to lead to the destruction of the law and the instatement of a new order. But if the imaginary "before" is inevitably figured within the terms of a prehistorical narrative that serves to legitimate the present state of the law or, alternatively, the imaginary future beyond the law, then this "before" is always already imbued with the self-justificatory fabrications of present and future interests, whether feminist or anti-feminist. The postulation of the "before" within feminist theory becomes politically problematic when it constrains the future to materialize an idealized notion of the past or when it supports, even inadvertently, the reification of a precultural sphere of authentic feminine. This recourse to an original or genuine femininity is a nostalgic and parochial ideal that refuses the contemporary demand to formulate an account of gender as a complex cultural construction. (36)

Because all utopian thought constitutes an imaginative attempt to escape historical determinism as well as historical contingency, there is a great temptation for feminist critics to discover in *The Blazing World,* or other early utopias by women, the evidence of a utopian past that articulates the longing for a utopian future. But whether we are gesturing toward a "precultural" or an extracultural utopian sphere of the feminine, we inevitably, as Butler suggests, mystify our own political and discursive origins and aims. Cavendish herself does not assume that she speaks for all women, or even for "All Noble and Worthy Ladies" to whom she dedicates a separate 1668 edition of *The Blazing World.* In the 1666 edition, addressing "The Reader" she simply declares, "I have made a world of my own: for which no body, I hope, will blame me, since it is in every one's power to do the like" (124).

Origins and Originality: (Self-)Invention and Utopia

It could be argued that Cavendish's reluctance to speak for others was born of her reluctance to be judged with others. The mythos of Cavendish as an entirely original and singular figure, without precedent or debt, does not find its origins in contemporary feminist criticism but in the artfully crafted publicity campaign designed and deployed by Margaret and William Cavendish to condition her reception. In *The Blazing World,* Cavendish dubs herself "Margaret the First," the title that Douglas Grant takes for his biography; and this is but one of her many self-bestowed titles.[49] Although, as Jean Gagen has pointed out, "At the time when Margaret Cavendish was exhorting women to seek and win honor in the public theater of the world, a well-defined feminist movement had been in existence in England and on the continent for more than a century," Cavendish, however, pretended or achieved a studious ignorance of the accomplishments of women of her own or previous generations.[50] In "An Epistle to My Readers," in *Natures's Pictures* (1656), she writes, "I have not read much in History to inform me of the past Ages. . . . for I fear I should meet with such of my Sex, that have out done all the glory I can aime at."[51] For Cavendish, history is not generated or constructed by a gendered or a genetic principle but through the singular performances of world-historical individuals.

Demonstrating her own qualifications was not a simple affair, as historical engagement and feminine retirement were not entirely reconcilable ideals. Abraham van Diepenbeke's striking portrait of Cavendish, which first appeared as a frontispiece to *Philosophical and Physical*

Studious She is and all Alone,
Most visitants, when She has none,
Her Library on which She lookes
It is her Head her Thoughts her Books.
Scorninge dead Ashes without fire
For her owne Flames doe her Inspire.

Figure 6. Margaret Cavendish. Frontispiece portrait from *Philosophical and Physical Opinions* (1655). By permission of The Huntington Library, San Marino, California.

Opinions (1655), offers an illuminating illustration of Cavendish's claim to historical singularity, portrayed as at once heroic and isolating (Figure 6). The engraving depicts the author in a library without books, left entirely to her own fertile imagination, with only her inkwell, pen, and paper at hand. Cavendish is encircled by cherubs who hover above her head with a laurel wreath, sparing her the labor (and the embarrassment) of being too evidently a self-crowned laureate. The balcony is inscribed with the following legend:

> Studious She is and all Alone
>   Most visitants, when She has none,
>   Her Library on which She looks
>   It is her Head her Thoughts her Books.
>   Scorning dead Ashes without fire
>   For her own Flames doe her Inspire.[52]

These lines reflect an often-repeated refrain in tributes to Cavendish by her husband and others, as well as in her own writing, which focuses on her originality and powers of invention. What is striking about this verse is its conflation of the physical and textual body into a singular, self-generating, phoenixlike form. While seeming to endorse Aristotle's opinion that "the female generates in herself," the verse transforms female physiology from a defect of nature to a theory of female poetic autonomy.[53]

Although the identification of the physical and poetic body has, as we have seen, a vexed and complicated reception, the association is one that Cavendish herself went to great lengths to reinforce and manipulate, both in her semi-autobiographical textual productions and in her artful self-presentations and fanciful comportment. The inventiveness of Cavendish's dress is amply documented (with varying degrees of fascination and contempt) in contemporary diaries and letters. John Evelyn in his diary found himself "much pleased, with the extraordinary fanciful habit, garb and discourse of the Duchess."[54] His wife, Mary Evelyn, was considerably less impressed, remarking, "Her main surpasses the imagination of poets. . . . her gracious bows, seasonable nods, courteous stretching out of her hands, twinkling of her eyes. . . . show what may be expected from her discourse, which is as airy, empty, whimsical, and rambling as her books, aiming at science, difficulties, high notions, terminating commonly in nonsense, oaths, and obscenity. . . . Never did I see a woman so full of herself, so amazingly vain and ambitious."[55] Mary Evelyn's association of Margaret Cavendish's extreme ambition with her airy, empty, whimsical, and rambling manner (both in person and in print) is precisely the sort of criticism that *The Blazing World* seems designed to disarm, if only by accepting the charges. In William Cavendish's prefatory poem to *The Blazing World,* for example, Margaret is compared favorably both to the ancients who divided the world into three parts, and to Columbus, who merely discovered a new world "lying in Time's shade":

> Then what are You, having no Chaos found
>> To make a World, or any such least ground?
>> But your creating Fancy, thought it fit
>> To make your World of Nothing, but pure Wit.
> Your Blazing-world, beyond the Stars mounts higher,
>> Enlightens all with a Celestial Fire.

Margaret Cavendish is cast here not as author of a world nowhere, but of a "World of Nothing" made of "pure Wit." But far from suggesting that her world is a trifling nothing, the paradox of praise William Cavendish develops in these lines describes his wife in a drama of creation ex nihilo. Far greater than a sublunary discoverer, Margaret Cavendish, out of empty air and pure whimsy, in her ramblings, which never leave the circuit of her thoughts, is a celestial maker of new worlds.

Notes

Introduction

1. Rosalie L. Colie, *The Resources of Kind: Genre-Theory in the Renaissance,* ed. Barbara K. Lewalski (Berkeley: University of California Press, 1973), pp. 19, 76–102. This description follows Plato's classification of poetry in the *Republic* (3.392 d) into description, imitation, and a third mode in which both these forms were mingled.
2. See, for example, Lyman Tower Sargent, *British and American Utopian Literature, 1516–1985: An Annotated, Chronological Bibliography* (New York: Garland, 1988), and Glenn Robert Negley, *Utopian Literature: A Bibliography with a Supplementary Listing of Works Influential in Utopian Thought* (Lawrence: Regents Press of Kansas, 1977). Of course, "personal" principles of selection reflect political commitments or assumptions as well. The once-customary exclusion of early modern women writers from utopian canons, for example, will be considered in Chapter 5.
3. The observation that native Utopians breed like rabbits explicitly makes an ironic joke of utopian reproduction. It is the description of l'abbaye de Thélème, with which Rabelais ends Gargantua's book, that comes closest to offering Rabelais's own utopian moment, inventing, as it does, its own origins.
4. *The Anatomy of Melancholy,* ed. Holbrook Jackson (New York: Random, 1977), p. 97.
5. See *The Shape of Utopia: Studies in a Literary Genre* (Chicago: University of Chicago Press, 1970), chap. 1.
6. "Defining the Literary Genre of Utopia: Some Historical Semantics, Some Genology, a Proposal and a Plea," *Metamorphoses of Science Fiction* (New Haven, Conn.: Yale University Press, 1979), p. 54.
7. *An Elusive Vision* (New York: Twayne Publishers, 1993), p. 12.
8. *A Rational Millennium: Puritan Utopias of Seventeenth-Century England and America* (Oxford: Oxford University Press, 1987), p. 14.

9. *The Political Unconscious: Narrative as a Socially Symbolic Act* (Ithaca, N.Y.: Cornell University Press, 1981), p. 9.

10. Georg Wilhelm Friedrich Hegel, *The Philosophy of History* (New York: Dover Publications, 1956), p. 26.

11. *The Content of the Form: Narrative Discourse and Historical Representation* (Baltimore: Johns Hopkins University Press, 1987), p. 61.

12. For a different approach to the relationship between early modern English utopian fiction and history, see Amy Boesky, *Founding Fictions: Utopias in Early Modern England* (Athens: University of Georgia Press, 1996). Boesky's provocative study appeared too late in the production of this book to allow me to respond adequately to its arguments.

Chapter One

1. Louis Marin, *Utopics: Spatial Play,* trans. Robert A. Vollrath (Atlantic Highlands, N.J.: Humanities Press, 1974).

2. In *The Ideologies of Theory: Essays 1971–1986,* vol. 2 (Minneapolis: University of Minnesota Press, 1988), p. 81. This essay originally appeared as "Naturalization [*sic*] and the Production of Utopian Discourse," *Diacritics* 7 (1977): 2–21.

3. These marks of history and Marxist theory are already featured by Marin himself, who situates them within a poststructuralist framework. Marin's interest in the history of "the neutral" (as a kind of utopian supplement) and "spatial play" challenges any simple divide between "theory" and "history" claimed in recent critical debates.

4. This gesture is particularly interesting in light of Jameson's own articulation of the interaction and intersection of philological stylistics and rhetorical analysis in "Criticism in History." The former, Jameson claims, is essentially "empirical and analytic" and "a middle class phenomenon," whereas the latter is "idealistic and speculative" and related to "an older and essentially precapitalist mode of linguistic organization." "Criticism in History," in *The Ideologies of Theory: Essays 1971–1986,* vol. 1 (Minneapolis: University of Minnesota Press, 1988; 1976), pp. 121–22. Jameson's theoretical utopianism is nowhere more evident than in this early essay: "Just as Marxism is both the end and the fulfillment of philosophy in general, so in much the same way it may be said to be both the end and the fulfillment of philosophies of history, and to demonstrate how the scattered and disparate events of history share common themes and common dilemmas, which link the toil and misery of Neolithic peoples to the most dramatic, as well as the most obscure, struggles of our own age" (133).

5. Richard Halpern has argued that Engels "values utopias because they generate 'stupendously grand thoughts and germs of thought'—because that is, they pave the way for theory." *The Poetics of Primitive Accumulation: English Renaissance Culture and the Genealogy of Capital* (Ithaca, N.Y.: Cornell University Press, 1991), p. 136.

6. Karl Mannheim, *Ideology and Utopia: An Introduction to the Sociology of Knowledge,* trans. Louis Wirth and Edward Shils (New York: Harcourt Brace Jovanovich, 1936), pp. 166–67.

7. Although Bloch is largely responsible for recuperating utopian thought for Marxism, his unsavory defense of Stalinism and the Moscow Show Trials is problematic for any historical consideration of the ideological function of that recuperation.

8. Although many New Leftists consider the new historicism an essentially conservative trend, it seems safe to generalize that the new historicists' explicit concern with power

and the politics of culture situate them well left in the general politics of the academy. Whatever their views on the possibilities of utopian practice, these critical schools are generally unified by their interest in exposing (however elusive, or inclusive) the mechanisms of ideology.

9. "Invisible Bullets," in *Shakespearean Negotiations: The Circulation of Social Energy in Renaissance England* (Berkeley: University of California Press, 1988), p. 65.

10. In *The New Historicism,* ed. Veeser (New York: Routledge, 1989), pp. 1–14.

11. Greenblatt has declared his preference of the term "cultural poetics" to the "new historicism," although both phrases trace their origins to his work.

12. *Renaissance Self-Fashioning: From More to Shakespeare* (Chicago: University of Chicago Press, 1980).

13. Greenblatt finds Utopia, on the other hand, utterly decided by history: "five years earlier or later More could not have written it" (58).

14. *The Art of Describing: Dutch Art in the Seventeenth Century* (Chicago: University of Chicago Press, 1983). Although Alpers's focus is on the seventeenth century, her observations on the connections between science and style trace their roots to the fifteenth and sixteenth centuries. For another interdisciplinary reading of Holbein's *Ambassadors,* here against Shakespeare's *Richard II,* see Ernest B. Gilman, *The Curious Perspective: Literary and Pictorial Wit in the Seventeenth Century* (New Haven, Conn.: Yale University Press, 1978), pp. 88–128.

15. See Alpers, pp. 244–45. The debate about whether perspective constituted a fundamentally subjective or objective scientific method for the construction of images is reflected in the writings of Alberti and Leonardo da Vinci and continues into the twentieth century. Panofsky's view that the convention established by geometric perspective is one among many possible conventions has been defended by Rudolf Arnheim, *Art and Visual Perception* (Berkeley: University of California Press, 1971); Gyorgy Kepes, *Language of Vision* (Chicago: P. Theobald, 1944); and Nelson Goodman, *Languages of Art: An Approach to a Theory of Symbols* (Indianapolis: Bobbs-Merrill, 1968). This view is contested by art historian E. H. Gombrich and psychologist M. H. Pirenne, who contend that geometric perspective is the scientifically accurate way of representing the three-dimensional world on a picture plane. See Erwin Panofsky, "Die Perspektive als 'Symbolische Form,'" in *Vortrage der Bibliotheck Warburg: 1924–25* (Leipzig-Berlin, 1927), pp. 258–330; E. H. Gombrich, "The 'What' and the 'How': Perspective Representation and the Phenomenal World," in *Logic and Art: Essays in Honor of Nelson Goodman,* ed. R. Rudner and I. Scheffler (Indianapolis: Bobbs-Merrill, 1972), pp. 129–49; M. H. Pirenne, "The Scientific Basis of Leonardo da Vinci's Theory of Perspective," *Journal for the Philosophy of Science* 3 (1952–53): 169–85.

16. On the Renaissance use of this figure, see Rensselaer Lee, *Ut Pictura Poesis* (New York: W. W. Norton, 1967). For a provocative critique of the new historicist method of "illustration," see Alan Liu, "The Power of Formalism: The New Historicism," *English Literary History* 56 (Winter 1989): 721–69.

17. "Psychoanalysis and Renaissance Culture," in *Literary Theory/Renaissance Texts,* ed. Patricia Parker and David Quint (Baltimore: Johns Hopkins University Press, 1986), pp. 210–224.

18. *The Order of Things: An Archeology of the Human Sciences* (New York: Random House, 1970), pp. 373–80.

19. Alan Liu has described both the tension and the emptiness of the new historicist paradigm: "A New Historicist paradigm holds up to view a historical context on one side, a

literary text on the other, and, in between, a connection of pure nothing. Or, rather, what now substitutes for history of ideas between context and text is the fantastic interdisciplinary nothingness of metaphor (more fully, the whole province of 'resemblances' Foucault charts in his 'Prose of the World' approach without its historical and theorized basis)" (743).

20. While I do not specifically address the British cultural materialists in this discussion, I will here mention Holstun's observation that cultural materialists "who tend to criticize the new historicist model of contained subversion, do not finally move very far from it." "Ranting at the New Historicism," *English Literary Renaissance* 19 (1989): 198. Jonathan Dollimore, for example, argues that "we can never find in a repressed subculture that most utopian of fantasies: an alternative to the dominant which is simultaneously subversive of it and self-authenticating." "Introduction: Shakespeare, Cultural Materialism, and the New Historicism," in *Political Shakespeare: New Essays in Cultural Materialism,* ed. Dollimore and Sinfield (Ithaca, N.Y.: Cornell University Press, 1985): 14–15.

21. It may very well be specious to distinguish politics per se and the relationship between politics and critical practice posited by various critical camps, but it seems worth pointing out that Marxists, cultural materialists, and new historicists are generally unified by a desire to challenge such distinctions.

22. Terry Eagleton, *Ideology: An Introduction* (London: Verso, 1991), pp. 1–2.

23. Eagleton, pp. 1–3.

24. "Renaissance Literary Studies and the Subject of History," *English Literary Renaissance* 16 (1986): 12.

25. See, most notably, *Discipline and Punish: The Birth of the Prison,* trans. Alan Sheridan (New York: Random House, 1979). Foucault's most direct remarks on utopian discourse can be found in his discussion of "heterotopia" in the beginning of *The Order of Things: An Archeology of the Human Sciences* (New York: Random House, 1970), which I discuss more fully in Chapter 3. For a Foucauldian reading of Bacon's *New Atlantis* (discussed in Chapter 4), see John Michael Archer, *Sovereignty and Intelligence: Spying and Court Culture in the English Renaissance* (Stanford: Stanford University Press, 1993), pp. 121–51.

Chapter Two

1. For a brilliant analysis of the rhetorical program of Italian Renaissance historians, see Nancy S. Struever, *The Language of History in the Renaissance: Rhetoric and Historical Consciousness in Florentine Humanism* (Princeton, N.J.: Princeton University Press, 1970).

2. One of the more influential and provocative examples is Elizabeth McCutcheon, "Denying the Contrary: More's Use of Litotes in the *Utopia,*" in *Essential Articles for the Study of Thomas More,* ed. R. S. Sylvester and G. P. Marc'hadour (Hamden, Conn.: Archon, 1977), pp. 263–74.

3. For example, Greenblatt's use of Holbein's anamorphism, or Harry Berger, Jr.'s reading of *Utopia* in the context of the technique of focused perspective: "The Renaissance Imagination: Second World and Green World," in *Second World and Green World: Studies in Renaissance Fiction-Making* (Berkeley: University of California Press, 1988), p. 31.

4. The editors of the Yale edition of Utopia, Edward Surtz and J. H. Hexter, have given the authoritative review in their introductions to *The Complete Works of St. Thomas More*, vol. 4 (New Haven, Conn.: Yale University Press, 1965); Page references to *Utopia* are taken from this edition and appear parenthetically in the text.

5. In addition to Greenblatt's and Jameson's readings of More, discussed earlier, notable recent work would include Amy Boesky's *Founding Fictions: Utopias in Early Modern England* (Athens: University of Georgia Press, 1996); Richard Halpern's *The Poetics of Primitive Accumulation: English Renaissance Culture and the Genealogy of Culture* (Ithaca, N.Y.: Cornell University Press, 1991); and Jeffrey Knapp's *An Empire Nowhere: England, America and Literature from "Utopia" to "The Tempest"* (Berkeley: University of California Press, 1992).

6. A particularly powerful treatment of the negative method of the "via negativa" is Richard Helgerson's "Inventing Noplace, or the Power of Negative Thinking," *Genre* 15 (1982): 101–21. Jeffrey Knapp reads *Utopia*'s negative engagement with history by demonstrating how this and a variety of other early modern English texts address the problem of the New World by representing England's imperial failures as a kind of otherworldly superiority.

7. This list should properly include those whose names head the prefatory letters and verse and who similarly participate in the fiction of *Utopia* by confirming its existence: Erasmus, John Froben, William Budé, Thomas Lupset, Jerome Busleyden, John Desmarais, and Gerald Geldenhauer.

8. *The Collected Works of Erasmus*, vol. 2, trans. R. A. B. Mynors and D. F. S. Thomson (Toronto: University of Toronto Press, 1975), pp. 147–48.

9. *The Collected Works of Erasmus*, vol. 3, trans. R. A. B. Mynors and D. F. S. Thomson, p. 89.

10. More's *Utopia*, like most utopias that follow, banishes the lawyer from the realm, notwithstanding More's own lawyerly training and practice.

11. "Of Sites and Parasites: The Centrality of the Marginal Anecdote in Book I of More's Utopia," *English Literary History* 54 (1987): 233, 242.

12. "More's Utopia and Uneven Development," *Boundary* 2, nos. 13.2–3 (1985): 234.

13. Fredric Jameson, "Of Islands and Trenches: Neutralization and the Production of Utopian Discourse," in *The Ideologies of Theory: Essays 1971–1986*, vol. 2 (Minneapolis: University of Minnesota Press, 1988), p. 94.

14. Although Marin produces a number of graphs, diagrams, and charts in *Utopics: Spatial Play*, he does not discuss the maps that accompany *Utopia* until a posthumously published essay: "Frontiers of Utopia: Past and Present," *Critical Inquiry* 19 (Winter 1993): 397–420. For an earlier discussion of the Utopian maps, see my "Mapping Out Ideology: The Case of Utopia," *Recherches sémiotiques/Semiotic Inquiry* 12 (1992): 73–94.

15. The origins of the two utopian maps are discussed later. The Yale editors regard as a confession of authorship Peter Giles's assertion in his letter to Jerome Busleyden (1 November 1516) that he had caused the Utopian alphabet to be added to the text, ostensibly shown to him while More was absent (23). His exclusive authorship is certainly a plausible, but not a necessary, assumption. In general, the theoretical implications of multiple authorship and collaboration in textual production among the humanists has not yet received the consideration it deserves.

16. The prefatory letters by Erasmus, William Budé, Jerome Busleyden, Peter Giles, and others participate in the fusion of fact and fancy by explicitly connecting the praiseworthiness of the textual Utopia to a demonstration of its actual existence.

17. See "Antibarbari," trans. Margaret Mann Phillips, in *The Collected Works of Erasmus,* vol. 23, ed. Craig R. Thompson (Toronto: University of Toronto Press, 1978), pp. 1–122. Erasmus's failure to defend eloquence in the *Antibarbarians* led John Colet to pay him the arch compliment, "Your book has quite persuaded me to abandon eloquence."

18. For an English translation, see Quirinus Breen, "The Correspondence of G. Pico della Mirandola and Ermolao Barbaro Concerning the Relation of Philosophy and Rhetoric," *Journal of the History of Ideas* 13 (1952): 392–412.

19. Frederic Seebohm discusses how John Colet, who was particularly influenced by the writings of "the Areopagite," and quoted them frequently in his own lectures, was brought to the painful conclusion that Grocyn was right. *The Oxford Reformers: John Colet, Erasmus and Thomas More* (London: Longmans, Green, 1896), pp. 61–93. On the Italian scholarship, see E. H. Wilkins, *Petrarch's Eight Years in Milan* (Cambridge, Mass.: Mediaeval Academy of America, 1958), no. 69, p. 226; John Monfasani, "Pseudo-Dionysus The Areopagite in Mid-Quattrocento Rome," in *Supplementum Festivum: Studies in Honor of Paul Oskar Kristeller* (Binghamton, N.Y.: Medieval and Renaissance Texts and Studies, 1987), pp. 189–219.

20. David Quint, whose discussion of humanist historicism informs my own, follows Kristeller and others in eliding the philological and rhetorical constituents of the humanist cultural program, although he points out Erasmus's emphasis in *The Praise of Folly* on "the historicism of humanist philology over the formalism of humanistic rhetoric." *Origin and Originality in Renaissance Literature: Versions of the Source* (New Haven, Conn.: Yale University Press, 1983), pp. xi, 9. On the humanist emphasis on rhetoric in the trivium, see also Paul O. Kristeller, "Humanism and Scholasticism"; Walter J. Ong, *Rhetoric, Romance and Technology* (Ithaca, N.Y.: Cornell University Press, 1971); Richard A. Lanham, *The Motives of Eloquence: Literary Rhetoric in the Renaissance* (New Haven, Conn.: Yale University Press, 1976); *Renaissance Humanism: Foundations, Forms, and Legacy,* vol. 3, "Humanism and the Disciplines," ed. Albert Rabil, Jr. (Philadelphia: University of Pennsylvania Press, 1988).

21. For a discussion of the maps' authorship, see *Complete Works,* vol. 4, pp. 276–77.

22. See *The Cosmographiae Introductio of Martin Waldseemüller in Facsimile,* ed. Joseph Fischer and Franz von Wieser, U.S. Catholic Historical Society Monograph 4 (1907; rpt., New York: Readex Microprint, 1966); see also *Circa 1492: Art in the Age of Exploration,* ed. Jay A. Levinson (New Haven, Conn.: Yale University Press, 1991), pp. 232–34.

23. The maps of Juan de la Cosa (who sailed aboard the Niña on Columbus's second voyage), Alberto Cantinto, and Giovanni Contarini, which predate Waldseemüller's map, also depict lands to the west of the West Indies but probably intended to represent China rather than America. See *Circa 1492,* pp. 230–31, 233; Peter Whitfield, *The Image of the World: 20 Centuries of World Maps* (Rohnert Park, Calif.: Pomegranate Artbooks, 1994), pp. 44–47. In 1508 the first edition of Ptolemy's "Geographia" to include the New World was printed in Rome. Johannes Schott's woodcut of 1513 is the most important of the new editions of Ptolemy. It included the "Tabula Terra Nova," the first map devoted to the delineation of the New World. See R. V. Tooley, *Maps and Map-Makers,* 4th ed. (London: B. T. Batsford, 1970), pp. 5–18; and P. D. A. Harvey, *The History of Topographical Maps: Symbols, Pictures and Surveys* (London: Thames & Hudson, 1980), p. 156.

24. Waldseemüller mistakenly believed that Vespucci had discovered the continent before Columbus. Although the name America stuck, in large part on the authority of this map, controversies continued to surround the authority of Vespucci's *Letters*. See *Letters from a New World: Amerigo Vespucci's Discovery of America*, ed. Luciano Formisano, trans. David Jacobson (New York: Marsilio, 1992).

25. Peter Barber, "England I: Pageantry, Defense, and Government: Maps at Court to 1550," in *Monarchs, Ministers, and Maps: The Emergence of Cartography as a Tool of Government in Early Modern Europe*, ed. David Buisseret (Chicago: University of Chicago Press, 1992), p. 27. See also Armando Cortesão, *The History of Portuguese Cartography* (Lisbon: Junta de Investigacoes do Ultramar, 1969–71), 1:248 (note 9), 2:52–73; Tony Campbell, "Portolan Charts from the Late Thirteenth Century to 1500," in *The History of Cartography*, vol. 1, ed. J. B. Harley and David Woodward (Chicago: University of Chicago, 1987), p. 410; *Circa 1492*, pp. 27–28, John Noble Wilford, *The Mapmakers* (New York: Random House, 1981), p. 38.

26. James A. Williamson, *The Cabot Voyages and Bristol Discovery under Henry VII* (Cambridge: Cambridge University Press, 1962), p. 220; Richard Hakluyt, *The Principal Navigations Voyages Traffiques and Discoveries of the English Nation*, ed. Irwin R. Blacker (New York: Viking, 1965), p. 17.

27. William Budé's letter to Thomas Lupset in the *parerga* describes Utopia as "undoubtedly" "one of the Fortunate Isles, perhaps close to the Elysian Fields" (12/13). The classical reference adds a double temporal location to Utopia as well.

28. R. A. Skelton, *Explorer's Maps: Chapters in the Cartographic Record of Georgraphical Discovery* (New York: Spring Books, 1958), fig. 40 and note p. 72. Skelton points out that although the maps carried by Columbus have not survived, "any seaman's chart drawn in Genoa would have shown him supposed islands in the Atlantic to serve as stepping-stones to the Indies" (pp. 52–53).

29. Raymond H. Ramsay, *No Longer on the Map: Discovering Places That Never Were* (New York: Viking Press, 1972), pp. 86–92; Donald S. Johnson, *Phantom Islands of the Atlantic* (New York: Walker & Co., 1994), pp. 113–22. The Catalan Atlas of 1375 turned the "insula de Brazil" into an atoll enclosing a lagoon, an image with striking parallels to Utopia's structure around a central harbor. The Atlantic island of Brazil continued to appear on maps through the nineteenth century.

30. The Yale editors of *Utopia* speculate that Utopian dye production may reflect shifting English textile export patterns. See pp. 426–27.

31. Brazil's place on the map was no more stable than the Isle of Brazil's during this period, as Spain and Portugal each claimed rights to the territory. This dispute was settled by papal arbitration when, in 1494, the Treaty of Tordesillas brought Brazil within the Portuguese sphere.

32. Barber, p. 27.

33. The intimate links between geography, astronomy, and astrology virtually guaranteed the occult status of maps despite their technical evolution. John Dee, who preferred Atlantis to America as the designation for the New World, had a life-long interest in maps—an interest noteworthy for combining the occult arts with scientific and classical learning. See E. G. R. Taylor, *Tudor Geography: 1485–1583* (London: Methuen, 1930), p. 99.

34. On the ceremonial use of maps as "props in court pageantry and propaganda," see Barber, pp. 26–27. Henry VIII was reported to have a world map mounted on the wall

behind his throne in the Painted Chamber at Westminster, and a number of other maps inherited from his father adorned his palaces. The pageant marking Katherine of Aragon's entry into London in 1501 included a cosmographical depiction of royal power.

35. For a brilliant discussion of the political and ideological import of Saxton's atlas, see Richard Helgerson, "The Land Speaks," in *Forms of Nationhood: The Elizabethan Writing of England* (Chicago: University of Chicago Press, 1992), pp. 105–47. Cartographic historian J. B. Harley has noted that while maps were still a relative novelty in Tudor society, they would become essential tools for rule by the second half of the sixteenth century. See *English Map-Making, Fifteen Hundred to Sixteen Fifty,* ed. Sarah Tyacke (London: Longwood Publishing, 1983), pp. 22–45. For a particularly lucid and well-documented discussion of the relationship of maps to governance in early modern England, see Peter Barber, "England II: Monarchs, Ministers, and Maps, 1550–1625," in *Monarchs, Ministers, and Maps,* ed. David Buissert (Chicago: University of Chicago, 1992), pp. 57–98.

36. See Marcel P. R. van den Broecke, *Ortelius Atlas Maps: An Illustrated Guide* ('t Goy, Netherlands: HES Publishers, 1996), p. 234.

37. See Cécile Kruyfhooft, "A Recent Discovery: Utopia by Abraham Ortelius," *The Map Collector* 16 (September 1981): 10–14; G. P. Marc'hadour, " 'M' for Map: Maps of Utopia," *Moreana* 19 (March 1982): 103–107. In this short review of Kruyfhooft's article is included J. Benedict Warren's provocative observation on the resemblance of the Utopian map to a map of the Aztec capital at Tenochtitlán that was printed with the Latin edition of Cortés's *Second Letter of Relation in Nuremberg* (1524). Warren speculates that the Utopian map may be the prototype (p. 106). Lorainne Stobbart uses the parallel as evidence that "the Utopia map was copied from a traditional Maya circular map," although this assertion is difficult to square with the dates of Cortés's, or any other voyager's, return from Mexico. *Utopia, Fact or Fiction?: The Evidence from the Americas* (Wolfeboro Falls, N.H.: Alan Sutton Publishing, 1992) p. 47.

38. This passage can be allied to Macrobian division of the world into climactic zones, which was thought to govern both physical and human geography.

39. For another reading of the connection in *Utopia* between time and space, history and geography, see Marin, p. 55 and passim.

40. R. F. Jones argues that "of the three inventions that impressed upon the Renaissance character. . . . —gunpowder, printing and the compass—the last appeared by far the most significant, not only because it was largely responsible for the discoveries that thrilled the age, but also because that mystery defied explanation and invited further study." *Ancients and Moderns,* 2d rev. ed. (St. Louis: Washington University Studies, 1961), p. 13.

41. For a history of its uses in classical times, see Erich Auerbach, "Figura," in *Scenes from the Drama of European Literature, Theory and History of Literature,* no. 9 (Minneapolis: University of Minnesota Press, 1984), pp. 11–76.

42. *Simulations,* trans. Paul Foss, Paul Patton, and Philip Beitchman (New York: Semiotext[e], 1983), p. 1. I thank David L. Clark and Manuel Utset for bringing this story and its retelling by Baudrillard to my attention.

43. Ortelius seems to have noted the revision of orientation in his Utopian map by confusing all the wind directions and placing *Occidens* on the right and *Oriens* on the left, thus reproducing Utopia as an inverted world.

44. The title cartouche to Ortelius's map of Utopia is structured in much the same way: "Utopiae Typus, Ex Narratione Raphaelis Hythlodaeus, Descriptione D. Thomae Mori, Delineatione Abarami Ortelii."

45. See *The King's Good Servant": Sir Thomas More 1477/8–1535*, ed. J. B. Trapp and Hubertus Schulte Herbrüggen (London: National Portrait Gallery, 1977), p. 41.

46. See *Complete Works*, vol. 4, p. clxxxix.

47. J. B. Harley, "Meaning and Ambiguity in Tudor Cartography," in *English Map-Making, Fifteen Hundred to Sixteen Fifty*, ed. Sarah Tyacke (London: Longwood Publishing, 1983) p. 23.

48. Claudio Guillen, "On the Concept and Metaphor of Perspective," in *Comparatists at Work: Studies in Comparative Literature*, ed. Stephen G. Nichols, Jr., and Richard B. Vowles (Waltham, Mass.: Blaisdell Publishing, 1968), p. 71.

49. *The Nature of the Four Elements*, The Tudor Facsimile Texts, ed. John S. Farmer (New York: AMS, 1908), A4v; rpt., *Six Anonymous Plays: 1500–1537*, Early English Dramatists ed. John S. Farmer (New York: Barnes & Noble, 1905; 1966), p. 8. Hereafter page numbers for both manuscript and reprint will be indicated parenthetically. For attribution of the anonymous play to Rastell, see A. W. Reed, *Early Tudor Drama* (London: Methuen, 1926), append. 1, pp. 187–201. Martin Waldseemüller's *Cosmographiae introductio* was an important source for Rastell as well as for More. See also M. E. Borish, "Source and Intention of *The Four Elements*," *Studies in Philology* 25 (1938): 149–63; George B. Parks, "The Geography of the Interlude of the Four Elements," *Philological Quarterly* 17 (1938): 251–62; Elizabeth M. Nugent, "Sources of John Rastell's *The Nature of the Four Elements*," *PMLA* 57 (1942): 74–88; George B. Parks's reply, "Rastell and Waldseemüller's Map," *PMLA* 58 (1943): 572–74; Johnstone Parr, "More Sources of Rastell's *Interlude of the Four Elements*," *PMLA* 60 (1945): 48–55; "John Rastell's Geographical Knowledge of America," *Philological Quarterly* 26 (1948): 229–40; E. J. Devereux, "John Rastell's Utopian Voyage," *Moreana* 13 (1976): 119–23.

50. Rastell observes the distinction between natura naturans (God or creating nature) and natura naturata (created nature) maintained by Aquinas in the *Summa Theologica* IIa–IIae 85, 6.

51. M. E. Borish has argued that Rastell depended on the 1515 edition of Gregor Reisch's "Margarita Philosophica," published in Strassburg by John Gruninger, which contains a large woodcut map of the world "Typvs universalis terre," based on the cartography of Martin Waldseemüller. The *Margarita* offers schematic representations of the world, and the seven liberal arts, in a history of the world from creation forward. In another illustration, suggestive for this study, Grammar, holding an alphabet, unlocks the door of the castle of the liberal arts.

52. For a biography of Rastell, see A. W. Reed, pp. 11–12.

53. Todorov discusses the almost automatic connection made between spiritual expansion and material conquest in the letters of Columbus. *The Conquest of America*, trans. Richard Howard (New York: Harper & Row, 1984), p. 44.

54. Jeffrey Knapp's chapter on More "take[s] seriously the possibility that More's overtly fictional new world inspired Rastell to seek a real one" (p. 21). My interest is to consider the two men's textual productions as very different responses to and representations of New World explorations and England's colonial destiny. Although we come to different conclusions, Knapp's argument about England's paradoxical relation to the New World will inform my own.

55. See Timothy D. Barnes, *Constantine and Eusebius* (Cambridge, Mass.: Harvard University Press, 1981), chap. 3, "The Rise of Constantine," pp. 28–43.

56. Barnes, p. 43 and note 146.

57. Quoted in *From Alexander to Constantine: Passages and Documents Illustrating the History of Social and Political Ideas, 336 B.C.–A.D. 337*, trans. by Ernest Barker (Oxford: Clarendon Press, 1956), p. 480.

58. R. W. Chambers describes the "underlying thought" of Utopia's pagan virtues as a reproach to its readers: "With nothing save Reason to guide them, the Utopians do this; and yet we Christian Englishmen, we Christian Europeans . . . !" *Thomas More* (New York: Harcourt & Brace, 1935), p. 128.

59. Berger, p. 31.

60. "Discourse in More's *Utopia:* Alibi/Pretext/Postscript," *ELH* 59 (1992): 290.

61. Freeman draws this master narrative from Jonathan Dollimore's Introduction to *Political Shakespeare,* ed. Jonathan Dollimore and Alan Sinfield (Manchester: Manchester University Press, 1985).

62. See *Complete Works,* vol. 2, p. 90. Richard S. Sylvester remarks in his Introduction to this volume how this image of the "grene world" "suggests not only the primal, chaotic world in which the conspirators worked out their plots, but also the youthful freshness and visionary opportunism with which they pursued their ambitions" (p. lxxxii).

63. Ernst Bloch's notion of "anticipatory illumination" is a useful analogue. See Jack Zipes, "Introduction: Toward a Realization of Anticipatory Illumination," in Ernst Bloch, *The Utopian Function of Art and Literature: Selected Essays,* trans. Jack Zipes and Frank Mecklenburg (Cambridge, Mass.: MIT Press, 1988), pp. xi–xliii.

64. Berger describes Utopia as a place where "time has no function and history no meaning" (68). Freeman remarks on "the text's duplicity in presenting history and myth as separate domains" (291). See also Hubertus Schulte Herbrüggen's assertion: "More does not deal with any such historicity, he is concerned with timeless structural principles. His Utopian world is, to the last detail, ideal and abstract." ("More's *Utopia* as Paradigm," in R. S. Sylvester and G. P. Marc'hadour, pp. 251–62). Michael Holquist argues that because utopias are written in the "subjunctive mood," the time they represent is "more utterly a convention than is even our artificial clock time" ("How to Play Utopia," *Yale French Studies* 41 [1969]: 112). For an argument that "Utopia is a highly time-conscious and singularly temperate country," see Elizabeth McCutcheon, "Time in More's Utopia," in *Acta Conventus Neo-Latini Turonesnsis,* ed. Jean-Claude Margolin (Paris: Vrin, 1980), 697–707.

65. For probable dates of composition of the two versions of *Richard III,* see *Complete Works,* vol. 2, pp. xiii–lxiv. Alison Hanham uses stylistic and thematic connections between *Utopia* and *Richard III* to mount a rather weakly supported and probably unnecessary argument for the earlier composition of *Utopia.* "Fact and Fantasy: Thomas More as Historian," in *Thomas More: The Rhetoric of Character: Essays presented at the Thomas More Quincentenary Symposium,* University of Otago (Dunedin, New Zealand: University of Otago Press, 1978), pp. 65–81. It is interesting to note that both Thomas More and Francis Bacon worked on their histories at roughly the same time that they constructed their utopian projects. For More, however, this was very early in his career, whereas Bacon began both projects when his political career was effectively over.

66. Wojciech Beltkiewicz suggested to me the possible relation of the two crosses to a divided church.

Chapter Three

1. Émile Pons assumes that More is author of the alphabet and tetrastichon. The Yale editors assume the author is Peter Giles (see *Complete Works,* vo. 4, p. 277, note 1811). I avoid the issue of exclusive authorship by treating the alphabet, the maps, the *parerga,* and the textual glosses as part of a complex collaborative project.

2. Asking Giles to settle this dispute, More declares, "Just as I shall take great pains to have nothing incorrect in the book, so if there is doubt about anything, I shall rather tell an objective falsehood than an intentional lie." Thus, taking accurate measure is used as the figure for truth-telling in a text that refuses comprehensible measure (*Complete Works,* vol. 4, p. 41).

3. "Humanism in England," in *Renaissance Humanism: Foundations, Forms and Legacy,* vol. 1, ed. Albert Rabil (Philadelphia: University of Pennsylvania Press, 1988), p. 14.

4. *De ratione studii,* trans. in Boyle, p. 52.

5. Johanna Drucker remarks that "attitudes towards language evolved in the Renaissance from the conviction that language could be analyzed for its perfection, as evidence of divine inspiration, to a realization that languages were embedded in human history, were inconsistent, imperfect, and subject to change." *The Alphabetic Labyrinth: The Letters in History and Imagination* (London: Thames & Hudson, 1995), p. 176.

6. While Émile Pons, the editors of the Yale edition, and others have traced the etymological origins of the transliterated Utopian words, I know of no reader who has remarked on the geometry of the Utopian letters. J. Duncan M. Derrett asserts that the curved Utopian letters, which correspond to the Roman "g" through "l," "have a distinctly South Asian appearance." But while these letters are the least geometrical in form, they may serve a different pictographic purpose than the one Derrett proposes, as they come closest to representing the shape of Utopia itself in varying orientations. See J. Duncan M. Derrett, "The Utopian Alphabet," *Moreana* 12 (1966): 61–65.

7. Thomas Nashe will use the quadrature as a figure for impossible tasks: "As much time as a man might have found out the quadrature of the circle in" ("Have with You to Saffron Walden" [1596]). John Donne cautions "Goe not thou about to Square eyther circle [God or thyself]" (Sermon 14, [1624]). The problem of the quadrature captured the imagination of such important Renaissance figures as Nicolas of Cusa and Joseph Scaliger but remained unsolved until the late eighteenth century, when F. Lindemann proved definitively that Euclidean tools could yield no answer. See Florian Cajori, *History of Mathematics* (New York: Chelsea Publishing, 1980), pp. 2, 17, 143; Morris Kline, *Mathematics in Western Culture* (London: Oxford University Press, 1953), pp. 50–51, 458.

8. Marin provides his reading of *Utopia* with a variety of possible (and yet inevitably impossible) Utopian figures based on the circular island and the quadrilateral city plan. See especially pp. 116–31.

9. Ralph Keen has examined what appears to be More's own annotated copy of *Euclid's Elements* to argue for More's particular knowledge of and interest in geometry. "Thomas More and Geometry," *Moreana* 86 (1985): 151–66. We also have the testimony of More's son-in-law and biographer, William Roper: "And so from time to time was he [More] by the prince advanced, continuing in his singular favor and trusty service twenty years and above—a good part whereof used the King upon holidays, when he had done his own devotions, to send for him into his traverse, and there

sometimes in matters of astronomy, geometry, divinity, and such other faculties, and sometimes of his worldly affairs, to sit and confer with him" ("The Life of Sir Thomas More," in *Two Early Tudor Lives,* ed. Richard S. Sylvester and Davis P. Harding [New Haven, Conn.: Yale University Press, 1962], pp. 201–202). Peter Giles's personal interest in geometry is harder to gauge, but the work of his close friend, Cuthbert Tunstall, author of "De arte supputandi," reminds us that geometry and mathematics were familiar features of humanist education. The Utopian educational system includes "musica, dialecticaque, ac numerandi & metiendi scientia." The Yale edition translates the last as "geometry" (157–58), but Keen points out that the phrase simply means "the ability to measure spaces" (152).

10. Keen, p. 153.

11. See Edward Grant, "Science and the Medieval University," in *Rebirth, Reform and Resilience: Universities in Transition 1300–1700,* ed. James M. Kittelson and Pamela J. Transue (Columbus: Ohio State University Press, 1984), p. 73.

12. "Concerning Lines, Angles and Figures," trans. David Lindberg, rpt., in *A Sourcebook in Medieval Science,* ed. Edward Grant (Cambridge, Mass.: Harvard University Press, 1974), pp. 385–88.

13. *Aristophanes,* vol. 2, Loeb Classical Library, trans. Benjamin Bickley Rogers (Cambridge, Mass.: Harvard University Press, 1924), p. 229. Hythlodaeus indicates that Aristophanes is first among the Greek poets read by the Utopians. Erasmus also gives him first place in "De ratione studii." More's debt to *The Birds* is elsewhere indicated by the name used for the Nephelogetes, or "cloud-begotten." Another possible source is Lucian's *Verae historia.*

14. Renaissance etymologies of "method" made clear the analogy by pointing out the component parts: *meta* (into/the middle of/in pursuit of) and *hodos* (the path). And much of Renaissance method was etymologically directed. See Marjorie O. Boyle, *Erasmus on Language and Method in Theology* (Toronto: University of Toronto, 1977), pp. 37–38, and Neal W. Gilbert, *Renaissance Concepts of Method* (New York: Columbia University Press), pp. 64–66.

15. Léon Herrmann finds the Utopian language defective in its omission of an equivalent for the letter Z, when the name of the Zapoletes would seem to require it. But as Elizabeth McCutcheon points out, this could be thematically explained by the fact that the Zapoletes "are certainly not part of the Utopian value system." *Moreana* 19 (1982): 4.

16. See *A Rational Millennium,* p. 65.

17. As one anonymous fifteenth-century text puts it: "Nil cifra significat sed dat signare sequenti." "The Crafte of Nombryinge," in *The Earliest Arithmetics in England,* Early English Text Society, vol. 68, ed. Robert Steele (London: Oxford University Press, 1922), p. 5. In the same volume, John of Holywood contends in "The Art of Nombrying" that "the .0. is clepede theta, or a cercle, other a cifre, other a figure of nought for nought it signyfiethe. Natheless she holdyng that place give the others for to signyfie" (p. 34).

18. *The Principle of Hope,* trans. Neville Plaice, Stephen Plaice and Paul Knight (Cambridge, Mass.: MIT Press, 1986), p. 165.

19. I disagree in this with Timothy J. Reiss, who finds the circular structure of *Utopia* to constitute a species of tautology or hole in discursive signification. See *The Discourse of Modernism* (Ithaca, N.Y.: Cornell University Press, 1982), pp. 108–14. James Holstun uses the more apt (if unabashedly anachronistic) figure of the Möbius strip to describe Utopia's circular design. See *A Rational Millennium,* pp. 57–58.

20. "In the first course, there was a shoulder of mutton, cut into an equilateral triangle, a

piece of beef into a rhomboides, and a pudding into a cycloid." *Gulliver's Travels* (Harmondsworth: Penguin, 1987), pp. 202–206.

21. Marjorie Hope Nicolson has shown how little Swift had to exaggerate, given the absurdity of some of the Royal Society's actual projects. See *Science and Imagination* (Ithaca, N.Y.: Cornell University Press, 1962), pp. 138–54.

22. Stewart, pp. 16–17.

23. Émile Pons's 1930 essay is still the most provocative reading of the function of the Utopian alphabet and verses.

24. For a detailed linguistic analysis of the Utopian verse, see Pons, p. 599. J. D. M. Derrett uses this allusion as one element of his case for the indological sources of the Utopia. See "Thomas More and Joseph the Indian," *Journal of the Royal Asiatic Society* (April 1962): 18–34.

25. See *Complete Works,* vol. 4, p. 278.

26. Léon Herrmann discovers French cryptograms warning against heresy embedded in the Utopian verse. *L'Utopien et le lanternois* (Paris: A. G. Nizet, 1981). For skeptical responses to Herrmann, see Elizabeth McCutcheon's untitled review, *Moreana* 19 (1982): 41–42, and, in the same issue, André Prévost's review article, "La Clef du mystère utopien," 35–39.

27. More's essentially etymological method would likely have been inspired by Plato's *Cratylus* (translated by Ficino). More seems to engage the dialogue's debate about natural and conventional names without clearly taking sides. The affiliation of philosophical (or scientific) method and etymology was continued in the Middle Ages through texts such as Isidore of Seville's *Etymologiae,* which was ultimately based on Stoic linguistic speculation. See W. Keith Percival, "Renaissance Linguistics: The Old and the New," *Studies in the History of Western Linguistics,* ed. Theodora Bynon and F. R. Palmer (London: Cambridge University Press, 1986), p. 63, and Neal Gilbert, *Renaissance Concepts of Method* (New York: Columbia University Press, 1960), pp. xiv–xv.

28. Pons, p. 590. Translation mine, with help from Tiane Donahue.

29. Because *grammatica* referred to the acquisition of Latin, Renaissance scholars understood all other languages, including their native tongues, as secondary or foreign with respect to grammar.

30. Hythlodaeus remarks that the Utopian language has a dual descent from Greek and Persian: "Their language, which in almost all other respects resembles the Persian, retains some traces of Greek in the names of their cities and officials" (180/181).

31. Renaissance theorists of translation, from Bruni to Dryden, stressed the importance of a translator's mastery of his own language. See Leonardo Bruni's "Preface to Aristotle's Ethics" and Dryden's "Preface to the Second Miscellany."

32. *Philosophical Investigations,* trans. G. E. M. Anscombe (New York: Macmillan, 1968), p. 13.

33. Erika Rummel observes in her analysis and comparison of Erasmus and More as translators that More is far more scrupulous about the literal than Erasmus in their parallel translations of Lucian. See "A Friendly Competition: More's and Erasmus' Translations from Lucian," in *Erasmus as a Translator of the Classics* (Toronto: University of Toronto Press, 1985), pp. 67–69.

34. Taking the Utopian language very seriously, polymath and historian of science Konrad Gesner (1516–1565) includes it in his survey of languages, *Mithridates* (1555; rpt., Aalen: Scientia Verlag, 1974). Although Gesner acknowledges the language as an invention (which he attributes to More rather than Giles), he nonetheless concludes his survey of world languages with the Tetrastichon ("Thomas Morus, Anglus, vir ingenio-

sus, Utopiae insulae a se confictae incolas lingua peculiari scribit uti, & characteres etiam fingit proprios" [rpt., pp. 234–35]). See Richard J. Schoeck, "Gesner on the Language of the Utopians," *Moreana* 17 (1980): 110–11.

35. *The Works of Francis Bacon,* vol. 3, ed. James Spedding, R. L. Ellis, and D. D. Heath (New York: Garret Press, 1968; 1857), p. 154.

36. Pons and Lupton identify this laureate poet with John Skelton, English poet laureate and adversary of More's friend John Lyly. Pons, p. 595; J. H. Lupton, "Introduction," *The Utopia of Sir Thomas More* (Oxford: Clarendon Press, 1895), p. cxiii.

37. For a Bakhtinian analysis of the polyphonic structure of *Utopia,* see Arthur Blaim, "More's *Utopia:* Persuasion or Polyphony?" *Moreana* 73 (1982): 5–20.

38. Nontheless, it is important to note that, for More, the defense of the translation of the classics was not identified with a defense of the vernacular.

39. See Leonardo Bruni: "It is a dangerous license to make a translator into a judge and arbiter. If translation be nothing else but the expression of one language in another, it is surely the duty of the translator neither to prophesy, nor to conjecture, nor to write according to his own judgment, nor to change the words to agree with some opinion of his own, but simply and straightforwardly, without any changes, to convey in his own language what was said in the other. Alteration is the translator's sin" (*The Humanism of Leonardo Bruni: Selected Texts,* trans. James Hankins [Binghamton, N.Y.: Medieval and Renaissance Texts and Studies, 1987], p. 207).

40. Although the place of logic in the trivium was consistently demoted by the humanists, the relative importance of grammar and rhetoric was not fixed; indeed, they seemed rather to be alternately characterized as the most inclusive and far-reaching of the liberal arts. In his "Oration on the Good Arts" (1484), Bartolomeo della Fonte argued for the preeminence of grammar as the branch of the *studia humanitatis* that contains all the others. See Charles Trinkaus, *The Scope of Renaissance Humanism* (Ann Arbor: University of Michigan Press, 1983), p. 58.

41. Letter to Dorp, Bruges, 21 October 1515; rpt., *St. Thomas More: Selected Letters,* ed. and trans. Elizabeth Frances Rogers (New Haven, Conn.: Yale University Press, 1961), p. 13. For Latin, see *The Correspondence of Thomas More,* ed. Elizabeth Frances Rogers (Princeton, N.J.: Princeton University Press, 1947), p. 32.

42. Eugenio Garin argues, "The expositions of the grammarians about the language of ancient texts began to involve all other texts and all other languages, i.e. institutions, habits, norms, procedures in logic and visions of the world." *Science and Civic Life in the Italian Renaissance,* trans. Peter Munz (New York: Doubleday, 1969), p. xi.

43. Garin, p. xi.

44. See Daniel Kinney, "More's Letter to Dorp: Remapping the Trivium," *Renaissance Quarterly* 34 (1981): 179–210.

45. Translated in Boyle, p. 37.

46. Steiner, *After Babel: Aspects of Language and Translation* (Oxford: Oxford University Press, 1975), p. 362.

47. Brian P. Copenhaver, "Translation, Terminology and Style in Philosophical Discourse," in *The Cambridge History of Renaissance Philosophy,* ed. Charles B. Schmitt and Quentin Skinner (Cambridge: Cambridge University Press, 1988), p. 90. On this controversy, see also Bruni, pp. 201–12.

48. *The Light in Troy* (New Haven, Conn.: Yale University Press, 1982), p. 51.

49. More's self-depiction as a rather passive and unassuming fellow causes many critics to employ the distinction between "author" More and "persona" More. I have always found such simple (and unnecessary) distinctions misleading, as the persona is not

simply an auditor but an author recording his role as an auditor. More seems to anticipate and implicate the "step back" this distinction assumes into the fabric of his fiction.
For another view, see Anthony Mortimer, "Hythlodaeus and Persona More: The Narrative Voices of Utopia," *Cahiers élisabéthains: Etudes sur la pré-Renaissance et la renaissance anglaises* 28 (October 1985): 23–35.

50. Leo Spitzer uses these terms to discuss similar techniques in Cervantes. "Linguistic Perspectivism in the *Don Quijote*," *Linguistics and Literary History: Essays in Stylistics*
(Princeton, N.J.: Princeton University Press, 1948), pp. 41–85.

51. *Complete Works*, vol. 4, note 114/7, p. 389.

52. *Complete Works*, vol. 4, p. 122, and note 122/10–13, p. 398.

53. Busleyden, one of Utopia's epistolary contributors, left in his will a fortune sufficient
to realize this important goal of the humanist educational campaign. See Peter R.
Allen, "Utopia and European Humanism: The Function of the Prefatory Letters and
Verses," *Studies in the Renaissance* 10 (1963): 93.

54. Leo Spitzer puts it nicely: "Thus we may conclude that, while, for the medieval world,
the procedures of polyonomasia and polyetymologia amounted to a recognition of the
working of the divine in the world, Cervantes [along with More, Erasmus, Rabelais,
and others] used the same devices in order to reveal the multivalence which words
possess for different human minds" (Spitzer, pp. 49–50).

55. The belief that all languages were descended from a single primordial and ono-
matopoetic language was generally accepted in the sixteenth century. See Percival, p.
63.

56. According to Harpsfield, More as chancellor gave a moving address before Parliament
in 1529: "The effect thereof was that the office of a Shepherd did most liuely resemble
the office and gouerment of a king" (Harpsfield, p. 58).

57. *Complete Works*, vol. 4, p. 128. See Holquist, pp. 106–23.

58. Barbara Johnson, "Translator's Introduction," Jacques Derrida, *Dissemination*
(Chicago: University of Chicago Press, 1981), p. xxxii.

59. *The Order of Things*, p. xviii.

60. Tom Moylan coins the term "critical utopia" to describe the self-conscious and self-
critical utopian fictions of the 1970s. But as in Foucault's analysis of heterotopia, Moylan's descriptions of the innovations of the self-conscious and self-reflexive "critical
utopia" are often better descriptions of what *Utopia* achieves than his own account of
"traditional utopias": "In each of the new utopias the society is shown with its faults,
inconsistencies, problems, and even denials of the utopians impulse in the form of the
persistence of exploitation and domination in the better place." *Demand the Impossible Science Fiction and the Utopian Imagination* (New York: Methuen, 1986).

61. Wittgenstein, p. 19.

62. "All such utopian voyages, or almost all, have a chapter on language where the author
most often displays a painstaking ingenuity" (Pons, p. 39).

63. Swift, p. 281. This would, of course, make the concept of fictions and literature virtually unthinkable, although we learn that the Houyhnhnms have a sort of poetry.

64. Edward Bellamy, *Looking Backward: 2000–1887* (Harmondsworth: Penguin, 1982),
p. 133.

65. The politics of linguistic omission brings to mind Orwell's dystopian *Nineteen Eighty-
four* and Oceania's reductive lexicon of Newspeak.

66. See, for example, Harry Berger, Jr., "Utopian Folly: Erasmus and More on the Perils of
Misanthropy," *English Literary Renaissance* 12 (1982): 271–90.

67. Hythlodaeus's model here is Plato. Hexter points out in his Introduction that in Di-

ogenes Laertius's *Lives of the Philosophers,* Plato refused to become a legislator for a new city because "they were opposed to equality of possessions" (*Complete Works,* 4: lxxxvii).

68. J. C. Davis has pointed out that many have exaggerated More's prominence or career prospects in 1516 when *Utopia* was first published. *"Utopia" and the Ideal Society: A Study of English Utopian Writing, 1516–1700* (Cambridge: Cambridge University Press, 1981).

69. "Rhetoric and Poetic in Thomas More's Utopia," *Humana Civilitas* no. 5, The Center for Medieval and Renaissance Studies, University of California, Los Angeles (Malibu, Calif.: Undena Publications, 1979); see also R. S. Sylvester, "Si Hythlodaeo Credimus: Vision and Revision in Thomas More's *Utopia,*" *Soundings* 51 (1968): 272–89, and William J. Kennedy, *Rhetorical Norms in Renaissance Literature* (New Haven, Conn.: Yale University Press, 1978), pp. 94–104.

70. *Praise of Folly,* trans. Clarence H. Miller (New Haven, Conn.: Yale University Press, 1979), p. 72.

71. Marin, p. 179.

72. Struever, p. 6.

73. "The Confutation of Tyndale's Answer," in *Complete Works,* vol. 8, part 1, p. 179. Noting More's fears, C. S. Lewis belies his own by remarking that in More's time (unlike the present day) "there was no real hope or fear that the paper states could be 'drawn into practice': the man engaged in blowing such bubbles did not need to talk as if he were on his oath" (*English Literature in the Sixteenth Century, Excluding Drama* [Oxford: Clarendon Press, 1954], p. 167).

Chapter Four

1. "The Plan of the Work," *The Great Instauration,* in *The Works of Francis Bacon,* vol. 4, ed. James Spedding, R. L. Ellis, and D. D. Heath (New York: Garrett Press, 1968; 1857), pp. 28, 32–33. All further citations from Bacon's work will refer to this edition by volume and page number.

2. For a different account of the *New Atlantis* as a foundation myth, see Amy Boesky, *Founding Fictions: Utopias in Early Modern England* (Athens: University of Georgia Press, 1996), esp. Introduction and chap. 2.

3. Only Howard White has devoted a book-length study to the *New Atlantis,* using the text as a guidebook to Bacon's political philosophy. White's exegesis relies exclusively on a system of material analogies. See *Peace among the Willows* (The Hague: Martinus Nijhoff, 1968). Several important Bacon scholars, including F. H. Anderson, Benjamin Farrington, and Paolo Rossi, give it little particular attention.

4. See, for example, Frank E. Manuel and Fritzie P. Manuel, *Utopian Thought in the Western World* (Cambridge, Mass.: Harvard University Press, 1979); J. C. Davis, *Utopia and the Ideal Society* (Cambridge: Cambridge University Press, 1981); and Northrop Frye, "Varieties of Literary Utopia," rpt., *Utopias and Utopian Thought,* ed. Frank E. Manuel (Boston: Beacon Press, 1965), pp. 25–49.

5. Readers concerned with the allegorical dimensions of the *New Atlantis* would include Frances Yates, *The Occult Philosophy in the Elizabethan Age* (London: Routledge & Kegan Paul, 1979), and *The Rosicrucian Enlightenment* (London: Routledge & Kegan Paul, 1972); Howard White; Judah Bierman; and Patricia Demers. Lewis Mumford,

who is quite sensitive to the utopia's oddities, uses them as a catalog of the reasons why the *New Atlantis* is not a real utopia at all. *The Story of Utopias* (New York: Viking Press, 1922; rpt., 1950), pp. 106–109.

6. *New Science, New World* (Durham, N.C.: Duke University Press, 1996), p. 96.

7. See Joseph Marie de Maistre, "Examin de la philosophie de Bacon," *Oeuvres completes,* vol. 6 (Lyon: Vitte et Perrussel, 1884–86; rpt., Geneva: Slatkine Reprints, 1979); Max Horkheimer and Theodor Adorno, "The Concept of Enlightenment," in *Dialectic of Enlightenment,* trans. John Cumming (New York: Herder & Herder, 1972).

8. Albanese, p. 98.

9. Spedding dates the work to 1624. That date was contested around the turn of this century with the discovery of some papers in the Harleian Charters quoting from an address given by Bacon before the houses of Parliament. These papers—in which the *New Atlantis* is twice mentioned—pushed the date of its composition back to some time between 1614 and 1617. The authenticity of the dates of these papers and their representation of Bacon was subsequently challenged, and the date suggested by Spedding has since been accepted by most scholars. For a full account of the controversy, see F. E. Held, Introduction, *Christianopolis* (New York: Oxford University Press, 1916), pp. 45–46. The reference to the Bensalemite officials refusing money with the expression "twice paid" offers the strongest textual evidence that Bacon wrote the *New Atlantis* after being found guilty for accepting bribes in 1621.

10. "Co-optation," in *The New Historicism,* ed. H. Aram Veeser (New York: Routledge, 1989), p. 171.

11. For an extensive study of the history of Bacon's reception and representation, see Nieves Mathews, *Francis Bacon: The History of a Character Assassination* (New Haven, Conn.: Yale University Press, 1996).

12. For example, Judah Bierman, "The *New Atlantis,* Bacon's Utopia of Science," *Papers in Language and Literature* 3 (1967): 99–110.

13. Eugene P. McCreary, "Bacon's Theory of the Imagination Reconsidered," *Huntington Library Quarterly* 36 (1973): 325.

14. Brian Vicker, ed. *English Science, Bacon to Newton* (Cambridge: Cambridge University Press, 1987), p. 34.

15. Judah Bierman, "*New Atlantis* Revisited," *Studies in the Literary Imagination* 4 (April 1971): 131.

16. Patricia Demers, "Bacon's Allegory of Science: The Theater of the *New Atlantis,*" *Journal of the Rocky Mountain Medieval and Renaissance Association* 4 (1983): 137.

17. Fish analyzes the ways in which the "experience" of the *Essays* corresponds with the method of scientific inquiry in *Self-Consuming Artifacts: The Experience of Seventeenth-Century Literature* (Berkeley: University of California Press, 1972). Michael Hattaway discusses how the aphorisms "connect to a notion of scientific hypothesis," while suggesting the ways in which Bacon was in fact "anti-method," in "Bacon and 'Knowledge Broken': Limits for Scientific Method," *Journal of the History of Ideas* 39 (1978): 183–97. Lisa Jardine has warned against judging Bacon "by our modern canons," exhorting students of literature to explore the connections of "what has become for us two separate cultures." *Francis Bacon: Discovery and the Art of Discourse* (London: Cambridge University Press, 1974), pp. 3–4. The new historicism has begun to make such connections its principal concern, although Bacon's presumed anti-literary, pro-science bias still informs his treatment in many recent studies.

18. *Francis Bacon and Modernity* (New Haven, Conn.: Yale University Press, 1986),

p. 196. Whitney himself goes on to offer a complex and provocative analysis of "the procedures" of the *New Atlantis.*

19. P. B. Shelley, "A Defense of Poetry," in *Shelley's Literary and Philosophical Criticism,* ed. John Shawcross (London: Henry Frowde, 1909; 1969), p. 127. Shelley's note directs us to the *Filium Labyrinthi* and the *Essay on Death* in particular.

20. L. C. Knights, "Bacon and the Seventeenth-Century Dissociation of Sensibility," in *Explorations* (New York: New York University Press, 1964), p. 109.

21. Nieve Mathews has pointed out that the phrase "dissociation of sensibility" and the historical argument locating an important change in the literary imagination in the first half of the seventeenth century were originally Hazlitt's, although he uses Bacon as an example of the "unified sensibility," a man who "united the powers of imagination and understanding in a greater degree than almost any other writer" (71).

22. For an excellent summary and analysis of the work of seventeenth- and eighteenth-century language reformers, see Murray Cohen, *Sensible Words: Linguistic Practice in England, 1640–1785* (Baltimore: Johns Hopkins Press, 1977).

23. For Eliot, it was not ultimately the New Science but the Civil War that served as the source of the irremediable rift that afflicted not only the English language but also English society itself. Eliot's comments linking the "dissociation of sensibility" to the Civil War were published in 1947, the same year that *Dialectic of Enlightenment* was published. See "Milton II," *Selected Prose of T. S. Eliot,* ed. Frank Kermode (New York: Harcourt Brace Jovanovich, 1975) pp. 265–74. For Bacon's impact on the Civil War, see Christopher Hill: "Bacon showed that science might be used for the relief of man's estate, to abolish poverty. Disregarded by the court in his lifetime, many of his works were first published, or published in English only after 1640." *The Collected Essays of Christopher Hill,* vol. 1 (Amherst: University of Massachusetts Press, 1985), p. 21.

24. For an important study particularly concerned with Bacon's modernity, see Timothy J. Reiss, *The Discourse of Modernism* (Ithaca, N.Y.: Cornell University Press, 1982).

25. Robert K. Merton, *Science, Technology and Society in Seventeenth-Century England* (New York: Howard Fertig, 1970); Ernest Tuveson, *Millennium and Utopia* (New York: Harper & Row, 1964); Charles Webster, *The Great Instauration: Science, Medicine and Reform, 1626–1660* (London: Gerald Duckworth, 1975).

26. John C. Briggs, *Francis Bacon and the Rhetoric of Nature* (Cambridge, Mass.: Harvard University Press, 1989); Charles Whitney, *Francis Bacon and Modernity* (New Haven, Conn.: Yale University Press, 1986).

27. Although his readings differ from my own, one critic who does make such connections is Jerry Weinberger, *Science, Faith, and Politics: Francis Bacon and the Utopian Roots of the Modern Age* (Ithaca, N.Y.: Cornell University Press, 1985). Although he overestimates Bacon's ultimate separation of religion and science, Christopher Hill is exceptional in linking the millennial aspect of Baconian thought to possibilities for historical transformation: "Bacon's ideas too contributed to millenarian optimism by giving men a sense of the possibility of historical change, akin to the sense of co-operating with God's purposes which Calvinists enjoyed" (21).

28. *The Language of Allegory* (Ithaca, N.Y.: Cornell University Press, 1979), pp. 66–67.

29. John Michael Archer, *Sovereignty and Intelligence: Spying and Court Culture in the English Renaissance* (Stanford, Calif.: Stanford University Press, 1993), p. 149.

30. Theodore Beza's notes on the New Testament (1594) interpreted Romans 11:25ff as signifying the future conversion of the entire Jewish people to Christ. The various editors of the Geneva Bible (1599 and after) followed this interpretation, as did the influ-

ential divines William Perkins, Robert Baille, and Hugh Broughton. See Peter Toon, ed., *Puritan Eschatology, 1600–1660* (London: James Clarke & Co., 1970), and Katharine Firth, *The Apocalyptic Tradition in Reformation Britain, 1530–1645* (Oxford: Oxford University Press, 1979).

31. For the story of Joab, see 2 Sam. 2:13ff and 1 Kings 1:1–2.

32. The complete passage describes the moment that prophecy is put aside and the labors of the faithful begin: "But thou O Daniel shut up the words and seal the book even to the end of time: many shall runne to and fro and knowledge shall be increased."

33. White, p. 52.

34. See note 19 of this chapter.

35. *The History of the World,* ed. C. A. Patrides (London: Macmillan, 1971), p. 70.

36. *The Philosophy of Francis Bacon* (Chicago: University of Chicago Press, 1948), p. 23.

37. For a detailed account of Bacon's fall, see Jonathan Marwil, *The Trials of Council: Francis Bacon in 1621* (Detroit: Wayne State University Press, 1976).

38. Archer, p. 1. Archer must modify Foucault's historical argument, which locates the emergence of a culture of surveillance in the eighteenth century. Archer rejects Foucault's "dichotomous periodization" (6) of sovereignty and surveillance to argue for their conjunction in the court culture of the English Renaissance.

39. It is a position that allowed for a great deal of representational latitude. Bacon in his essay "Of Simulation and Dissimulation" asserts, "The best composition and temperature is to have openness in fame and opinion, secrecy in habit; dissimulation in seasonable use; and a power to feign if there be no remedy" (6.389).

40. *Philo,* Loeb Classical Library, trans. F. H. Colson and G. H. Whitaker (Cambridge, Mass.: Harvard University Press, 1934), p. 207.

41. Bacon uses Bensalem's secrecy to reverse the political teaching of Plato's Ring of Gyges myth in Book 2 of the *Republic.* Where Plato's myth indicates that invisibility spawns complete lawlessness, Bacon's suggests that invisibility is the key to national security and peace.

42. *James I and the Politics of Literature: Jonson, Shakespeare, Donne, and Their Contemporaries* (Stanford, Calif.: Stanford University Press, 1983), p. 65.

43. In *The History of Henry VII,* Bacon emphasizes the issue of political counterfeits as the greatest threat to Henry's political legitimacy and security in two royal impersonators, Sambert Symnell and Perkin Warbeck, who counterfeited Edward Plantagenet and Richard, duke of York, respectively.

44. Archer, p. 140.

45. For two early feminist readings of Bacon's feminine construction of nature, see Carolyn Merchant's critique in *The Death of Nature* (San Francisco: Harper & Row, 1980), and Evelyn Fox Keller's defense in "Baconian Science: A Hermaphroditic Birth," *Philosophical Forum* 11. 3 (1980): 299–308.

46. For an excellent study of the Renaissance iconology of cherubim available to Bacon, see Elizabeth McCutcheon, "Bacon and the Cherubim: An Iconographical Reading of the *New Atlantis,*" *English Literary Renaissance* 2 (1972): 334–55.

47. *The Faerie Queene,* ed. Thomas P. Roche (New York: Penguin, 1979), p. 376. All other references to Spenser are from this edition and are cited by book, canto, and line.

48. J. P. Zetterberg, "Echoes of Nature in Salomon's House," *Journal of the History of Ideas* 43 (1982): 179. On Bacon's rejection of the Aristotelian definition of art as an inferior and mimetic art, see also Paolo Rossi, *Philosophy, Technology, and the Arts in the Early Modern Era,* trans. Salvator Attanasio (New York: Harper & Row, 1970), p. 137.

49. "To Fashion a Gentleman: Spenser and the Destruction of the Bower of Bliss," in *Renaissance Self-Fashioning,* pp. 157–92.

50. Archer detects in the Tirsan's wife a suggestion of Queen Elizabeth as "the repressed memory of the feminized image of sixteenth-century English sovereignty" (149).

51. Philip Sidney, *A Defense of Poetry,* ed. Jan Van Dorsten (Oxford: Oxford University Press, 1966; rpt. 1978), p. 24.

52. Aristotle, "Nichomachean Ethics," in *The Works of Aristotle,* vol. 9, trans. W. D. Ross (London: Oxford University Press, 1940), I.iii.5. On the interplay of knowledge and action, see also the first aphorism of Book 1 of the *Novum Organum:* "Man, being the servant and interpreter of Nature, can do and understand so much and so much only as he has observed in fact or in thought of the course of nature; beyond this he neither knows anything nor can do anything" (4.47).

53. See in the *Novum Organum* (4.212) where Bacon faults Galileo for his hypothesis regarding the motion of the Earth. It is remarkable that Bacon is more scientifically backward in his scientific utopia than the authors of two contemporary hieratic Christian utopias: Campanella conjectures about the Earth's rotation as a possibility in *La Citta del sole,* and Andreae accepts it in *Christianopolis.* On Bacon's views of his contemporaries' scientific achievements, see Nell Eurich, *Science in Utopia: A Mighty Design* (Cambridge, Mass.: Harvard University Press, 1967), pp. 134–44.

54. See in the *Novum Organum* (4.59) where Bacon faults William Gilbert for creating a world system based on his "toy," the magnet. See also the *Novum Organum* (4.65) and *Historia Naturalis and Experimentalis* (2.13–14).

55. Bacon never mentions Johannes Kepler's work, although Kepler had dedicated his *Harmonice Mundi* to King James while Bacon was lord chancellor.

56. Although William Harvey was Bacon's personal physician and used the inductive method in his research on the circulatory system, Bacon makes no reference to his accomplishments in his works. See Eurich, pp. 136–37.

57. Introduction, *Francis Bacon: A Selection of His Works,* ed. Sidney Warhaft (New York: Odyssey Press, 1965), pp. 9–10.

58. Glanvill calls his elaboration: *Bensalem, being a description of a catholick and free spirit both in religion and learning. In a continuation of the story of the Lord Bacon's New Atlantis* (London, 1675). For another seventeenth-century continuation, see *New Atlantis begun by Lord Verulam, Viscount St. Albans and continued by R.H. Esquire wherein is set forth a platform of Monarchical Government . . .* (London: John Cooke, 1660). R.H.'s defense of monarchy suggests how far it departs from its original. R.H. will declare in his preface that his text is "in defense of good laws" (1).

59. Sprat, p. xii.

60. To The Royal Society, rpt., Sprat, prefatory verse, n.p.

61. *A Critical Edition of Abraham Cowley's "Davideis,"* ed. Gayle Shadduck (New York: Garland Press, 1987). On Cowley's shortcomings even as an epic poet, see Thomas Greene, *The Descent from Heaven: A Study in Epic Continuity* (New Haven, Conn.: Yale University Press, 1963), pp. 366–73.

62. M. M. Bakhtin, "Epic and Novel," in *The Dialogic Imagination,* ed. Michael Holquist, trans. Caryl Emerson and Michael Holquist (Austin: University of Texas, 1981), p. 13.

63. See Marjorie Nicolson's chapter, "The Scientific Background of Swift's Voyage to Laputa," in *Science and Imagination* (Ithaca, N.Y.: Cornell University Press, 1962), pp. 110–54.

Chapter Five

1. Makin includes Cavendish in a catalog of learned women: "The present Dutchess of New Castle, by her own Genius, rather than any timely Instruction, over-tops many grave Gown-Men," in "An Essay to Revive the Antient Education of Gentlewomen" (1673). Rpt., Augustan Reprint Society, no. 202, William Andrews Clark Memorial Library, ed. Paula L. Barbour (Los Angeles: University of California, 1980). p. 10. Makin's image of a "world in flame" is suggestive for Amy Boesky's reading of *The Blazing World* in the context of the Great Fire of 1666. *Founding Fictions: Utopias in Early Modern England* (Athens: University of Georgia Press, 1996), pp. 128–33.
2. *The Blazing World and Other Writings,* ed. Kate Lilley (London: Penguin, 1994).
3. Samuel Pepys, *The Diary of Samuel Pepys,* vol. 9, ed. Robert Latham and William Matthews (Berkeley: University of California, 1970–79), p. 123; Dorothy Osborne, *Letters from Dorothy Osborne to Sir William Temple,* ed. Kingsley Hart (London: Folio Society, 1968), p. 58.
4. *A Room of One's Own* (New York: Harcourt Brace Jovanovich Press, 1929; 1957), pp. 64–65.
5. "The Reenchantment of Utopia and the Female Monarchical Self: Margaret Cavendish's Blazing World," *Tulsa Studies in Women's Literature* 11 (1992): 230.
6. Cavendish describes General History as "mechanical," "profitable for Travellers, Navigators and Merchants." National History, which she terms "political," she declares "pernicious, by reason it teaches subtil Policies, begets Factions, not onely between particular Families and Persons, but also between whole Nations and great Princes" (n.p.).
7. "Trembling Texts: Margaret Cavendish and the Dialectic of Authorship," *English Literary Renaissance* 24.1 (Winter 1994): 184–210.
8. In the Preface to *The Blazing World,* Cavendish finds it convenient to describe fancy in generic (that is, masculine) terms, rather than to claim it as a peculiarly feminine strategy for representation: "fictions are an issue of man's fancy, framed in his own mind, according as he pleases" (123).
9. Prefatory epistle "To His Grace the Duke of Newcastle," in *The Life of. . . . William Cavendish* (London: A Maxwell, 1667), n.p. William Cavendish wrote a prefatory epistle to Margaret Cavendish's *Philosophical and Physical Opinions* to "justifie the Lady Newcastle, and Truth against falsehood, laying those false and malicious aspersions to her, that she was not Author of her Books" (London: J. Martin & J. Allestrye, 1655), n.p.
10. For an authoritative discussion of the topos of the woman-on-top in early modern European culture, see Natalie Zemon Davis, "Women on Top," in *Society and Culture in Early Modern France* (Stanford, Calif.: Stanford University Press, 1975), pp. 124-51. Although the woman-on-top was predominately invoked as a figure for social disorder, Davis's argument that sexual inversions could "undermine as well as reinforce" (131) hegemonic authority demonstrates that the topos left some room for play. Lisa T. Sarasohn examines the use of the "world turned upside down" topos in Cavendish's scientific works in "A Science Turned Upside Down: Feminism and the Natural Philosophy of Margaret Cavendish," *Huntington Library Quarterly* 47 (1984): 289–307.
11. See, for example, Janet Todd, "She was not the first woman to publish fictional material and she was certainly not the first to publish. But she was the first to use published

fictions to create a fantastic, wish-fulfilling, compensatory world." In *The Sign of Angellica: Women, Writing and Fiction, 1660–1800* (New York: Columbia University Press, 1989), p. 68.

12. Elliott argues that "in the Saturnalia. . . . release is the sanctioned way to the Golden Age. Here is a clue to what the Golden Age actually is: a time or a condition in which limitation and renunciation do not exist." *The Shape of Utopia* (Chicago: University of Chicago Press, 1970), p. 15. Even in saturnalian inversion, however, Elliott tends to assume a stable (that is, masculine) subject position.

13. *Collected Dialogues,* ed. Edith Hamilton and Huntington Cairns (Princeton, N.J.: Princeton University Press, 1982), pp. 691–96. Although women serve as guardians in the *Republic,* the arguments used to defend this proposition depend on traditional notions of women as breeding stock and as prizes for masculine performance. Holding "women in common" posits a utopian sharing of women as property. It suggests neither the imagined abolishment of property nor the elevation of women to equal partners in the ideal republic.

14. Even Hall's anti-feminist satire suggests an unsettling narrative of women's real lives, as when he describes Viraginia as a land of exiles: "Very few Viraginians were born here, but they flock here from every other place in the world, either driven here because their husbands are extremely ferocious or exiled here voluntarily because their husbands were extremely cruel and jealous" (61). Despite the pathos of this passage, the general argument of the book is that men are responsible for their women and must blame themselves for their "natural" misbehavior.

15. *Discovery of a New World* is also the title used by John Wilkins for his 1614 meditation on the possibility of life on the moon, a text that offers another obvious source for Cavendish. Aphra Behn, like Cavendish, was interested in the discovery narrative as a source for feminist speculation, and she similarly called her translation of M. de Fontenelle's *Entretiens sur la pluralité des mondes Discovery of a New World* (1688).

16. There are, of course, a number of exemplary warrior women in Renaissance literature, but these are often paired with and opposed to evil Amazons whose defeat defines their goodness, a model Cavendish sees determined to avoid. See Simon Shepherd, *Amazons and Warrior Women: Varieties of Feminism in Seventeenth-Century Drama* (Brighton, England: Harvester Press, 1981), p. 13.

17. "The Subject of Utopia: Margaret Cavendish and Her Blazing World," in *Utopian and Science Fiction by Women,* ed. Jane L. Donawerth and Carol A. Kolmerten (Syracuse, N.Y.: Syracuse University Press, 1994), p 18.

18. Todd, p. 56.

19. Mendelson remarks that "the Duchess of Newcastle did not conceal her contempt for women of the lower orders; her utopian fantasies had reference only to titled women like herself." *The Mental World of Stuart Women* (Amherst: University of Massachusetts Press, 1987), p. 6. Jean Gagen assumes Cavendish's heroines are transparent self-portraits, "for the Duchess of Newcastle was her own favorite character, and she stalked through her plays and narratives in numerous transparent disguises." "Honor and Fame in the Works of the Duchess of Newcastle," *Studies in Philology* 56 (1959): 532–33.

20. "Embracing the Absolute: The Politics of the Female Subject in Seventeenth-Century England," *Genders* 1 (Spring 1988): 25.

21. I will consider below the ramifications of the dematerialization of the female body with respect to Cavendish's discourse of natural history.

22. Frank E. Manuel and Fritzie P. Manuel, *Utopian Thought in the Western World* (Cambridge, Mass.: Harvard University Press, 1979).

23. "Psycho-Analytic Notes on an Autobiographical Account of a Case of Paranoia" (1911), in *The Standard Edition of the Complete Psychological Works of Sigmund Freud,* vol. 12, trans. and ed. James Strachey (London: Hogarth, 1958), pp. 3–82.

24. Although several of Cavendish's plays do feature cross-dressing, *The Blazing World,* in fact, does not; and the practice of cross-dressing on stage must be regarded, after all, as a dramatic commonplace.

25. Freud's emphasis on Schreber's disappointment in remaining childless as a precipitating factor in his illness may also cause the Manuels to link the doctor and the duchess, although, once again, in diagnostic terms, neither their physical inability to give birth nor their emotional responses to finding themselves childless are in any way comparable.

26. In "Toward a Psychological History of Utopias," Frank E. Manuel states with confidence that "if one avoids solipsistic manifestations and restricts oneself primarily to those utopias which have won a measure of public acceptance (and become at least a folie à deux), the maincurrents of utopian feeling, the dreams shared widely enough to be social utopias with a general history can be identified. Some dreams express so forcefully a poignant longing of masses of men that their words reverberate for centuries." In *Utopias and Utopian Thought,* ed. Frank E. Manuel (Boston: Beacon Press, 1967), p. 69.

27. Despite his acidic criticisms of Cavendish's writing, Pepys wrote gushingly in his diary: "The whole story of this Lady is a romance, and all she doth is romantic" (Pepys 8.163).

28. The heroine of Cavendish's *Assaulted and Pursued Chastity,* for example, rejects romances, declaring that "their impossibilities makes them ridiculous to reason; and in youth they beget wanton desires, and amorous affections" (54).

29. I am indebted to Jaya Mehta for pointing out to me the Petrarchan inversion. For a fascinating discussion of the recurrent motif of arctic landscapes in feminist utopian literature, see Naomi Jacobs, "The Frozen Landscape in Women's Utopian and Science Fiction," in *Utopian and Science Fiction by Women: Worlds of Difference,* ed. Jane L. Donawerth and Carol A. Kolmerten (Syracuse, N.Y.: Syracuse University Press, 1994), pp. 190–204.

30. Samuel Pepys records that on 7 November 1667 he attended the first performance of the Dryden-Davenant *Tempest* at which the king "and a great many great ones" were also present (Pepys 8.521). William Davenant was a friend of the Cavendishes; he had served on Newcastle's staff as lieutenant general of ordnance in 1642, and associated with them in exile on the Continent. He most likely introduced Dryden to the Cavendishes, which ultimately resulted in the dramatic collaboration between Dryden and William Cavendish on *Sir Martin Mar-All,* first produced in August 1667.

31. Pepys compares Dryden's *Tempest* with *The Sea Voyage* in an entry dated 25 March 1668 (Pepys 9.133). For comments on Shakespeare's play, see 7 November 1667 (Pepys 8.521).

32. *The Works of John Dryden,* vol. 10, ed. Maximillian E. Novak (Berkeley: University of California Press, 1970), p. 6.

33. "Transmuting Othello: Aphra Behn's Oroonoko," in *Cross Cultural Performances: Differences in Women's Re-Visions of Shakespeare,* ed. Marianne Novy (Urbana: University of Illinois Press, 1993), p. 16.

34. Cavendish's biographer, Douglas Grant, notes that her criticism of Shakespeare is "one of the earliest of Shakespeare critiques, and is also an excellent piece of shrewd and enthusiastic writing" (114).

35. Whatever its resemblance to *Othello, Oroonoko*, of course, acknowledges no particular literary debt to Shakespeare, as Behn claims to be writing from personal knowledge.

36. For an analysis of the extensive political applications of Aesop's *Fables* in the Renaissance, see Annabel M. Patterson, *Fables of Power: Aesopian Writing and Political History* (Durham, N.C.: Duke University Press, 1991).

37. Although "satire" and "satyr" have distinct etymologies, sixteenth- and seventeenth-century grammarians often mistakenly linked them.

38. "Blazing Worlds: Seventeenth-Century Women's Utopian Writing," in *Women, Texts and Histories, 1575–1760*, ed. Clare Brant and Diane Purkiss (New York: Routledge, 1992), p. 119. See also Lilley's introduction to *The Blazing World* (xxv–xxvi).

39. *The Works of Francis Bacon*, vol. 3, ed. James Spedding, R. L. Ellis, and D. D. Heath (New York: Garrett Press, 1968; 1857), p. 162.

40. *The Death of Nature: Women, Ecology and the Scientific Revolution* (San Francisco: Harper & Row, 1980; 1989), p. xix.

41. *Gender Trouble: Feminism and the Subversion of Identity* (New York: Routledge, 1990), p. 35.

42. *The Blazing World* was first published in 1666 during an outbreak of the plague in London.

43. On William Cavendish's desire for sons and her own views on childrearing, see Margaret Cavendish's *CCXI Sociable Letters* (London: William Wilson, 1664): "A Woman hath no such reason to desire Children for her Own Sake for first her Name is Lost to her Particular, in her Marrying, for she quits her own, and is named as her Husband; also her Family, for neither Name nor Estate goes to her Family according to the Laws" (pp. 183–84).

44. *The Matter of Revolution: Science, Poetry, and Politics in the Age of Milton* (Ithaca, N.Y.: Cornell University Press, 1996), p. 188.

45. Devon L. Hodges, *Renaissance Fictions of Anatomy* (Amherst: University of Massachusetts Press, 1985), p. 2. Hodges notes the transformations of the signification of anatomy, from dissection, to "the science of bodily structure," to its use as a trope.

46. Tinkler, p. 243; Aristotle, *Rhetoric*, 1.3.

47. "Good Fortune is such an Idol of the World, and is so like the golden Calfe worshipped by the Israelites, that those Arch-Rebels never wanted Astrologers to foretel them good success in all their Enterprises, nor Poets to sing their Praises, nor Orators for Panegyricks; nay, which is worse, nor Historians neither, to record their Valour in fighting, and Wisdom in Governing" (Preface, n.p.).

48. Donawerth and Kolmerten, the editors of the collection in which Khanna's essay appears, argue that women's utopian fiction offers "a continuous literary tradition in the West from the seventeenth-century to the present day" (i). Somewhat paradoxically, however, Donawerth and Kolmerten understand this as a "lost tradition" that their volume is an attempt to reconstruct: "Although these women writers may only have known one or two other texts by women in this tradition—and early writers may each have reinvented the form—from our vantage point we are able to piece together the squares to see the design of this history as a whole" (i). The parataxis of patchwork in the image that Donawerth and Kolmerten select to describe their project suggests

the tensions between understanding this tradition as patchwork or as a seamless continuity.

49. *Margaret the First: Biography of Margaret Cavendish, Duchess of Newcastle, 1623–1673* (Toronto: University of Toronto Press, 1957).

50. "Honor and Fame in the Works of the Duchess of Newcastle," *Studies in Philology* 56 (1959): 525.

51. In an assertion of loyalty rather than fact, Mistress Toppe, formerly Elizabeth Chaplain, Cavendish's maid, writes "Madam, You are not onely the first English Poet of your Sex, but the first that ever wrote this way." See her dedicatory letter to *Poems and Fancies* (1653).

52. The verse is unsigned, but Douglas Grant has attributed it to William Cavendish. See *Margaret the First*, p. 143. William Cavendish does claim the dedicatory verse introducing his wife's 1662 *Playes*, with similar sentiments celebrating her as a self-created Phoenix rising out of Terence's and Plautus's ashes.

53. Aristotle, *De generatione animalium*, 1.2 [716a 13]; see also Ian Maclean, *The Renaissance Notion of Woman* (Cambridge: Cambridge University Press, 1980), p. 30.

54. *The Diary of John Evelyn*, vol. 3, ed. E. S. de Beer (Oxford: Clarendon Press, 1955) p. 478.

55. Letter to Bohun, rpt., *The Diary of John Evelyn*, vol. 4, pp. 8–9.

Bibliography

Albanese, Denise. *New Science, New World*. Durham, N.C.: Duke University Press, 1996.

Alberti, Leon Battista. *On the Art of Building in Ten Books*. Translated by Joseph Rykwert, Neil Leach, and Robert Tavernor. Cambridge: MIT University Press, 1988.

Allen, Peter R. "Utopia and European Humanism: The Function of the Prefatory Letters and Verses." *Studies in the Renaissance* 10 (1963): 91–107.

Alpers, Svetlana. *The Art of Describing: Dutch Art in the Seventeenth Century*. Chicago: University of Chicago Press, 1983.

Altman, Joel, B. *Tudor Play of Mind: Rhetorical Inquiry and the Development of Elizabethan Drama*. Berkeley: University of California Press, 1978.

Ames, Russell. *Citizen Thomas More and His Utopia*. Princeton, N.J.: Princeton University Press, 1949.

Anderson, F. H. *The Philosophy of Francis Bacon*. Chicago: University of Chicago Press, 1948.

Andreae, Johann Valentin. *Christianopolis: An Ideal State of the Seventeenth Century*. Translated by F. E. Held. New York: Oxford University Press, 1916.

Archer, John Michael. *Sovereignty and Intelligence: Spying and Court Culture in the English Renaissance*. Stanford, Calif.: Stanford University Press, 1993.

Aristophanes. *The Birds*. Translated by Benjamin Bickley Rogers. Cambridge, Mass.: Harvard University Press, 1924.

Aristotle. *The Works of Aristotle*. 11 vols. Translated by W. D. Ross. London: Oxford University Press, 1940.

Arnheim, Rudolf. *Art and Visual Perception*. Berkeley: University of California Press, 1974.

Astell, Ann W. "Rhetorical Strategy and the Fiction of Audience in More's Utopia." *Centennial Review* 29 (Summer 1985): 302–19.

Auerbach, Erich. "Figura." In *Scenes from the Drama of European Literature*. Minneapolis: University of Minnesota Press, 1984, pp. 11–76.

Bacon, Francis. *The Works of Francis Bacon.* 14 vols. Edited by James Spedding, Robert Leslie Ellis, and Douglas Denon Heath. New York: Garrett Press, 1968.

Bakhtin, M. M. *Dialogic Imagination.* Edited by Michael Holquist. Translated by Caryl Emerson and Michael Holquist. Austin: University of Texas, 1981.

Barber, Peter."England I: Pageantry, Defense, and Government: Maps at Court to 1550." In *Monarchs, Ministers, and Maps: The Emergence of Cartography as a Tool of Government in Early Modern Europe,* edited by David Buisseret. Chicago: University of Chicago Press, 1992.

Barker, Ernest, ed. and trans. *From Alexander to Constantine: Passages and Documents Illustrating the History of Social and Political Ideas, 336 B.C.–A.D. 337.* Oxford: Clarendon Press, 1956.

Barnes, Timothy D. *Constantine and Eusebius.* Cambridge, Mass.: Harvard University Press, 1981.

Baudrillard, Jean. *Simulations.* Translated by Paul Foss, Paul Patton, and Philip Beitchman. New York: Semiotext(e), 1983.

Bellamy, Edward. *Looking Backward: 2000–1887.* Harmondsworth: Penguin, 1982.

Berger, Harry Jr. *Second World and Green World: Studies in Renaissance Fiction-Making.* Berkeley: University of California Press, 1988.

———. "Utopian Folly: Erasmus and More on the Perils of Misanthropy." *English Literary Renaissance* 3 (1982): 271–90.

Bevington, David M. "The Dialogue in *Utopia:* Two Sides to the Question." *Studies in Philology* 58 (1961): 496–509. Reprinted as "The Divided Mind." In *Twentieth Century Interpretations of Utopia,* edited by William Nelson. Englewood Cliffs, N.J.: Prentice-Hall, 1968.

Bierman, Judah. "The *New Atlantis,* Bacon's Utopia of Science." *Papers in Language and Literature* 3 (1967): 99–110.

———. "*New Atlantis* Revisited." *Studies in the Literary Imagination* 4 (April 1971): 121–42.

Blaim, Artur. "More's *Utopia:* Persuasion or Polyphony?" *Moreana* 73 (1982): 5–20.

Bleich, David. "More's *Utopia:* Confessional Modes." *American Imago* 28 (1971): 24–52.

Bloch, Ernst. *The Principle of Hope.* 3 vols. Translated by Neville Plaice, Stephen Plaice, and Paul Knight. Cambridge, Mass.: MIT Press, 1986.

———. *The Utopian Function of Art and Literature: Selected Essays.* Translated by Jake Zipes and Frank Mecklenburg. Cambridge, Mass.: MIT Press, 1988.

Bodin, Jean. *The six bookes of a commonweale.* A facsimile reprint of the 1606 English translation of *Les Six livres de la république* (1576). Edited by Kenneth Douglas McRae. Cambridge, Mass.: Harvard University Press, 1962.

Boesky, Amy. *Founding Fictions: Utopias in Early Modern England.* Athens: University of Georgia Press, 1996.

Borish, M. E. "Source and Intention of *The Four Elements.*" *Studies in Philology* 25 (1938): 251–62.

Boyle, Marjorie O. *Erasmus on Language and Method in Theology.* Toronto: University of Toronto Press, 1977.

———. *Rhetoric and Reform: Erasmus' Civil Dispute with Luther.* Cambridge, Mass.: Harvard University Press, 1983.

Breen, Quirinus. "The Correspondence of G. Pico della Mirandola and Ermolao Barbaro Concerning the Relation of Philosophy and Rhetoric." *Journal of the History of Ideas* 13 (1952): 392–412.

Briggs, John C. *Francis Bacon and the Rhetoric of Nature.* Cambridge, Mass.: Harvard University Press, 1989.

Broecke, M. P. R. van den. *Ortelius Atlas Maps: An Illustrated Guide.* 't Goy, Netherlands: HES Publishers, 1996.

Bruni, Leonardo. *The Humanism of Leonardo Bruni: Selected Texts.* Binghamton, N.Y.: Medieval and Renaissance Texts and Studies, 1987.

Buisseret, David, ed. *Monarchs, Ministers, and Maps: The Emergence of Cartography as a Tool of Government in Early Modern Europe.* Chicago: University of Chicago Press, 1992.

Burton, Robert. *The Anatomy of Melancholy.* Edited by Holbrook Jackson. New York: Random House, 1977.

Butler, Judith. *Gender Trouble: Feminism and the Subversion of Identity.* New York: Routledge, 1990.

Cajori, Florian. *History of Mathematics.* New York: Chelsea Publishing, 1980.

Calvino, Italo. *Invisible Cities.* Translated by William Weaver. New York: Harcourt Brace Jovanovich, 1974.

Campanella, Tommaso. *La Città del sole: dialogo poetico/The City of the Sun: A Poetical Dialogue.* Translated by Daniel J. Donno. Berkeley: University of California Press, 1981.

Campbell, Tony. "Portolan Charts from the Late Thirteenth Century to 1500." In *The History of Cartography,* vol. 1, edited by J. B. Harley and David Woodward, pp. 371–463. Chicago: University of Chicago Press, 1987.

Caspari, Fritz. *Humanism and the Social Order in Tudor England.* Chicago: University of Chicago Press, 1954.

Cavendish, Margaret. *"The Blazing World" and Other Writings.* Edited by Kate Lilley. London: Penguin, 1994.

———. *CCXI Sociable Letters.* London: William Wilson, 1664.

———. *The life of the Thrice Noble, High and Puissant Prince William Cavendishe, Duke, Marquess, and Earl of Newcastle. . . . written by the Thrice Noble, Illustrious, and Excellent Princess, Margaret, Duchess of Newcastle, his wife.* London: A. Maxwell, 1667.

———. *Philosophical and Physical Opinions.* London: J. Martin & J. Allestrye, 1655.

Certeau, Michel de. *The Writing of History.* Translated by Tom Conley. New York: Columbia University Press, 1988.

Chambers, R. W. *Thomas More.* New York: Harcourt Brace, 1935.

Cohen, Murray. *Sensible Words: Linguistic Practice in England, 1640–1785.* Baltimore: Johns Hopkins University Press, 1977.

Cohn, Norman. *Pursuit of the Millennium: Revolutionary Millenarians and Mystical Anarchists of the Middle Ages.* Revised and expanded edition. New York: Oxford University Press, 1970.

Colie, Rosalie, L. *Paradoxia Epidemica: The Renaissance Tradition of Paradox.* Princeton, N.J.: Princeton University Press, 1966.

———. *The Resources of Kind: Genre Theory in the Renaissance.* Edited by Barbara K. Lewalski. Berkeley: University of California Press, 1973.

Copenhaver, Brian P. "Translation, Terminology and Style in Philosophical Discourse." In *The Cambridge History of Renaissance Philosophy,* edited by Charles B. Schmitt and Quentin Skinner, pp. 77–110. Cambridge: Cambridge University Press, 1988.

Cortesão, Armando. *The History of Portuguese Cartography.* 2 vols. Lisbon: Junta de Investigações do Ultramar, 1969–71.

Cowley, Abraham. *A Critical Edition of Abraham Cowley's "Davideis."* Edited by Gayle Shadduck. The Renaissance Imagination, 22. New York: Garland, 1987.

Davis, J. C. *Utopia and the Ideal Society: A Study of English Utopian Writing 1516–1700.* Cambridge: Cambridge University Press, 1981.

Davis, Natalie Zemon. *Society and Culture in Early Modern France.* Stanford, Calif.: Stanford University Press, 1975.

Dean, Leonard F. "Sir Francis Bacon's Theory of Civil History Writing." In *Essential Articles for the Study of Francis Bacon,* edited by Brian Vickers, pp. 211–35. Hamden, Conn.: Archon Books, 1968.

Demers, Patricia. "Bacon's Allegory of Science: The Theater of the *New Atlantis.*" *Journal of the Rocky Mountain Medieval and Renaissance Association* 4 (1983): 135–48.

DeMolen, Richard L., ed. *Essays on the Works of Erasmus.* New Haven, Conn.: Yale University Press, 1978.

Derret, J. D. M. "Thomas More and Joseph the Indian." *Journal of the Royal Asiatic Society* (April 1962): 18–34.

———. "The Utopian Alphabet." *Moreana* 12 (1966): 61–65.

Derrida, Jacques. *Dissemination.* Translated by Barbara Johnson. Chicago: University of Chicago Press, 1981.

———. *Of Grammatology.* Translated by Gayatri Chakravorty Spivak. Baltimore: Johns Hopkins University Press, 1974.

Devereux, E. J. "John Rastell's Utopian Voyage." *Moreana* 13 (1976): 119–23.

Dollimore, Jonathan. "Introduction: Shakespeare, Cultural Materialism, and the New Historicism." In *Political Shakespeare: New Essays in Cultural Materialism,* edited by Jonathan Dollimore and Alan Sinfield. Ithaca, N.Y.: Cornell University Press, 1985.

Donawerth, Jane L., and Carol A. Kolmerten, eds. *Utopian and Science Fiction by Women: Worlds of Difference.* Syracuse, N.Y.: Syracuse University Press, 1994.

Donner, H. W. *Introduction to "Utopia."* Freeport, N.Y.: Books for Library Press, 1969.

Drucker, Johanna. *The Alphabetic Labyrinth: The Letters in History and Imagination.* London: Thames & Hudson, 1995.

Dryden, John. *The Works of John Dryden.* Vol. 10. Edited by Maximillian E. Novak. Berkeley: University of California Press, 1970.

Eagleton, Terry. *Ideology: An Introduction.* London: Verso, 1991.

Elliott, Robert. C. *The Shape of Utopia: Studies in a Literary Genre.* Chicago: University of Chicago Press, 1970.

Erasmus, Desiderius. *Antibarbari.* Translated by Margaret Mann Phillips. In *Collected Works of Erasmus.* Vol. 23. Edited by Craig R. Thompson. Toronto: University of Toronto Press, 1978.

———. *Collected Works of Erasmus.* 86+ vols. General Editors Peter G. Bietenholz, B. M. Corrigan, et al. Toronto: University of Toronto Press, 1974.

———. *Opus Epistolarum Des. Erasmi Roterdami*. 7 vols. Edited by P. S. Allen. Oxford: Clarendon Press, 1906–58.

———. *Praise of Folly*. Translated and edited by Clarence H. Miller. New Haven, Conn.: Yale University Press, 1979.

Eurich, Nell. *Science in Utopia: A Mighty Design*. Cambridge, Mass.: Harvard University Press, 1967.

Evelyn, John. *The Diary of John Evelyn*. 6 vols. Edited by E. S. de Beer. Oxford: Clarendon Press, 1955.

Farrington, Benjamin. "Francis Bacon after His Fall." *Studies in the Literary Imagination* 4 (April 1971): 143–58.

———. *Francis Bacon, Philosopher of Industrial Science*. New York: H. Schuman, 1949.

———. *The Philosophy of Francis Bacon: An Essay on Its Development from 1603–1609 with New Translations of Fundamental Texts*. Liverpool: Liverpool University Press, 1964.

Ferguson, Margaret W. "Transmuting Othello: Aphra Behn's *Oroonoko*." In *Cross-Cultural Performances: Differences in Women's Re-Visions of Shakespeare*, edited by Marianne Novy, pp. 1–14. Urbana: University of Illinois Press, 1993.

Firth, Katharine. *The Apocalyptic Tradition in Reformation Britain 1530–1645*. Oxford: Oxford University Press, 1979.

Fish, Stanley E. *Self-Consuming Artifacts: The Experience of Seventeenth-Century Literature*. Berkeley: University of California Press, 1972.

Fleisher, Martin. *Radical Reform and Political Persuasion in the Life and Writings of Thomas More*. Geneva: Librairie Droz, 1973.

Foucault, Michel. *Discipline and Punish: The Birth of the Prison*. Translated by Alan Sheridan. New York: Random House, 1979.

———. *The Order of Things: An Archeology of the Human Sciences*. Translation of *Les Mots et les choses*. New York: Random House, 1970.

Fowler, Alastair. *Kinds of Literature: An Introduction to the Theory of Genres and Modes*. Cambridge, Mass.: Harvard University Press, 1982.

Fox, Alistair. *Utopia: An Elusive Vision*. New York: Twayne Publishers, 1993.

Freeman, John. "Discourse in More's Utopia: Alibi/Pretext/Postscript." *English Literary History* 59 (1992): 289–311.

Freud, Sigmund. "Psycho-Analytic Notes on an Autobiographical Account of a Case of Paranoia" (1911). In *The Standard Edition of the Complete Psychological Works of Sigmund Freud*, vol. 12, translated and edited by James Strachey. London: Hogarth Press, 1958.

Frye, Northrop. "Varieties of Literary Utopia." In *Utopias and Utopian Thought*, edited by Frank Manuel. Boston: Beacon Press, 1967.

Gagen, Jean. "Honor and Fame in the Works of the Duchess of Newcastle." *Studies in Philology* 56 (1959): 519–38.

Gallagher, Catherine. "Embracing the Absolute: The Politics of the Female Subject in Seventeenth-Century England." *Genders* 1 (Spring 1988): 24–39.

Garin, Eugenio. *Science and Civic Life in the Italian Renaissance*. Translated by Peter Munz. New York: Doubleday, 1969.

Geoghegan, Vincent. *Utopianism and Marxism*. New York: Methuen, 1987.

Gesner, Konrad. *Mithridates de differentiis linguarum tum veterum tum quae hodie apud diversas nationes in toto orbe terrarum in usu sunt* (1555). Facsimile with Introduction by Manfred Peters. Aelen: Scientia Verlag, 1974.

Gilbert, Neal. *Renaissance Concepts of Method.* New York: Columbia University Press, 1960.

Gilman, Ernest B. *The Curious Perspective: Literary and Pictorial Wit in the Seventeenth Century.* New Haven, Conn.: Yale University Press, 1978.

Glanvill, Joseph. *Bensalem, being a description of a catholick and free spirit both in religion and learning. In a continuation of the story of the Lord Bacon's New Atlantis.* London, 1675.

Goldberg, Jonathan. *James I and the Politics of Literature.* Stanford, Calif.: Stanford University Press, 1989.

Gombrich, E. H. "The 'What' and the 'How': Perspective Representation and the Phenomenal World." In *Logic and Art: Essays in Honor of Nelson Goodman,* edited by R. Rudner and I. Scheffler, pp. 129–49. Indianapolis: Bobbs-Merrill, 1972.

Graff, Gerald. "Co-optation." In *The New Historicism,* edited by H. Aram Veeser, pp. 168–81. New York: Routledge, 1989.

Grafton, Anthony, and Lisa Jardine. *From Humanism to the Humanities.* Cambridge, Mass.: Harvard University Press, 1986.

Grant, Douglas. *Margaret the First: A Biography of Margaret Cavendish, Duchess of Newcastle, 1623–1673.* Toronto: University of Toronto Press, 1957.

Grant, Edward. "Science and the Medieval University." In *Rebirth, Reform and Resilience: Universities in Transition 1300–1700,* edited by James M. Kittelson and Pamela J. Transue, pp. 68–102. Columbus: Ohio State University Press, 1984.

————., ed. *A Source Book in Medieval Science.* Cambridge, Mass.: Harvard University Press, 1974.

Greenblatt, Stephen. "Invisible Bullets." In *Shakespearean Negotiations: The Circulation of Social Energy in Renaissance England,* pp. 21–65. Berkeley: University of California Press, 1988. Originally appeared in *Glyph* 8 (1981): 40–61.

————. "Psychoanalysis and Renaissance Culture." In *Literary Theory/Renaissance Texts,* edited by Patricia Parker and David Quint, pp. 210–24. Baltimore: Johns Hopkins University Press, 1986.

————. *Renaissance Self-Fashioning: From More to Shakespeare.* Chicago: University of Chicago Press, 1980.

————. "Towards a Poetics of Culture." In Veeser, pp. 1–14. Originally appeared in *Southern Review* (Australia) 20 (1987): 3–5.

Greene, Thomas M. *The Descent from Heaven: A Study in Epic Continuity.* New Haven, Conn.: Yale University Press, 1963.

————. *The Light in Troy: Imitation and Discovery in Renaissance Poetry.* New Haven, Conn.: Yale University Press, 1982.

Guillen, Claudio. "On the Concept and Metaphor of Perspective." In *Comparatists at Work: Studies in Comparative Literature,* edited by Stephen G. Nichols, Jr., and Richard B. Vowles, pp. 28–90. Waltham, Mass.: Blaisdell Publishing, 1968.

Hakluyt, Richard. *Hakluyt's Voyages: The Principal Navigations, Voyages, Traffiques, and Discoveries of the English Nation.* Edited by Irwin R. Blacker. New York: Viking Press, 1965.

Hall, Joseph. *Another World and Yet the Same.* Translated and edited by John Millar Wands. New Haven, Conn.: Yale University Press, 1981.

Halpern, Richard. *The Poetics of Primitive Accumulation: English Renaissance Culture and the Genealogy of Capital.* Ithaca, N.Y.: Cornell University Press, 1991.

Hanham, Alison. "Fact and Fantasy: Thomas More as Historian." In *Thomas More: The Rhetoric of Character.* Essays presented at the Thomas More Quincentenary Symposium University of Otago, 1978. Edited by Alistair Fox and Peter Leech, pp. 65–81. Dunedin, New Zealand: University of Otago, 1978.

Hansot, Elizabeth. *Perfection and Progress: Two Modes of Utopian Thought.* Cambridge, Mass.: MIT Press, 1974.

Harley, J. B. "Meaning and Ambiguity in Tudor Cartography." In *English Map-Making, Fifteen Hundred to Sixteen Fifty,* edited by Sarah Tyacke, pp. 22–45. London: Longwood Publishing, 1983.

Harrison, John L. "Bacon's View of Rhetoric, Poetry and the Imagination." In *Essential Articles for the Study of Francis Bacon,* edited by Brian Vickers, pp. 253–71. Hamden, Conn.: Archon Books, 1968.

Harpsfield, Nicholas. *The Life and death of Sir Thomas Moore, knight, sometymes Lord high chancellor of England, written in the tyme of Queene Marie by Nicholas Harpsfield, L.D.. Ed. Elsie Vaughn Hitchcock.* Early English Text Society, 186. London: Oxford University Press, 1932.

Harvey, P. D. A. *The History of Topographical Maps: Symbols, Pictures and Surveys.* London: Thames & Hudson, 1980.

Hattaway, Michael. "Bacon and 'Knowledge Broken'" Limits for Scientific Method." *Journal of the History of Ideas* 39 (1978): 183–97.

Hegel, Georg Wilhelm Friedrich. *The Philosophy of History.* New York: Dover Publications, 1956.

Helgerson, Richard. *Forms of Nationhood: The Elizabethan Writing of England.* Chicago: University of Chicago Press, 1992.

———. "Inventing Noplace, or the Power of Negative Thinking." *Genre* 15 (1982): 101–21.

Herbrüggen, Hubertus Schulte. "More's Utopia as Paradigm." In *Essential Articles for the Study of Thomas More,* edited by R. S. Sylvester and G. P. Marc'hadour, pp. 251–62. Hamden, Conn.: Archon Books, 1977.

Herrmann, Léon. *L'Utopien et le lanternois.* Paris: A. G. Nizet, 1981.

Hes, Willy. *Ambrosius Holbein.* Strassburg: Heitz and Mündel, 1911.

Hill, Christopher. *The Collected Essays of Christopher Hill: Volume One: Writing and Revolution in 17th-Century England.* Amherst: University of Massachusetts Press, 1985.

Holquist, Michael. "How to Play Utopia: Some Brief Notes on the Distinctiveness of Utopian Fiction." *Yale French Studies* 41 (1968): 106–123.

Holstun, James. "Ranting at the New Historicism." *English Literary Renaissance* 19.2 (1989): 189–225.

———. *A Rational Millennium: Puritan Utopias of Seventeenth-Century England and America.* New York: Oxford University Press, 1987.

Horkheimer, Max, and Theodor W. Adorno. *Dialectic of Enlightenment.* Translated by John Cumming. New York: Herder & Herder, 1972.

Howell, Wilbur Samuel. *Poetics, Rhetoric, and Logic: Studies in the Basic Disciplines of Criticism.* Ithaca, N.Y.: Cornell University Press, 1975.

Jacobs, Naomi. "The Frozen Landscape in Women's Utopian and Science Fiction." In *Utopian and Science Fiction by Women: Worlds of Difference,* edited by Jane L. Donawerth and Carol A. Kolmerten, pp. 190–204. Syracuse, N.Y.: Syracuse University Press, 1994.

Jameson, Fredric. "Criticism in History." In *The Ideologies of Theory: Essays, 1971–1986,* vol. 1, pp. 119–36. Minneapolis: University of Minnesota Press, 1988; 1976.

———. "Of Islands and Trenches: Neutralization and the Production of Utopian Discourse." In *Ideologies of Theory: Essays, 1971–1986,* vol. 2, pp. 75–101. Theory of History and Literature, 49. Minneapolis: University of Minnesota Press, 1988. Originally appeared as "Of Islands and Trenches: Naturalization [*sic*] and the Production of Utopian Discourse." *Diacritics* (Summer 1977): 2–21.

———. *The Political Unconscious: Narrative as a Socially Symbolic Act.* Ithaca, N.Y.: Cornell University Press, 1981.

Jardine, Lisa. *Francis Bacon: Discovery and the Art of Discourse.* London: Cambridge University Press, 1974.

Johnson, Donald S. *Phantom Islands of the Atlantic.* New York: Walker & Co., 1994.

Jones, Richard Foster. *Ancients and Moderns: A Study of the Rise of the Scientific Movement in Seventeenth-Century England.* 2d rev. ed. St. Louis: Washington University Studies, 1961.

Kateb, George. *Utopia and Its Enemies.* New York: Free Press of Glencoe, 1963.

Kautsky, Karl. *Thomas More and His Utopia.* New York: Russell & Russell, 1959.

Khanna, Lee Cullen. "The Subject of Utopia: Margaret Cavendish and Her Blazing World." In *Utopian and Science Fiction by Women,* edited by Jane L. Donawerth and Carol A. Kolmerten, pp. 15–34. Syracuse, N.Y.: Syracuse University Press, 1994.

Keen, Ralph. "Thomas More and Geometry." *Moreana* 86 (1985): 151–66.

Keller, Evelyn Fox. "Baconian Science: A Hermaphroditic Birth." *Philosophical Forum* 11.3 (1980): 299–308.

Kendrick, Christopher. "More's Utopia and Uneven Development." *Boundary* 2, nos. 13.2–3 (1985): 233–66.

Kennedy, William J. *Rhetorical Norms in Renaissance Literature.* New Haven, Conn.: Yale University Press, 1978.

Kepes, Gyorgy. *Language of Vision.* Chicago: P. Theobald, 1944.

Kermode, Frank. *The Genesis of Secrecy: On the Interpretation of Narrative.* Cambridge, Mass.: Harvard University Press, 1979.

———. *The Sense of an Ending: Studies in the Theory of Fiction.* London: Oxford University Press, 1966.

Kinney, Arthur. "Rhetoric and Poetic and Thomas More's *Utopia.*" *Humana Civilitas* 5. The Center for Medieval and Renaissance Studies, University of California, Los Angeles. Malibu: Undena Publications, 1979.

Kinney, Daniel. "More's Letter to Dorp: Remapping the Trivium." *Renaissance Quarterly* 34 (1981): 179–210.

Kline, Morris. *Mathematics in Western Culture.* London: Oxford University Press, 1953.

Knapp, Jeffrey. *An Empire Nowhere: England, America, and Literature from "Utopia" to "The Tempest."* Berkeley: University of California Press, 1992.

Knights, L. C. "Bacon and the Seventeenth-Century Dissociation of Sensibility." In *Explorations: Essays in Criticism Mainly on the Literature of the Seventeenth Century*. New York: New York University Press, 1964.

Kristeller, Paul, "Humanism and Scholasticism in the Italian Renaissance." *Byzantion* 17 (1944–45): 346–74. Reprinted in *Studies in Renaissance Thought and Letters* (1956) and *Renaissance Thought: The Classic, Scholastic, and Humanist Strains* (1961).

Kruyfhooft, Cécile. "A Recent Discovery: Utopia by Abraham Ortelius." *The Map Collector* 16 (September 1981): 10–14.

Lanham, Richard A. "More, Castiglione, and the Humanist Choice of Utopias." In *Acts of Interpretation: The Text in Its Contexts: 700–1600*, edited by Mary J. Carruthers and Elizabeth D. Kirk. Norman, Okla.: Pilgrim, 1982.

———. *The Motives of Eloquence: Literary Rhetoric in the Renaissance*. New Haven, Conn.: Yale University Press, 1976.

Lee, Rensselaer, W. *"Ut Pictura Poesis": The Humanistic Theory of Painting*. New York: Norton, 1967.

Leslie, Marina. "Gender, Genre, and the Utopian Body in Margaret Cavendish's *Blazing World*." *Utopian Studies* 7.1 (1996): 6–24.

———. "Mapping Out Ideology: The Case of Utopia." *Recherches sémiotiques/Semiotic Inquiry* 12 (1992): 73–94.

Levenson, Jay A., ed. *Circa 1492: Art in the Age of Exploration*. New Haven, Conn.: Yale University Press, 1991.

Lewis, C. S., ed. *English Literature in the Sixteenth Century, Excluding Drama*. Oxford: Oxford University Press, 1954.

Lilley, Kate. "Blazing Worlds: Seventeenth-Century Women's Utopian Writing." In *Women, Texts and Histories, 1575–1760*, edited by Clare Brant and Diane Purkiss, pp. 102–33. New York: Routledge, 1992.

Liu, Alan. "The Power of Formalism." *English Literary History* 56 (Winter 1989): 721–67.

Lucian. *The Works of Lucian*. 4 vols. Translated by H. W. Fowler and F. G. Fowler. Oxford: Clarendon Press, 1905.

Lupton, J. H. Introduction. *The Utopia of Sir Thomas More*. Oxford: Clarendon Press, 1895.

Lyons, John D., and Stephen G. Nichols, eds. *Mimesis: From Mirror to Method, Augustine to Descartes*. Hanover, N.H.: University Press of New England, 1982.

McCreary, Eugene P. "Bacon's Theory of the Imagination Reconsidered." *Huntington Library Quarterly* 36 (1973): 317–26.

McCutcheon, Elizabeth. "Bacon and the Cherubim: An Iconographical Reading of the *New Atlantis*." *English Literary Renaissance* 2 (1972): 334–55.

———. "Denying the Contrary: More's Use of Litotes in the Utopia." In *Essential Articles for the Study of Thomas More*, edited by R. S. Sylvester and G. P. Marc'hadour, pp. 263–74. Hamden, Conn.: Archon Books, 1977.

———. "Thomas More, Raphael Hythlodaeus and the Angel Raphael." *Studies in English Literature* 9 (1969): 21–38.

———. "Time in More's *Utopia*." In *Acta Conventus Neo-Latini Turonensis*, edited by Jean-Claude Margolin, pp. 697–707. Paris: Vrin, 1980.

McKeon, Richard. "Renaissance and Method in Philosophy." In *Studies in the History of Ideas,* pp. 37–114. New York: Columbia University Press, 1935.

Maclean, Ian. *The Renaissance Notion of Woman: A Study in the Fortunes of Scholasticism and Medical Science in European Intellectual Life.* Cambridge: Cambridge University Press, 1980.

Maistre, Joseph Marie, comte de. "Examin de la philosophie de Bacon." In *Oeuvres completes,* vol. 6. Lyon: Vitte et Perrussel, 1884–86; rpt., Geneva: Slatkine Reprints, 1979.

Makin, Bathsua. *An Essay to Revive the Antient Education of Gentlewomen.* Edited by Paula L. Barbour. The Augustan Reprint Society, 202. William Andrews Clark Memorial Library. Los Angeles: University of California, 1980.

Mannheim, Karl. *Ideology and Utopia: An Introduction to the Sociology of Knowledge.* Translated by Louis Wirth and Edward Shils. New York: Harcourt Brace Jovanovich, 1936.

Manuel, Frank E. "Toward a Psychological History of Utopias." In *Utopias and Utopian Thought,* pp. 69–98.

——., ed. *Utopias and Utopian Thought.* Boston: Beacon Press, 1967.

Manuel, Frank E., and Fritzie P. Manuel. *Utopian Thought in the Western World.* Cambridge, Mass.: Harvard University Press, 1979.

Marin, Louis. "Frontiers of Utopia: Past and Present." *Critical Inquiry* 19 (Winter 1993): 397–420.

——. *Utopics: Spatial Play.* Translated by Robert A. Vollrath. Atlantic Highlands, N.J.: Humanities Press, 1984. Originally published as *Utopiques: Jeux d'espace.* Paris: Editions de Minuit, 1973.

Marius, Richard. *Thomas More: A Biography.* New York: Alfred A. Knopf, 1984.

Marks, Elaine, and Isabelle de Courtivron, eds. *New French Feminisms: An Anthology.* New York: Schocken, 1980.

Marwil, Jonathan. *The Trials of Council: Francis Bacon in 1621.* Detroit: Wayne State University Press, 1976.

Massing, Jean Michel. "Observations and Beliefs: The World of the Catalan Atlas." In *Circa 1492: Art in the Age of Exploration,* edited by Jay A. Levenson, pp. 27–33. New Haven, Conn.: Yale University Press, 1992.

Mathews, Nieves. *Francis Bacon: The History of a Character Assassination.* New Haven, Conn.: Yale University Press, 1996.

Mazzeo, Joseph Anthony. *Renaissance and Revolution: Backgrounds to Seventeenth-Century English Literature.* New York: Pantheon, 1967.

Mendelson, Sara Heller. *The Mental World of Stuart Women.* Amherst: University of Massachusetts Press, 1987.

Merchant, Carolyn. *The Death of Nature: Women, Ecology, and the Scientific Revolution.* San Francisco: Harper & Row, 1980.

Merton, Robert K. *Science, Technology and Society in Seventeenth-Century England.* New York: Howard Fertig, 1970.

Michael, Ian. *English Grammatical Categories and the Tradition to 1800.* London: Cambridge University Press, 1970.

Miller, William E. "Double Translation in English Humanistic Education." *Studies in the Renaissance* 10 (1963): 163–74.

Monfasani, John. "Pseudo-Dionysius the Areopagite in Mid-Quattrocento Rome." In

Supplementum Festivum: Studies in Honor of Paul Oskar Kristeller, pp. 189–219. Binghamton, N.Y.: Medieval and Renaissance Texts and Studies, 1987.

Montrose, Louis. "Renaissance Literary Studies and the Subject of History." *English Literary Renaissance* 16 (1986): 5–12.

More, Thomas. *The Correspondence of Sir Thomas More.* Edited by Elizabeth Frances Rogers. Princeton, N.J.: Princeton University Press, 1947.

————. *Richard II.* In *The Complete Works of St. Thomas More.* Vol. 2. Edited by Richard S. Sylvester. New Haven, Conn.: Yale University Press, 1963.

————. *Selected Letters.* Translated and edited by Elizabeth Frances Rogers. New Haven, Conn.: Yale University Press, 1961.

————. *Utopia.* In *The Complete Works of St. Thomas More.* Vol. 4. Edited by Edward Surtz, S.J., and J. H. Hexter. New Haven, Conn.: Yale University Press, 1963.

Mortimer, Anthony. "Hythlodaeus and Persona More: The Narrative Voices of Utopia." *Cahiers elisabethains: Etudes sur la pre-renaissance et la renaissance anglaises* 28 (October 1985): 23–35.

Moylan, Tom. *Demand the Impossible: Science Fiction and the Utopian Imagination.* New York: Methuen, 1986.

Mumford, Lewis. *The Story of Utopias.* New York: Viking Press, 1922; 1962.

Münster, Sebastian, and Hans Holbein, "Typus Cosmographicus Universalis." From *Novus Orbis Regionum* (1532). Reprinted in *The Mapping of the World: Early Printed World Maps, 1472–1700,* edited by Rodney W. Shirley, Plate 61, p. 74. London: Holland Press, 1983.

Nadel, George H. "History as Psychology in Francis Bacon's Theory of History." In *Essential Articles for the Study of Francis Bacon,* edited by Brian Vickers, pp. 236–52. Hamden, Conn.: Archon Books, 1968.

Negley, Glenn Robert. *Utopian Literature: A Bibliography with a Supplementary Listing of Works Influential in Utopian Thought.* Lawrence: Regents Press of Kansas, 1977.

Nicolson, Marjorie Hope. *Science and Imagination.* Ithaca, N.Y.: Great Seal Books, 1962.

Nugent, Elizabeth M. "Sources of John Rastell's The Nature of the Four Elements." *PMLA* 57 (1942): 74–88.

Ong, Walter J. *Rhetoric, Romance, and Technology.* Ithaca, N.Y.: Cornell University Press, 1971.

Orgel, Stephen. "Affecting the Metaphysics." In *Twentieth-Century Literature in Retrospect,* edited by Reuben A. Brower. Cambridge, Mass.: Harvard University Press, 1971.

Orwell, George. *Nineteen Eighty-four.* New York: Oxford University Press, 1984.

Panofsky, Erwin. "Die Perspektive als 'Symbolische Form.'" In *Vortrage der Bibiotheck Warburg: 1924–25,* 258–330. Leipzig-Berlin, 1927.

————. *Renaissance and Renascences in Western Art.* Uppsala: Almquist and Wiskell, 1960.

————. "Renaissance of Renascences?" *Kenyon Review* 6 (1944): 201–36.

Parks, George B. "The Geography of the Interlude of the Four Elements." *Philological Quarterly* 17 (1938): 251–62.

————. "Rastell and Waldseemüller's Map." *PMLA* 58 (1943): 572–74.

Patrides, C. A. *The Phoenix and the Ladder: The Rise and Decline of the Christian View of History.* Berkeley: University of California Press, 1964.

Patterson, Annabel, M. *Fables of Power: Aesopian Writing and Political History.* Durham, N.C.: Duke University Press, 1991.

Pepys, Samuel. *The Diary of Samuel Pepys.* 8 vols. Edited by Robert Latham and William Matthews. Berkeley: University of California Press, 1970–79.

Percival, W. Keith. "Renaissance Linguistics: The Old and the New." In *Studies in the History of Western Linguistics,* edited by Theodora Bynon and F. R. Palmer, pp. 56–68. Cambridge: Cambridge University Press, 1986.

Perlette, John M. "Of Sites and Parasites: The Centrality of the Marginal Anecdote in Book I of More's Utopia." *English Literary History* 54 (1987): 231–52.

Philo. *On Dreams.* Loeb Classical Library. Translated by F. H. Colson and G. H. Whitaker. Cambridge, Mass.: Harvard University Press, 1934.

Plato. *The Collected Dialogues.* Edited by Edith Hamilton and Huntington Cairns. Princeton, N.J.: Princeton University Press, 1961.

Pons, Émile. "Les Langues imaginaires dans le voyage utopique." *Revue de littérature comparée* 10 (1930): 589–607.

Prévost, André. "La Clef du mystère utopien." *Moreana* 19 (1982): 35–39.

Prior, Moody, E. "Bacon's Man of Science." *Journal of the History of Ideas* 15 (1954): 348–70.

Quilligan, Maureen. *The Language of Allegory.* Ithaca, N.Y.: Cornell University Press, 1979.

Quint, David. *Origin and Originality in Renaissance Literature: Versions of the Source.* New Haven, Conn.: Yale University Press, 1983.

Quintillian. *Education of an Orator.* 2 vols. Translated by John Selby Watson. London: Henry G. Bohn, 1856.

Rabelais, François. *Oeuvres complètes.* 2 vols. Edited by Pierre Jourda. Paris: Garnier Frères, 1962.

Rabil, Albert, ed. *Renaissance Humanism: Foundations, Forms, and Legacy.* 3 vols. Philadelphia: University of Pennsylvania Press, 1988.

Ralegh, Sir Walter. *The History of the World.* Ed. C. A. Patrides. London: Macmillan, 1971.

Ramsay, Raymond H. *No Longer on the Map: Discovering Places That Never Were.* New York: Viking Press, 1972.

Rastall, John. *The Nature of the Four Elements.* The Tudor Facsimile Texts. Edited by John S. Farmer. New York: AMS, 1908. Reprinted in *Six Anonymous Plays: 1500–1537.* New York: Barnes & Noble, 1905; 1966.

Reed, A. W. *Early Tudor Drama.* London: Methuen, 1926.

Reiss, Timothy J. *The Discourse of Modernism.* Ithaca, N.Y.: Cornell University Press, 1982.

R.H. *New Atlantis begun by Lord Verulam and continued by R.H.* London, 1660.

Rogers, John. *The Matter of Revolution: Science, Poetry, and Politics in the Age of Milton.* Ithaca, N.Y.: Cornell University Press, 1996.

Roper, William. "The Life of Sir Thomas More." In *Two Early Tudor Lives,* edited by Richard. S. Sylvester and Davis P. Harding. New Haven, Conn.: Yale University Press, 1962.

Rossi, Paolo. *Francis Bacon: From Magic to Science.* Translated by Sacha Rabin-ovitch. London: Routledge & Kegan Paul, 1968.

————. *Philosophy, Technology, and the Arts in the Early Modern Era.* Translated by Salvator Attanasio. New York: Harper & Row, 1970.

Rummel, Erika. *Erasmus as a Translator of the Classics.* Toronto: Toronto University Press, 1985.

Sarasohn, Lisa T. "A Science Turned Upside Down: Feminism and the Natural Philos-ophy of Margaret Cavendish," *Huntington Library Quarterly* 47 (1984): 289–307.

Sargent, Lyman Tower. *British and American Utopian Literature, 1516–1985: An An-notated, Chronological Bibliography.* New York: Garland, 1988.

Schoeck, Richard J. "Gesner on the Language of the Utopians." *Moreana* 17 (1980): 110–11.

————. "Humanism in England." In *Renaissance Humanism: Foundations, Forms and Legacy,* vol. 2, edited by Albert Rabil, Jr., pp. 5–38. Philadelphia: University of Pennsylvannia Press, 1988.

————. " 'A Nursery of Correct and Useful Institutions': On Reading More's *Utopia* as Dialogue." *Moreana* 22 (1969): 19–32.

Seebohm, Frederic. *The Oxford Reformers: John Colet, Erasmus, and Thomas More.* London: Longmans, Green, 1896.

Seigel, Jerrold. *Rhetoric and Philosophy in Renaissance Humanism.* Princeton, N.J.: Princeton University Press, 1968.

Shakespeare, William. *The Tempest.* Edited by Robert Langbaum. Harmondsworth, England: Penguin, 1987.

Shelley, P. B. "A Defense of Poetry." In *Shelley's Literary and Philosophical Criticism,* edited by John Shawcross. London: Henry Frowde, 1909.

Shepherd, Simon. *Amazons and Warrior Women: Varieties of Feminism in Seven-teenth-Century Drama.* Brighton, England: Harvester Press, 1981.

Sherman, Sandra. "Trembling Texts: Margaret Cavendish and the Dialectic of Author-ship." *English Literary Renaissance* 24.1 (Winter 1994): 184–210.

Shirley, Rodney W. *The Mapping of the World: Early Printed World Maps, 1472–1700.* In *Cartographica.* Vol. 9. London: Holland Press, 1983.

Sidney, Philip. *A Defence of Poetry.* Edited by Jan Van Dorsten. Oxford: Oxford Uni-versity Press, 1978.

Skelton, R. A. *Explorer's Maps: Chapters in the Cartographic Record of Geographical Discovery.* New York: Praeger, 1958.

Skinner, Quentin. "Sir Thomas More's Utopia and the Language of Renaissance Hu-manism." In *The Languages of Political Theory in Early Modern Europe,* edited by Anthony Pagden. Cambridge: Cambridge University Press, 1987.

Sonnino, Lee, A., ed. *A Handbook to Sixteenth-Century Rhetoric.* London: Routledge & Kegan Paul, 1968.

Spenser, Edmund. *The Faerie Queene.* Edited by Thomas P. Roche. New York: Pen-guin, 1979.

Spitzer, Leo. "Linguistic Perspectivism in the *Don Quijote.*" In *Linguistics and Literary History: Essays in Stylistics.* Princeton, N.J.: Princeton University Press, 1948.

Sprat, Thomas. *The History of the Royal Society.* Edited by Jackson I. Cope and Harold Whitmore Jones. Saint Louis: Washington University Press, 1958.

Steiner, George. *After Babel: Aspects of Language and Translation.* Oxford: Oxford University Press, 1975.

Stewart, Susan. *Nonsense: Aspects of Intertextuality in Folklore and Literature.* Baltimore: Johns Hopkins University Press, 1979.

Stobbart, Lorainne. *Utopia, Fact or Fiction?: The Evidence from the Americas.* Wolfeboro Falls, N.H.: Alan Sutton Publishing, 1992.

Struever, Nancy S. *The Language of History in the Renaissance: Rhetorical and Historical Consciousness in Florentine Humanism.* Princeton, N.J.: Princeton University Press, 1970.

Suvin, Darko. "Defining the Literary Genre of *Utopia:* Some Historical Semantics, Some Genology, a Proposal and a Plea." In *Metamorphoses of Science Fiction,* pp. 37–62. New Haven, Conn.: Yale University Press, 1979.

Swift, Jonathan. *Gulliver's Travels.* Harmondsworth, England: Penguin, 1987.

Sylvester, R. S. "A Part of His Own: Thomas More's Literary Personality in His Early Works." *Moreana* 15 (1967): 29–42.

———. "Si Hythlodaeo Credimus: Vision and Revision in Thomas More's *Utopia.*" In *Essential Articles for the Study of Thomas More,* edited by R. S. Sylvester and G. P. Marc'hadour. Hamden, Conn.: Archon Books, 1977.

Taylor, E. G. R. *Tudor Geography: 1485–1583.* London: Methuen, 1930.

Tinkler, John F. "Bacon and History." In *The Cambridge Companion to Bacon,* edited by Markku Peltonen, pp. 232–59. Cambridge: Cambridge University Press, 1996.

Todd, Janet. *The Sign of Angellica: Women, Writing, and Fiction, 1660–1800.* New York: Columbia University Press, 1989.

Todorov, Tzvetan. *The Conquest of America: The Question of the Other.* Translated by Richard Howard. New York: Harper & Row, 1984.

Tooley, R. V. *Maps and Map-Makers.* 4th ed. London: B. T. Batsford, 1970.

Toon, Peter. *Puritans, The Millennium and the Future of Israel: Puritan Eschatology, 1600–1660.* London: James Clarke & Co., 1970.

Trapp, J. B., and Hubertus Schulte Herbrüggen, eds. "The King's Good Servant": Sir Thomas More 1477/8-1535. Ipswich: Boydell Press, 1977.

Trevor-Roper, Hugh. "Sir Thomas More and Utopia." In *Renaissance Essays: 1400–1620,* pp. 24–58. Chicago: University of Chicago Press.

Trinkaus, Charles. *In Our Image and Likeness: Humanity and Divinity in Italian Humanist Thought.* 2 vols. London: Constable, 1970.

———. *The Scope of Renaissance Humanism.* Ann Arbor: University of Michigan Press, 1983.

Trubowitz, Rachel. "The Reenchantment of Utopia and the Female Monarchical Self: Margaret Cavendish's *Blazing World.*" *Tulsa Studies in Women's Literature* 11 (1992): 229–45.

Tuveson, E. L. *Millennium and Utopia: A Study in the Background of an Idea of Progress.* New York: Harper & Row, 1964.

Tyacke, Sarah, ed. *English Map-Making, Fifteen Hundred to Sixteen Fifty.* London: Longwood Publishing Group for the British Library, 1983.

Veeser, H. Aram., ed. *The New Historicism.* New York: Routledge, 1989.

Vespucci, Amerigo. *Letters from a New World: Amerigo Vespucci's Discovery of Amer-*

ica. Translated by David Jacobson. Edited by Luciano Formisano. New York: Marsilio, 1992.

Vickers, Brian, ed. *English Science, Bacon to Newton*. Cambridge: Cambridge University Press, 1987.

————., ed. *Essential Articles for the Study of Francis Bacon*. Hamden, Conn.: Archon Books, 1968.

Waldseemüller, Martin. *The Cosmographiae Introductio of Martin Waldseemüller in Facsimile*. Edited by John and Franz von Wieser. Catholic Historical Society Monograph 4. New York, 1907.

Wallace, Karl W. *Francis Bacon on the Nature of Man*. Urbana: University of Illinois Press, 1967.

Warhaft, Sidney. Introduction. *Francis Bacon: A Selection of His Works*. New York: Odyssey Press, 1965.

————. "The Providential Order in Bacon's New Philosophy." *Studies in the Literary Imagination* 4 (April 1971): 49–64.

Webster, Charles. *The Great Instauration: Science, Medicine, and Reform 1626–1660*. London: Gerald Duckworth & Co., 1975.

Weinberger, J. "Science and Rule in Bacon's Utopia: An Introduction to the Reading of the *New Atlantis*." *American Political Science Review* 70 (1976): 866–72.

————. *Science, Faith, and Politics: Francis Bacon and the Utopian Roots of the Modern Age*. Ithaca, N.Y.: Cornell University Press, 1985.

White, Hayden. *The Content of the Form: Narrative Discourse and Historical Representation*. Baltimore: Johns Hopkins University Press, 1987.

White, Howard. *Peace among the Willows*. The Hague: Martinus Nijhoff, 1968.

Whitney, Charles. *Francis Bacon and Modernity*. New Haven, Conn.: Yale University Press, 1986.

Wilde, Oscar. "The Soul of Man under Socialism." In *Complete Works,* edited by Vyvyan Holland, pp. 1079–1104. London: Collins, 1966; 1983.

Wilford, John Noble. *The Mapmakers: The Story of the Great Pioneers in Cartography from Antiquity to the Space Age*. New York: Random House, 1981.

Wittgenstein, Ludwig. *Philosophical Investigations*. Translated by G. E. M. Anscombe. New York: Macmillan, 1968.

Woodward, David. "Maps and the Rationalization of Geographic Space." In *Circa 1492: Art in the Age of Exploration,* pp. 83–87. New Haven, Conn.: Yale University Press, 1991.

Woolf, Virginia. *A Room of One's Own*. New York: Harcourt Brace Jovanovich, 1929; 1957.

Yates, Frances. *The Occult Philosophy in the Elizabethan Age*. London: Routledge & Kegan Paul, 1979.

————. *The Rosicrucian Enlightenment*. London: Routledge & Kegan Paul, 1972.

Zetterberg, J. Peter. "Echoes of Nature in Salomon's House." *Journal of the History of Ideas* 43 (April–June 1982): 179–94.

Index